ISBN 978-1-330-60259-1
PIBN 10081107

FB &c Ltd, Dalton House, 60 Windsor Avenue, London, SW19 2RR.
Company number 08720141. Registered in England and Wales.

THE

SCOT ABROAD

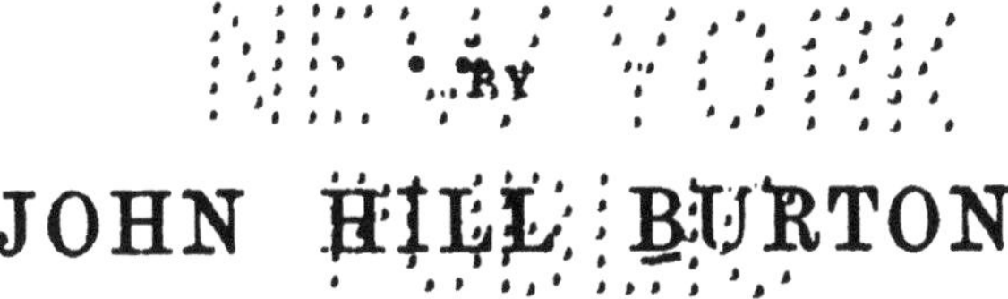

BY

JOHN HILL BURTON

AUTHOR OF 'THE BOOK-HUNTER,' ETC.

IN TWO VOLUMES

VOL. I.

WILLIAM BLACKWOOD AND SONS
EDINBURGH AND LONDON
MDCCCLXIV

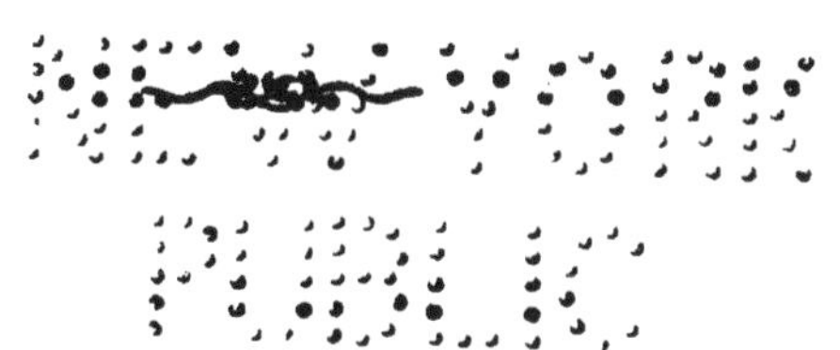

THE growth of these two volumes is similar to that of their predecessor, 'The Book-Hunter,' which was received with unexpected favour.

The Author had at various times, through periodical literature and otherwise, offered some suggestions on the existence and character of certain unexplored recesses in historical literature. He found himself backed by friendly advisers in the opinion that it would be worth while to go over the ground more systematically, bring his suggestions to clearer conclusions, and see how far they could be assorted in systematic groups. The project was rendered all the more attractive by the new light thrown into corners previously obscure by the noble collection of documents issued under the direction of the Master of the Rolls in this country, and the investigations of accomplished archæologists abroad. The Author found that the result could neither be reached in so brief a time nor packed in so small a compass as he expected, since new vistas, ever opening up, lured him farther on. The book thus greatly changed its nature after the title had been announced. But although the whole first volume, given up to an account of 'The Ancient League with France,' is passed before 'The Scot Abroad' strictly commences, yet the title is not so illogical as it may seem, since the whole book refers to the relations of Scotland and Scotsmen with foreign countries.

To go abroad merely for the purpose of dealing with one's countrymen dispersed in foreign lands, may appear as egregious an instance of nationality as any of those which the Author has hunted up for the amusement of his reader. He pleads as his excuse that, having devoted the time at his disposal to the reconstruction, from the beginning, of the History of Scotland in its present received shape, he has been tempted to leave from time to time the beaten road, and follow up the nearest openings into districts where he could wander at large, free from the responsibilities for exhaustive completeness which attend on history-making. He will be glad if the good-natured reader takes his offering in the same spirit, and treats it as a holiday ramble through some secluded scenes in history and literature.

CONTENTS OF VOLUME I.

THE ANCIENT LEAGUE WITH FRANCE.

Chapter I.

Chapter II.

Chapter III.

Chapter IV.

Chapter V.

THE

ANCIENT LEAGUE WITH FRANCE.

Chapter I.

The Charlemagne and Achaius Question settled—The War of Independence—The established Quarrel with Scotland and England—Its Consequence in the League with France—Wallace's Share in the Transaction—The old Treaties—Social Life in France during the Hundred Years' War—The Constable Buchan—The Battles of Baugé, Crevant, and Verneuil—The Establishment of the Scots Guard—Some of their Feats.

HAVE long thought that the story of the old League between France and Scotland is so significant of national character, is so fruitful in romantic personal incident, and held so powerful an influence on the destinies of Europe, that an account of it could not

Chapter III.

Chapter IV.

Chapter V.

THE

ANCIENT

LEAGUE WITH FRANCE.

Chapter I.

The Charlemagne and Achaius Question settled—The War of Independence—The established Quarrel with Scotland and England—Its Consequence in the League with France—Wallace's Share in the Transaction—The old Treaties—Social Life in France during the Hundred Years' War—The Constable Buchan—The Battles of Baugé, Crevant, and Verneuil—The Establishment of the Scots Guard—Some of their Feats.

HAVE long thought that the story of the old League between France and Scotland is so significant of national character, is so fruitful in romantic personal incident, and held so powerful an influence on the destinies of Europe, that an account of it could not fail of interest in the hands of any one content merely to tell the facts and briefly explain the political conditions out of which they arose. Its own proper interest is so deep and true as to gain rather than lose when its history is stripped of the remote antiquity and other fabulous decorations by which enthusiastic national historians have attempted to enhance it. We are told how the Emperor Charlemagne, having resolved to establish a vast system of national or imperial education, looked around for suitable professors to teach in his universities; and perceiving Scotland to be the most learned of nations, and the most likely to supply him with the commodity he desired, he forthwith entered into a league with Achaius, the then ruling monarch of that ancient kingdom. Such is the account of the origin of the League with France, as told by Boece and our other fabulous chroniclers, and courteously accepted on the side of France by Mezeray and his brethren, who seem gladly to welcome so valuable a piece of authentic information. No doubt one finds, on minute inquiry, that, contemporary with the reign of the Charlemagne of France and the Kaiser Karl of the Germans, there flourished a chief—or a king, if you will—called Eochy or Auchy, holding sway over some considerable portion of the Celtic people of the west, and probably living in a sort of craal built of mud and wattles. But that the Emperor ever knew of his existence is not very probable; and instead of receiving an embassy from Charlemagne as a contemporary monarch seeking the friendship of an honoured and powerful fellow-sovereign, Eochy doubtless owed it to his own insignificance, and his distance from the centre of European power, that he was not called upon to acknowledge the supreme authority of him who had resumed the empire of the world.

In reality, it spoils the interest and significance of the alliance to attempt to trace it farther back than those political conditions which, four hundred years later, gave it efficient purpose. These were the war of independence against the dominion of England, and the contemporary claims of the English kings on the succession to the throne of France. These concurring sources of contest rendered the League the most natural thing in the world. It enabled the kings of the house of Valois to fight their battle on British ground without sending an army there; it provided to the Scots, whenever they could safely leave their homes, an opportunity for striking a blow at the enemy and oppressor of their land.

To see the influence of this adjustment, not only on the nations immediately concerned, but on Europe at large, let us look a little more closely into details. Taking any old-established state, with a fixed natural boundary and distinct institutions of its own, it is difficult to realise in the mind the same area of territory and its people at a time when neither the boundaries nor the institutions existed. Our natural indolence makes us lean on these specialties as a means of obtaining clearness at an easy price to the intellect; and rather than leave them and grope at the truth, we carry them back step by step, until they have gone infinite ages beyond their real beginning. There is retribution for this as for other instances where indolent reliance supersedes independent judgment. Those of our historians who have had too much honesty to go headlong into the accepted fables of their predecessors, have had cruel difficulties in identifying ancient Scotland. At one time they find the territories of some Saxon king stretching to the Tay; at another, the King of Scots reigns to the Humber, or farther. It would have saved them a world of trouble and anxiety to come at once to the conclusion that Scotland was nowhere—that the separate kingdom marked off against England by a distinct boundary on the physical globe, as well as by a moral boundary of undying hatred, did not then exist.

A common language stretched along from north to south, varying perhaps in its substance and tone by imperceptible degrees in the ears of the travelling stranger, as the language of each of the two countries now does. Unfortunately, this simple view brings us to the verge of a perilous controversy. There are some topics which the temper and reason of the human race seem not to have been made strong enough to encounter, so invariably do these break down when the topics in question are started. Of such is the question, To which of the great classes of European languages did that of the people called Picts belong? The contest, like a duel with revolvers over a table, has been rendered more awful by the narrowness of the field of battle, since some time ago the world possessed just one word, or piece of a word, said to be Pictish, and now one of the most accomplished antiquarians of our day has added another.

Keeping clear of this scene of peril, let us content ourselves with the obvious fact, that at an early age the eastern and northern parts of what now is Scotland were peopled by a race of very pure Teutonic blood and tongue. They formed a portion of that brotherhood of Saxon states, among which the amalgamations and splittings, and the drifting-in of fresh swarms among old settlers, make so complex and confused a web of Anglo-Saxon history. It would happen, in these gains and losses of territory, that some ambitious Bretwalda of the south would extend his dominion or his influence far northward; and from such incidents the pedants of the feudal law, who could not look beyond their own forms and nomenclature into the conditions of an age when there was neither feudality nor a Scotland to be feudalised, invented a feudal superiority in the Saxon kings over the kingdom of Scotland.

The conquest of the south, of course, changed its position towards the north. England became Normanised, while Scotland not only retained her old Teutonic character, but became a place of refuge for the Saxon fugitives. The remnants of Harold's family—the old royal race of England—came among the other fugitives to Scotland, and took up their position there as an exiled court awaiting their restoration, and looking to their brethren of Scotland to aid them in effecting it. At the head of these princely exiles was Edward the Ætheling. His sister, the renowned St Margaret, married Malcolm the King of the Scots, who thus became more than ever the hope of the Saxon party. The names of their children have a thoroughly Anglo-Saxon sound: Edgar, the eldest, who succeeded to the throne; Edward, named after his maternal relation the Confessor; Edmond, and Ethelred. King Malcolm, in his marriage, is not to be altogether viewed as having, with chivalrous generosity, made a home for a persecuted princess in the only way in which such an arrangement could be decorously accomplished. He had hopes of solid results from the brilliant connection, and made a bold effort to render them good by an invasion of England; for there can be little doubt that Harding is right when he says of that fierce raid into Cumberland which ended in the battle of the Standard, that "King Malcolm of Scotland warred in England for his wife's right, pretending that she was right heir of England."

During the interval of two hundred years between their invasion of England and their invasion of Scotland, the Normans had been gradually extending their social influence northward. As the flower of chivalry and the leaders of fashion they were personally popular in Scotland, where many of them became favourites at court, and formed rich matrimonial alliances. It is possible that the wise men of the day may have deemed it a good policy to plant in the country offshoots of that mighty race who seemed destined to rule mankind wherever they went; but if they thought that they would thus establish a Norman aristocracy, who in time would have a patriotic interest in the soil, and protect it from the designs of the aggrandising kings of England, their policy in the course of events turned out to be a failure.

In the mean time the country saw chiefly the bright side of the Norman character; for it is observable that the settlers had not so deeply rooted themselves as to cover the land with those castles which are everywhere the most remarkable and enduring memorials of their presence. Fortresses, no doubt, existed before their day, but these were generally mounds or ramparts, within which people inhabited open dwellings of wood, turf, or wattles. The Norman was the first to plant the feudal castle—a building comprising within its four thick stone walls a rich man's dwelling, a fortress, and a prison, signifying that he who built it intended to consume the fruit of the soil, to make war upon his enemies, and to administer his own justice among the people. The castles scattered over Europe not only show how far the Normans have penetrated, as the shingle on the beach marks the height of the tide; but their various architectural types indicate, like those of fossils in geology, the historical period of deposit. The annalists tell us how, after William's arrival, England was covered with Norman strongholds; and that country is rich in remains of the earliest type of castle—the great square block, destitute of the later adjunct of flanking works, and the round arch, marking the lingering predominance of Roman forms. If there ever were castles of this sort in Scotland, they were at least so rare that no specimen now remains—at least I can find none after diligent search. On the other hand, of the later and richer type of feudal architecture — the pointed Gothic buildings with outworks, peculiar to the reigns of the Edwards—there are many fine specimens. The same phenomena may be seen in Ireland and Wales. Over all three countries the tide of Norman conquest had rolled; and though in Scotland the tide was driven back, it left these characteristic relics behind.

Luckily for England, and for the liberties of the world, there were elements of national strength which in the end worked the tyranny of Norman rule out of the constitution. Of the misery which the Saxon people had to endure under the earliest Plantagenet monarchs we have scanty traces, for such things are not with safety committed to writing; but what we have is sufficiently expressive. Perhaps the following, taken from that sober unobtrusive narrative, the 'Saxon Chronicle,' may suffice for this occasion :—

"They cruelly oppressed the wretched men of the land with castle-works. When the castles were made, they filled them with devils and evil men. Then took they those men that they imagined had any property, both by night and by day, peasant men and women, and put them in prison for their gold and silver, and tortured them with unutterable torture, for never were martyrs so tortured as they were. They hanged them up by the feet, and smoked them with foul smoke; they hanged them by the thumbs, or by the head, and hung fires on their feet; they put knotted strings about their heads, and writhed them so that it went to the brain. They put them in dungeons in which were adders and snakes and toads, and killed them so. Some they put in a 'crucet hûs'—that is, in a chest that was short and narrow and shallow—and put sharp stones therein, and pressed the man therein, so that they brake all his limbs. In many of the castles were (instruments called) a 'loathly and grim;' these were neck-bonds, of which two or three men had enough to bear one. It was so made, that is (it was) fastened to a beam; and they put a sharp iron about the man's throat and his neck, so that he could not in any direction sit, or lie, or sleep, but must bear all that iron. Many thousands they killed with hunger. I neither can nor may tell all the wounds or all the tortures which they inflicted on wretched men in this land; and that lasted the nineteen winters while Stephen was king, and ever it was worse and worse. They laid imposts on the towns continually, and called it 'censerie.' When the wretched men had no more to give, they robbed and burned all the towns, so that thou mightest well go all a day's journey and thou shouldst never find a man sitting in a town, or the land tilled. Then was corn dear, and flesh, and cheese, and butter; for there was none in the land. Wretched men died of hunger; some went seeking alms who at one while were rich men; some fled out of the land." *

This is set down to the reign of Stephen, just about the time of the battle of the Standard, and about half-way between the conquest of England and the war of resistance in Scotland. Seeing this going on more or less for two hundred years, it is not wonderful that the Scots, continuing and flourishing under their old Saxon institutions, were grimly resolved to fight to the death against such a rule. The representative of this national feeling was the renowned William Wallace. Of him so much old romance and modern nonsense has been uttered that cautious people are apt to shun his name in history, as, like Arthur, Merlin, Roland, and Odin, that of a mythical person not susceptible of articulate identification. But few historical

---

* 'Saxon Chronicle:' Record Edition, ii. 230, 231.

figures come out so distinctly and grandly when stripped of the theatrical properties. He was a skilful and brave general, an accomplished politician, and a public man of unstained faith and undying zeal.

Nor is it at all necessary, in vindicating his fame, utterly to blacken those who would not co-operate with him. The Normans, who had acquired recent wealth and rank in Scotland, were not zealous in standing up for the independence of the people of the country and their protection from Norman tyranny—how could they be expected to be so? One name among them has been consigned to eminent historical infamy, and for centuries has borne the burden of the ardent hatred of all true-hearted Scots—the elder Baliol. I remember our being taught at school carefully to avoid confounding his name with another specially dedicated to infamy—the Belial of Scripture. It is lucky for those who thus lie under historical ban that they are generally beyond the condition of suffering, either in body or spirit, from the execrations heaped upon their memory. And if we should say that even the fame of the departed has a right to be protected from injustice—to receive due praise if its owner has done service to mankind, and at least quiet oblivion if he has done no harm—a more easy consolation for the injustice done comes in the reflection that, under the same name, the demon of the historians is a different being from the harmless commonplace man who owned the name in the flesh. So this Baliol, while in history he stands forth as the foul betrayer of his country's independence—as traitor to the vile allegiance he had sold himself to—as guilty of every political crime which historical magniloquence can express—was, in the flesh, a very ordinary sort of man, who, in agreeing to do homage for a territory to the monarch who had preferred him to it, acted on much the same principle as the holder of a snug office at the present day who sides with the statesman who has appointed him to it. And if he was at one time, under sore temptation, guilty of tampering with his allegiance, he did the best he could afterwards to put matters right. Looking to the social and political conditions of him and his class, it would be difficult to find a proposition that would have seemed more preposterous to them than that they should sacrifice the prospects of a good fief for the preservation either of a separate nationality or the liberties of a truculent, self-willed people. The Bruces themselves belonged to the same set; but ere the grandson of the original claimant gained his great victory, the lapse of a quarter of a century of animosity may have nourished a sense of nationality towards the people for whom he fought; and even if he was, after all, only the Norman adventurer, who saw a grand career of ambition as the leader of a people who would not be enslaved, he fairly won the crown he wore.

The battle of Bannockburn, in being the conclusive act which relieved Scotland from the domination of the English King, became also the crisis at which France and Scotland became united in fast friendship. This friendship had been growing during the war of independence, but it could exist as a permanent European institution only after that was over. And at this point arises one of those occasions for rendering history distinct by unravelling minor confusions, which sometimes bring those who do the work of unravelling under suspicion as lovers of paradox. We shall all the more clearly understand the nature and tendency of the alliance by starting with the fact that, before a thorough external union with France, Scotland cast forth certain French characteristics which had found their way into the elements of her political and social condition. The rule of the Normans was the rule of a race who had made themselves French; however rapidly, among a kindred Teutonic people, they were returning to their old Norse character. Of the Norman families which had established themselves in the country, Scotland retained but a small minority after the war of independence, for the obvious reason that the great majority had cast their lots with their natural leader, the King of England. The topographical antiquary, tracing the history of the early ownership of estates in Scotland, sees the change expressed with a distinctness plainer than any historical narrative. The early charters are rich in such a courtly Norman nomenclature as De Quincey, De Vere, De Vipont, D'Umfraville, Mortimer, and De Coucy. When order is restored, and the lands are again recorded as having lords, there are Johnstons, Bells, Armstrongs, Scots, Kerrs, Browns, and suchlike, telling at once of their native Saxon origin. The loss of their estates, indeed, was a substantial grievance to the Norman holders, who would not relinquish them without a struggle; and in their effort to get them back again, under Edward Baliol, whom they had set up as King of Scotland for that purpose, they were very nearly successful in crushing the newly-bought independence of the land.

Thus the extinction of the English rule had at first the effect of removing French elements out of Scotland. In England, the language of France, being the language of the Court, became that of the law, in which it has left to our own day some motley relics, remaining imbedded in it like grotesque organic remains. If, along with the influx of Normans, their language may have at one time been creeping into legal practice in Scotland, the efforts of the Edwards to enforce the English forms of law throughout the country made their technicalities especially odious. All the way from the border to the Highland line, the people, high and low, came to speak in very pure Teutonic; for it is curious that the language of the Lowland Scots has not received the slightest tinge from close contact with the Celtic. Whatever it may have been among the common people, the literary language of England became afflicted with Gallicisms; and so it came to pass that Barbour sang the liberation of his country from the English kings in purer English, according to the canon of the present day, than his contemporary Chaucer, whose more finished verses are not so easily read by Englishmen as those of the Aberdonian. England in the end outgrew these French elements, but Scotland cast them forth at once. And we shall find that, however close became the intimacy of the two nations, and however powerful the influence of the greater on the destinies of the less, the symptoms of that influence were ever external and superficial—it never penetrated to the national heart. After the expulsion of the English—or, more properly, of the Normans—from the north, it becomes a key-note in French history that England is to be fought from Scotland; while, on the English side of European history, the response is that everything must be right on the Border before it will be prudent to send an expedition to the Continent.

When we have a clear hold on those great national conditions of which the League was an inevitable result, it is of less moment to know the minute particulars about the dates and tenor of the treaties, and the statesmen who negotiated them. But these too have their interest. The first name practically connected with them is Wallace's; and there is some reason, besides his renown as a warrior, and an organiser and governor of his fellow-men, to award to him the reputation of a successful diplomatist. The legendary chroniclers, such as Blind Harry the minstrel, tell us that he frequented France; that he became a respected friend and a favoured counsellor of the French monarch; that he performed valorous feats on French soil, and that he chased pirates on French waters. These stories have been discredited by the grave, to whom it did not commend them that one of his feats was the hunting and slaying of a lion in Guienne. But there is an odd tenacity of life in the fundamentals of even the most flagrant legends about the Scottish hero. Few names have been so saturated with nonsense in prose and verse; and the saturation seems to be ceaseless, having developed a formidable access in our own very times. Yet when we come to documents and other close quarters, we generally realise in some shape or other almost all the leading events of his wonderful legendary career. The statements of the graver of the old Scots historians are sufficient to convince the man who has worked hardest of all in clearing up the history of the League, that he was received at the French Court.* For those of narrower faith there is one little scrap of what lawyers call real evidence, worth more than all the narratives of the chroniclers. When Wallace was

* "Il se réfugia en France, où il fut honorablement accueilli et traité par le Roi."—Michel, Les Ecossais en France, i. 46.

apprehended and taken to London for trial, after the fashion of dealing with other criminals he was searched, and the articles in his possession duly removed and inventoried. Among these were letters of safe-conduct from King Philip—his French passport, in short; a valuable piece of evidence, had any been needed, of practices hostile to the King of England.* That he should, at the Court of Philip, have forgotten the great cause to which he was devoted is an inadmissible supposition; and he is at least as likely as any one to have suggested that the common interest of France and Scotland lay in enmity towards England.

But we find more distinct traces of Wallace having dealt with France through a diplomatic agent. When he held the office of Governor of Scotland, like every other man in power he required conformity in those who worked with him; and when they would not conform, displaced them. If he needed an excuse for strong measures, he had it in the urgency of the question at issue—the preservation of the national independence. Accordingly, he drove out the primate who leaned to the Norman side, and got William Lamberton, a partisan of the national independence, elected Archbishop of St Andrews. Certain articles presented against this

* Palgrave, 'Documents and Records illustrating the History of Scotland, and the Transactions between the Crowns of Scotland and England,' cxcv.

archbishop to his ecclesiastical superior, the Pope, by King Edward, bear that—

"Being thus made bishop, Lamberton continued at the Court of France with other the great men of Scotland, the King's enemies, labouring continually to do all the harm and injury in his power against his liege lord, until the peace was finally concluded between France and England. And after the conclusion of such treaty, he, Lamberton, by letters-patent under his seal, urged and excited the prelates, earls, barons, and all the commonality of Scotland (these being the King's enemies), to carry on the war vigorously until the bishop and the other lords in France could return to Scotland. . . . Moreover, the bishop addressed his special letters, sealed with his seal, to the traitor Wallace, and prayed that, for the love of him the bishop, he, Wallace, would do all possible hurt and damage to the King of England. And Lamberton also wrote to his officers in Scotland to employ a portion of his own provision for the sustenance of Wallace." *

Soon afterwards Scotland was too effectually subdued to hold independent diplomatic relations abroad. In a curious way, however, the thread of the negotiations so begun may be traced through the intervening confusions, until the whole was resumed when France and Scotland could speak to each other both as separate independent kingdoms,

---

* Palgrave, clxv.

and both having deep cause of enmity against England.* In the mean time, between Philip of France and Edward of England there was enacted a series of feudal pedantries which were the farce to the tragedy going on in Scotland, Edward reversing his position, and acting the truculent vassal. Both affairs arose out of those curious conditions of the feudal system which made monarchs do homage to each other for the sake of little additions to their available territories. Thus had the King of the Scots done homage at Windsor for the fief of Huntingdon and several other benefices held within the kingdom of England; and so, when the opportunity came, the King of England called this homage-doing King his vassal. In like manner, Edward himself acknowledged the feudal superiority of the King of France in respect to his Continental possessions. So it came to pass that, as some English sailors committed acts of piracy against French subjects, Philip of France called on Edward of England to come to Paris and do homage, and stand trial for misconduct as a disobedient vassal to his liege lord, just as Edward himself had called on Baliol to come to Windsor. But the total disproportion between the demand and the power to enforce it made the

* In one of the monkish chronicles (Lanercost, 182) it is narrated that, when Edward had penetrated, in 1296, as far as Aberdeen, he there found emissaries from Philip of France, with letters to Baliol and to many leading men of Scotland.

summons of the French King ridiculous. It would have been a sight to behold the countenance of the fierce and determined long-legged Edward when he received it. The foolish bravado brought on the first English war in France, making way for those which followed it. The French were too glad to get out of the affair by the treaty of 1303; but, hard pressed as they then were, they tried to keep true faith with their friends of Scotland. Somewhat to the surprise of Edward, they introduced the Scots, their good allies, as a party to the negotiations; and when Edward said that if there ever were an alliance of Scotland and France his vassal Baliol had freely resigned it, the French told him that Baliol, being then a prisoner of war, was no free agent, and could renounce nothing for the kingdom of Scotland. This time, however, the support of France availed nothing, for Scotland was speedily afterwards blotted for a time out of the list of independent nations.

It is under the year 1326—twelve years after the battle of Bannockburn—that in Rymer's great book of treaties we read the first articulate treaty between France and Scotland. There the French monarchs came under obligation to those of Scotland, "in good faith as loyal allies, whenever they shall have occasion for aid and advice, in time of peace or war, against the King of England and his subjects." On the part of the Scots kings it is stipulated that they shall be bound "to make war upon the kingdom of England with all their force, whensoever war is waged between us and the King of England." In 1371, when the alliance was solemnly renewed, a hundred thousand gold nobles were advanced to Scotland on curious and shrewd conditions. The money was to be employed for the ransom of King David from custody in England. Should, however, the Pope be pleased to absolve the Scots Government of that debt, then the gold nobles were to be employed in making war against England. When proffers were made to France for a separate truce, not including Scotland, they were gallantly rejected. On the other hand, when Scotland was sorely tempted by the Emperor Maximilian, and by other potentates from time to time, to desert her ally France, she refused. It endeared the alliance to both nations to sanctify it with the mellowness of extreme antiquity, and references to its existence since the days of Charlemagne find their way even at an early period into the formal diplomatic documents.

There are two sides in the history of an alliance as in that of a war. Of the history of the ancient League, however, the first chapter belongs almost entirely to France. Some Scotsmen went thither and influenced the political condition of the country long before France impressed the policy of Scotland. It will clear the way for what follows, to take a glance at the social condition of the land to which the Scots refugees flocked, after their country had established itself in hostile independence of the Plantagenet kings. In later times people have been accustomed to seek the politics of France in Paris, giving little heed to the provinces; but at the accession of the house of Valois, the contrast between the eminence of the one and the insignificance of the other was still greater.

Paris was at that time, indeed, as much beyond any other European capital in extent, in noble buildings, and in luxurious living, as it is now beyond the secondary towns of France. The fruitfulness of the reigning family provided it with a little mob of native royalties, who made it so attractive that not only did all the great feudatories of the crown flock thither, but even independent monarchs preferred playing the courtier there to reigning in their own dingy capitals. One finds the kings of Navarre, of Sicily, and of Bohemia perpetually in the way, and turning up upon the surface of history when anything notable occurs in the French Court; they could not tear themselves from the attractions of the place.

The populousness and luxurious living of Paris are attested in a not pleasant or dignified fashion by the large number of butchers necessary to supply the city. They formed, when combined, a sort of small army; large enough, however, to be estimated by the thousand. They were often used as a powerful but a dangerous political engine. By bullying bravado and violence they held a sort of corporate power when almost everything else of the kind had been annihilated. This power they used according to their nature. It was they who did the professional part of the business when the prisons were broken open by the Burgundian party, and the throats of the prisoners cut, making a scene in the year 1418 which was exactly repeated in the year 1792.

The allusion to these brutes brings one naturally from the concentration of luxury, wealth, and rank in Paris, to the horrible abyss by which it was all surrounded. It is difficult to conceive the wretchedness and degradation of France at that time—still more difficult, when it is fully realised, to understand by what steps the great nation of Henry IV. and Louis XIV.—the still greater nation of later times—arose to such a height of lustre and triumph. Whatever other elements were at work in the long eventful regeneration, it may surely be permitted to our national pride to count that the infusion of Scottish blood into the veins, as it were, of the country, must have had some share in the change.

There was at that time throughout the land neither sturdy independence nor affectionate, trusting dependence. Everything was thoroughly wrong. The great showed their superiority only in acts of injustice, insult, and cruelty; the poor were servile and abject in subjection, and brutal, treacherous, and ungrateful when the iron rule was for a moment evaded. A sort of mortifying process was killing all the elements of independent constitutional action one by one, and approaching the heart. The jurisdictions and privileges which the municipalities had inherited from the Roman Empire were crushed out.

The lower feudatories were absorbed one by one, and the higher followed. By a curious fatality it fell to the family of Valois to unite the characteristic defects of a centralised despotism with those of an oligarchy. The great provinces came gradually one by one into the hands of the King; but instead of being united to the crown so as to make a compact and symmetrical empire, they were given to the princes of the blood and their descendants.

Hence arose a class of nobles or territorial aristocracy, who formed a separate caste, looking down upon and bearing enmity to all owners of territory who were not of the blood-royal. Such were the lords of Burgundy, Orleans, Anjou, Bourbon, Berri, La Marche, and a crowd of others. The tendency of things was towards not only a divine right in the crown to govern, but a divine right in the blood-royal to possess all things. The law was gradually withdrawing its protection from those who were not either themselves of the royal stock, or protected in a sort of clientage by one of the princes of the blood. Men in the highest places who did not belong to the sacred race might be pitched from their chairs of state to the dungeon or the scaffold, with that reckless celerity which characterises the loss of influence in Eastern despotisms.

One of the few men in that disastrous period who was enabled to afford to France some of the services of a real statesman was the Sieur de Montagu. He had been raised to influence under Charles V., and became Comptroller of Finances under his mad successor, Charles VI. He was a little, smooth-spoken, inoffensive man, who had the art of making friends; and few positions would have appeared in any tolerably well-governed state more firm and unassailable than his. He had two brothers invested with rich bishoprics, one of them also holding civil office, and rising to be Chancellor of France; while his daughters were married into the first families among the nobles of France below the rank of royalty.

Of course he had not neglected the opportunity which a supervisance of the wretched and ruined finances of the nation afforded him for enlarging and consolidating his own fortunes. He had enormous wealth to fall back upon should he ever be driven from office. In too fatal a reliance on the security of his position, he made an imprudent display of his worldly goods, on the occasion of the advancement of one of his brothers from the shabbyish bishopric of Poitiers to the brilliant see of Paris. Montagu resolved to give an entertainment, and to do the thing in style. The company who were invited and who attended proved at once his greatness and his popularity. The list of distinguished guests would dazzle the eyes of the most fashionable penny-a-liner of the 'Morning Post.' It included the King and Queen of France, the King of Navarre, and the royal dukes in a bundle. They were feasted from a service of gold and silver such as, it was significantly remarked, none of their own palaces could produce.

The magnificence of an entertainment is not always so exceedingly satisfactory to the entertained as the confiding landlord expects it to be. On this occasion one of the guests—John the Fearless, Duke of Burgundy—took offence at the profuse magnificence which surrounded him, and argued himself into the conclusion that it would more aptly become his own palace than the hotel of the parvenu.

A few days afterwards, when Montagu was decorously walking to morning mass with one of his bishop brothers, Pierre des Essarts the Prevôt of Paris crossed his path and laid a hand on his shoulder. The great statesman, highly indignant at such a familiarity, cried out, "Ribaud, es-tu si hardi que de me toucher?" but Essarts had a warrant, and in fact the affair was serious. Montagu was arrested and thrown into a dungeon in the Petit Chatelet. The next step was to get up a feasible accusation against him. Doubtless his methods of amassing money, like those of every other statesman of the day, would not stand a very severe scrutiny; but proceedings in this direction would be slow, petty, and inconclusive; and as any chance might turn the tables in the victim's favour, it was necessary to get up something more astounding, odious, and conclusive. He was therefore charged with sorcery and magic; and, to bring the accusation to a definite and practical conclusion, it was alleged that by these illegal arts he had produced the King's insanity. He was put to the torture, and, after giving his tormentors hard work, he confessed whatever they pleased. The instruments being removed, he retracted, and appealed to his dislocated wrists and wrenches of the body, ending in hernia, as the real causes of his confession. But he was in hands where his wealth, not the punishment of a guilty man, was wanted.

The affair had to be got over before the King should have a lucid interval; so the tortured mangled body was relieved of its miseries by the headsman's axe. The King, when the lucid interval came, was indignant at the usage his faithful servant had received: but there was no remedy. John the Fearless was not the man to loose his grip on what he had touched, and, unless the head could also have been restored to its old owner, how was restoration to be made of the estates?

It is one of the most significant marks of a Providence overruling the affairs of man, that such acts are calculated, in some shape or other, to retaliate on their doers. When the princes of the blood established practices of cruelty and perfidy, they were unable absolutely to exempt themselves, and establish as an unfailing rule that the consequent calamities should be restricted entirely to inferior persons. The Dukes of Burgundy and of Orleans, the King's nearest relations, were rivals for that supreme power which somebody or other must wield in the name of the madman. The former took a short way of settling the question. Orleans was murdered in the streets of Paris by the direction of Burgundy. The clergy and the savans of the day were called upon to applaud the deed as a wholesome act of tyrannicide. The opportunity was a good one for propitiating clerical influences. It was the time when rival popes were bidding for support, and stretching points with each other; so, what the one scrupled at, the other was delighted to oblige with. The sinuosities of the discussion on the slaughter of Orleans, influenced as they were by the duplex action of the Popedom and the oscillations of the two contending civil parties, would make an amusing history of ups and downs. To-day a consistory applauds the act as a service to God and the King—next a synod brings the consistory to task for maintaining a doctrine so revolting; and, anon, a higher authority justifies the consistory and rebukes the synod.

This affair caused great uneasiness throughout the whole privileged class of royal scions. Attacking and killing one of their own number in the open street was treating him no better than a common seigneur, or even a roturier. The Duke of Burgundy should not have acted so by one of themselves—it was an ungentlemanly thing. Upon the other hand, were he to be subjected to legal responsibility for what he had done, this would involve the admission that the royal class could be liable to the jurisdiction of the ordinary tribunals—an alternative too horrible and preposterous to be indulged in for a moment. Altogether the question was indeed in a fix.

The end illustrated the spirit expressed in the Psalms, "Bloody and deceitful men shall not live out half their days." The death of their leader did not immediately ruin the Orleanists, who continued the struggle under his relation the Count of Armagnac. Year after year went on the ceaseless contest, each up and down alternately, while their wild struggle crushed and ruined every surrounding object they came in contact with. Nor when Henry V. was thundering at the gate could they hear the warning voice of conquest over the horrid din of their own quarrels, or relax their hold of each other to turn an arm against the invader.

To be sure, they met and tried to come to an understanding. One meeting was held on an island in a small lake with a barrier across it, so that but few could be assembled on either side, and these few could not touch each other. The results of this meeting were not very satisfactory, but the next was more conclusive. It was held on the long bridge of Montereau, where the Yonne meets the Seine. A complex barrier was erected to obviate treachery. The Orleanists, however, had the last handling of it, and the Duke of Burgundy, with the small body of attendants admitted on the bridge, found themselves somehow face to face with the Orleanists, while a bar clicked behind them and cut off their communication. John the Fearless made the best of things, clapped his greatest enemy, Tanguy du Chatel, on the shoulder, and called him a good guarantee for his safety. As he knelt to the young Dauphin, the hilt of his sword incommoded him, and he touched it to move it aside. Those who surrounded him, waiting the first good opportunity for their work, pretended that they believed he was drawing his sword, and immediately hacked him to pieces. Comines drew from this incident the moral that rival kings and great heads of parties should not attempt to hold personal interviews. The temptation on such occasions to settle all old scores by a single *coup*, he counted too great for ordinary flesh and blood.

While such was the nature of things at the top of the social tree, to convey an impression of the wretchedness and degradation at its other extremity is beyond the power of general terms. The details themselves make the reader at last callous with their weary monotony of torture, starvation, and slaughter. The stories told to inflame the *sans-culottes* of the Revolution—how that a feudal lord coming home from the chase would rip up the *ventres* of a couple of serfs, and warm his feet in their reeking vitals—such things were no exaggeration of the reality, and, indeed, no imagination could exaggerate it. From the frequency with which whole districts are rendered pestilential by the thousands of dead, starved, or slaughtered, one wonders how the land kept up its population, and how the scanty remnant of inhabitants had heart to renew the race, and bring into the world fresh victims of such horrors. When Henry V. came over to make his conquest, his captains excited curiosity at first, until they knew better the habits of the country, by abstaining from an established practice both of Orleanists and Burgundians, which required that when any peasant had been caught, and compelled to act as guide, to bury the dead, or perform any enforced services, he should, when no longer of use, be stripped of any clothing worth removing, and then be hung up by the heels before a fire, where, whether with the refinement of basting or not, he was roasted until he gave the clue to any hoard of silver pieces he might have saved, or until he died, if he could or would give no such clue.

The English victories in the hundred years' war, which seem so astounding, are but natural results to those who are in the habit of contemplating, through contemporary documents, the abjectness of the French peasantry or villainage of the period. The great masses brought into the field were so far from being trained to war, either as soldiers of the crown or followers of their seigneurs, that they were denied the use of arms, unless when marshalled in an army. The English bow and bill men were, on the other hand, sturdy knaves, well fed, free within certain limits, and expert at handling their weapons. In fact, between them and their Norman masters, after the lapse of centuries, a sort of surly compact had been formed as between those who knew each other to be sterling stuff, for they were kindred in character, and had both sprung from the same hardy Scandinavian stock. The English bow and bill men were nearly as good as mailed men-at-arms; and one of these fully equipped and mounted was among a crowd of serfs like a ship of war in a fleet of fishing-boats—he could go about unharmed, slaughtering all he could come at, until he became tired. So little of common cause was there between them, that the French men-at-arms on some provocation would set to slaughtering among their starving crowd of followers, or would let the enemy do so without taking umbrage. The Captal of Buch gained great honour by a bloody attack on a large body of the Jacques, who were doing no creditable work, certainly, yet it was on his own side. In their great battles with the English invaders, the French men-at-arms were nearly as much occupied in chastising their own serfs as in fighting with the enemy; and at Agincourt the leaders would not condescend to act at the head of their men, but formed themselves into a separate battel, apart from the great mass, who became consequently a chaotic crowd, not only useless but detrimental. According to a very offensive practice of those chivalrous times, the chances of safety to a vanquished foe depended on what he was likely to fetch in ransom; in some instances a rich or royal captive was in danger from a contest among his captors for the monopoly of his capture and the corresponding ransom-money. Alas for the poor French serf! there was little chance of making anything of *him;* nor, in the distracted state of the country, was he worth preserving as a slave. He was put to the most valuable use when his carcass manured the ground on which he fell.

So much for the social condition of the French people during the early part of the hundred years' war with the English kings. To the political condition of France as a nation, and one of the European community, perhaps the best key may be found in the remark of Sismondi, that the contest was not in its origin a national one between France and England. It was a question of disputed succession, in which the competitors for the crown were the only persons ostensibly interested. The nobles took their side according to their calculations, founded on interest or connection, as the smaller European princes have done in the great wars of later times. As to the serfage, if they thought at all, the tendency of their thoughts would probably be that they could not be more miserable than they were, whoever was their king; and we may be pretty sure that they did not attempt to solve the question about the prevalence of the old Salic code within the soil of France. In fact, the invaders, accustomed to treat their neighbours at home as fellow-beings, were, as we have seen, kinder to the poor peasantry than their armed countrymen. But a conquering class or race will ever become insolent and exasperating; and, after a time, the oppression and insolence of the invaders sent the healthy blood of patriotism to the heart of the people, where it aroused that cohesive natural energy which swept the enemy from the land, and made France the great empire it became.

With the Scots, on the other hand, the war, though waged on French soil, was national from the beginning. It was thus the fortune of their allies to secure a body of men-at-arms who were not only brave men and thoroughly-trained soldiers, but who brought with them still higher qualities in that steadfast faith which had been hardened on the anvil of a war for national freedom. Nominally entering the French service as mercenary troops, there never were soldiers less amenable to the reproachful application of that term. Of all the various elements which a French army then contained—among the Italian and German hirelings—among native men-at-arms who had been fighting but the other day against their existing leader and cause, and might in a few days do so again—among the wretched serfage who were driven into the field and did not even know what side they were on—among all these, the Scots alone had a cause at heart. France was the field on which they could meet and strike the Norman invaders who had dealt so much oppression on their paternal soil, and had run up so long an account of injuries and cruelties ere they were driven forth. The feeling, no doubt, was an unamiable one, according to modern ethics. It came to nothing that can be expressed in gentler language than the Scot's undying hatred of his neighbour to the south of the Tweed. The many terrible incidents in the long war of Scottish independence testify the sincerity of this hatred. But as motives went in those days, it was among the most sterling and honest going, and served to provide the French kings with a body of men hardy and resolute, steady and true; and possessing so specially these qualities, that even Louis XI.—perhaps of all monarchs whose character is well known to the world the most unconfiding and most sceptical of anything like simple faith and honesty—was content, amid all his shifting slippery policy and his suspicions and precautions, to rely implicitly on the faith of his Scots Guard.

The English army had been twelve years in occupation. Agincourt had been fought, the infant heir of the house of Lancaster had been proclaimed at Paris with the quiet decorum that attends the doings of a strong government, when Scotland resolved to act. In 1424, John Stewart, Earl of Buchan, arrived in France with a small army of his fellow-countrymen. Accounts of the numbers under his command vary from 5000 to 7000. This seems but a small affair in the history of invasions, but, looking at the conditions under which it was accomplished, it will turn out to be a rather marvellous achievement. It is only necessary to look at the map of Europe to see that from whichever side of our island the Scots attempted to approach France, they must pass through the narrow seas in which England even then professed to have a naval superiority. A steamer now plies from Leith to Dunkirk for the benefit of those who prefer economy and a sea voyage to a railway journey; but from the union of the crowns down to the establishment of that vessel a year or two ago, the idea of going from Scotland to France otherwise than through England would have been scouted. The method of transferring troops, too, in that period, was by galleys, rowed by galley-slaves, little better than mere rafts for sea-going purposes, and ever requiring in foul weather to hug the shore. Scotland could not have afforded vessels to transport this force ; it was taken in hand by France, Castile and Aragon offering, as we are told, to assist with forty vessels.

Henry V. of England, then ruling in France, naturally felt the seriousness of an infusion of such fresh blood into the distracted and ruined country ; and he instructed his brother, the Duke of Bedford, acting as viceroy, to put on the screw at all the English seaports, and do whatever the old traditional prerogatives of the crown, in purveying vessels and seamen, was capable of doing, in order that a force might be raised to intercept the Scots expedition. Bedford lost the opportunity, however. The Scots troops debarked at La Rochelle, and, passing towards the valley of the Loire, encamped at Chatillon.

These rough northern foreigners were not received by the natives without invidious criticism. Two or three instances occur in which the simple parsimony of the commissariat of the Scots camp has astonished the people of more luxurious countries. But it became a second nature with the wandering man-at-arms to bear enforced starvation at one time, and compensate it by superfluous indulgence at another. The Scots probably took their opportunity in a country which, desolated though it was by warfare, was a Garden of Eden after their own desolate bogs, and they earned for themselves the designation of *sacs à vin et mangeurs de moutons.*

But an opportunity occurred for wiping off such a reproach. The Scots and some French, all under the command of Buchan, approached the old town of Baugé, in Anjou, on one side of the stream of the Cauanon, while Clarence and the great English host were encamped on the other. The Scots, just in time to save themselves, discovered their danger. The English were crossing the river by a narrow bridge when Buchan came up and fought the portion of the army which had crossed over. As M. Michel remarks, it was the same tactic that enabled Wallace to defeat Surrey and Cressingham at Stirling—it might also be described as a seizing of the opportunity that was afterwards so signally missed at Flodden. Then took place one of those hand-to-hand conflicts, in which the highest-spirited and best-mounted knights of the age encountered in a mingled turmoil of general battle and single combat. The great host meanwhile struggled over, and was attacked in detail. It was a victory attended, from its peculiar conditions, with more than the average slaughter of the conquered. In the words of Monstrelet, "The Duke of Clarence, the Earl of Kyme (?), the Lord Roos, Marshal of England, and, in general, the flower of the chivalry and esquiredom, were left dead on the field, with two or three thousand fighting men."

Henry V. was naturally provoked by a defeat that so strongly resembled those he had been accustomed to inflict; and his anger, sharpened by grief for the death of his brother, tempted him into one of those unworthy acts which great conquerors sometimes commit when thwarted by defeat. He had then in his possession the young King of the Scots, James I. With his consent, or in his name, an instruction was issued to the Scots army no longer to fight in the cause of France against England. Buchan protested that the orders of a monarch not at freedom were of no avail. Henry then thought fit to treat the Scots as rebels, not entitled to the courtesies of war. To make the case more clear, he took his captive to France. James was in the English camp when Melun was taken, and therefore Henry hanged twenty Scotsmen found among the garrison. On the surrendering of Meaux, too, there were especially excluded from the conditions of the capitulation all the Welsh, Irish, and Scotch—as if all these were alike rebels.

It is generally said that Buchan got the baton of High Constable of France as a reward for the victory of Baugé, though Monstrelet speaks of him as Constable when he fought it. At all events, he held this high office—an office so very high that his poor countrymen at home cannot have easily seen to the top of it. We are told that, in court precedence, it ranked next after the blood-royal; that an insult to the holder of it, being equivalent to one on royalty itself, was similarly punished; and that he was the highest military authority in the kingdom, having at his disposal all its warlike resources—the commander-in-chief, in short. Moreri, who tells us this, also, to be sure, tells us that when a king of England dies, the lord mayor of London acts as interim king until another is fairly settled on the throne; but it is to be presumed that Moreri had a better knowledge of the practices on the banks of the Seine than of those on the banks of the Thames. In this country we are familiar with the title chiefly through the great names coupled with it—the Constable de Luxemburg, the Constable Montmorenci, Du Guesclin, and the terrible Bourbon. Among such names, to stumble on the Constable Buchan sounds quite homely, as we say in Scotland. The constabulary was considered too formidable an office to be always full, and seems to have been reserved for emergencies, like the Roman dictatorship; and that hour of emergency and of destitution of native spirit must have been dark indeed, when its highest dignity, and also the custody of the honour of the nation, were together conferred upon a stranger. The dignity was balanced by princely domains and castles stretching over the territory between Avranches and Chartres. These the new-comer seems to have almost taken into his own hand, for the French authorities speak of his putting himself in possession of the castle at Chartres after the battle of Baugé.

After that battle Buchan was joined by his father-in-law, Archibald Earl of Douglas, who brought with him a reinforcement of four or five thousand Scots. Douglas, among other honours and substantial rewards, was invested with the great dukedom of Touraine. There was almost a rivalry in the royal munificence to the two leaders, and their followers were not forgotten, as we shall afterwards see; but they left on bloody battle-fields a record that their honours and emoluments were well paid for, and but briefly enjoyed. Though Baugé had taught the wholesome doctrine to the French that their enemies were not unconquerable, and had put the house of Valois in sufficient heart to renew the struggle, it was yet uphill work. In the battle of Crevant in 1424 the Scots were the chief sufferers. In one brief sentence Monstrelet testifies to their devotedness, and narrates their fate: "The English and Burgundians won the day and the field; the greater part of the Scots, amounting to three thousand, who were in the front ranks, were either killed or taken."*

The remnant of the Scots auxiliaries, though thus thinned and weakened, bore the chief weight of the bloody battle of Verneuil a year afterwards.† This is one of the many battles in which defeat has been attributed to misunderstandings and mistakes among allies, for there were there men of three nations on one side—French, Lombards, and Scots. Wherever the blame lay, the penalty was paid by the Scots, of whom all but a few lay dead where they fought. It has been said that their fate was of their own seeking, for, on meeting face to face with their mortal enemies of England, they sent Bedford a message that they would neither spare nor be spared—neither give nor take quarter.‡ Buchan,

---

* 'Monstrelet,' by Johns, vi. 48.

† Siamondi says of the marshalling of the French army, "Les Ecossais, qui faisoient le nerf de leur armée."—xiii. 34.

‡ "Un écrivain contemporain, se faisant l'écho d'un bruit répandu à l'époque, signale la fierté écossaise comme la principale cause du désastre de Verneuil, qu'il considère comme un événement heureux pour la France : 'Les Écossais,' dit-il, 'sont d'habitude ardents et solides au combat, mais téméraires et fiers à l'excès.' Puis, après un récit sommaire de cette journée, il continue ainsi : 'C'était un spectacle affreux à contempler que celui des monceaux de cadavres entassés et pressés sur ce champ de bataille, là surtout où la lutte avait eu lieu avec les Écossais ; car pas un d'eux ne fut épargné à titre de captif. . . . . La cause de cet acharnement et de ce carnage sans merci fut la fierté des Écossais : avant l'engagement, le Duc de Bedford leur

the High Constable, and Douglas, the Duke of Touraine, were found among the dead. They had not given their lives an utterly vain sacrifice to the cause of their adoption. Though Verneuil is counted among the English victories, it had no resemblance to the sweeping triumphs of Crecy, Poitiers, and Agincourt. It was so tough an affair, and was so near to the defeat of Bedford and Salisbury, that they became really alarmed about the stability of the supremacy of the house of Lancaster in France.

We cannot rightly estimate the influence over the destinies of Europe of the events which severed Scotland from England and allied her to France, without remembering that it was long the aim of every powerful European monarch to follow the example of Charlemagne, and restore the Roman Empire. People have been so much occupied in discussing the religious hierarchy bequeathed to the world by the old Empire, that they seem to have forgotten how much of its political organisation remained to influence mankind. Roman institutions, in fact, live and influence our everyday habits and customs, and many of our greatest political organisations have their root in the established practice of

---

ayant envoyé demander quelles seraient les conditions du combat, ils répondirent qu'ils ne voulaient pas, ce jour-là, faire de prisonniers aux Anglais, ni que les Anglais leur en fissent; réponse qui, en allumant contre eux la fureur de l'ennemi, les fit exterminer.' "—Michel, i. 148, quoting from Meyer, 'Annales Rerum Belgicarum.'

the Empire. It is there, for instance, that we shall find how, in European diplomacy and international law, there are rules obeyed by nations, obligations performed by them, and rights exacted by them, without any paramount authority to enforce obedience. The paramount authority existed once in the person of the Emperor of the world; and though it has departed, the practices and traditions which kept the various states of Europe together have remained in force, and have been worked by "the great powers," who may be said to hold the functions of the old Empire in a sort of commission. It is observable that at the present day the established rules of diplomacy have scarcely extended beyond the bounds of the old Empire, except by including Russia; but though the greater part of the Russian territory was beyond the pale, there is no court in Europe where the traditions of the Empire are so religiously maintained as in that of Russia—where, indeed, the ambition which made the monarchs of the middle ages aim at the restoration of the empire of the world is believed still to guide the policy of the house of Romanoff. We cannot get the Oriental nations to accept of our system of diplomacy, except by sheer force. An ambassador they count an intruder and a spy, and they preserve no treaty which they can break. Even in the American States, where diplomacy and international law are studied more than anywhere else, it seems impracticable to apply those old traditional rules called the laws of war and peace, which have kept Europe together.

The municipalities which have so deeply influenced the history of Europe are a section of the institutions of the Empire. There are towns whose existing governments were given to them by the Cæsars; and it was a signal testimony to the vitality of these institutions, that in the late reconsolidation of Italy they formed the means of dovetailing together the fragments which had been so long separated. In some countries the Justinian collections are the only absolute authorities in the law—in all they have more or less a place. In England even, for all the abuse it has met with from the common lawyers, the civil law has an acknowledged place in Equity, the Ecclesiastical Courts, and the Admiralty jurisdiction; and large masses of it have, surreptitiously and under false names, been brought into the sacred precinct of the common law itself. It would be difficult to say of the laws which adjust rights and obligations between man and man in England, whether one would find a greater quantity in the Statutes at Large than in the Pandects.

The political machinery of the Imperial system, though broken into fragments, remained in its several parts so compact and serviceable for centuries as to be available for consolidating the power of Napoleon. It may easily be understood, then, how readily it would serve any monarch of the thirteenth or fourteenth century who felt strong enough to use it. Hence these monarchs were not merely excited by vague notions of influence and conquest with indefinite results, but saw a distinct, recognised office, supreme among worldly monarchies in dignity and power, which had been held of old, and might be aspired to again, as a legitimate object of ambition. The double-eagle in the achievement, figurative of the conjoined empires of the East and of the West, indicates powers which have some time or other aspired at the empire of the world—at renewing the conditions under which Cæsar could decree "that all the world should be taxed."

It is curious to see how the newly-grown feudal system, with its fictions and pedantries—its rights of property and possession, for instance, as separated from its rights of superiority—aided the influence of the Imperial organisation in the hands of clever and vigilant princes. A troublesome territory would be handed over by a great king to some smaller neighbour, who, nearer the spot, was better able to govern it, and who, if it were not handed over to him, might take it. He came under obligation to do homage for it to the giver, but the practical result of this obligation would depend on subsequent events. If generation after generation of his house were gradually acquiring such fiefs, they might soon possess a power sufficient to defy the feudal superior. On the other hand, the practice of doing homage for a part of their possessions might taint a decaying house with the sense of inferiority, and bring them in at last for homage for the whole. When Edward I. summoned Baliol to come to Windsor and give account of his conduct, and when that same Edward was himself cited by Philip of France to kneel before him and answer for certain piracies committed by Englishmen, the feudal formalities were the same, but behind them were certain realities which made the two affairs very different. Thus Europe presented to the able and ambitious among her monarchs two kinds of apparatus of aggrandisement. In the one, a vassal house, gaining fief after fief, would work its way to the vitals of a monarchy, and extinguish its life; in the other, a great power would crush one by one its smaller neighbours, by gradually enlarging the prerogative of the lord paramount.

Whoever would wish to see this sort of game played with the most exquisite skill and the most curious turns of luck, should study closely the history of the absorption of Burgundy into France. In our own country the play was more abrupt and rough. It was handled with a brute force, which succeeded in Ireland and Wales, but drove Scotland to effective resistance. The significance of this resistance was not limited to this island. The Normans were then bearing it with a high hand over all the nations of Europe. If the Empire was to be restored, he who should be chief among the Norman rulers would be the man to restore it. Had Henry V. been King of all Britain, it would have been the most natural of effects to such a cause that he should also have been undisputed King of France; and with such a combination of powers in his hand, what was to prevent him from being the successor of Charlemagne? The battle of Bannockburn was the ostensible blow which broke this chain of events. It was not the only interruption which Norman aggrandisement had then to encounter. Only twelve years earlier than Bannockburn, the Flemings had gained a popular victory over the chivalry of France at Courtrai; within a year after the defeat of Edward, the Swiss bought their independence in the terrible battle of Morgarten. The coincidence is not purely incidental. The three battles were types of a general revulsion against Norman aggrandisement arising in the hearts of the oppressed in various parts of Europe.

As part of an empire which included France and Scotland, with whatever else so much power might enable its owner to take, it is hard to say how it would have fared with the liberties of England, governed perhaps from Paris rather than London; and some have thought that the enjoyers of these liberties owe a debt to the victors at Bannockburn.

Everybody has heard of the famous Scots Guard of France. The same authorities that carry back the League to the days of Charlemagne, make him the founder of this force. It is a pity that we have no distinct account of its origin, and can only infer from historical probabilities that Claude Fauchet is right in saying that it was formed out of that remnant of the Scots who survived the slaughter at Verneuil, and did not desire to return home.* If Charles VII. was not the founder of the Guard, it is pretty certain that he adjusted its organisation as a permanent institution of the French Court. This easy, lucky monarch was so thoroughly the parent of the Scots Guard, that they wept for him in a demonstrative manner, which induced an old chronicler to say—

> "Et les Escossoys hault crioient
> Par forme de gemissement."

The Scots Guard consisted of one hundred gensdarmes and two hundred archers. They had a captain who was a high officer of state. The first captain of the Guard who appears in history—and probably the first person who held the office—was John Stewart, lord of Aubigné, the founder of a great Scots house in France, of which more hereafter. By a chivalrous courtesy the appointment to this high office was confided to the King of Scots. This was an arrangement, however, that could not last. As the two nations changed their relative position, and the Guard began to become Scots only in name, it became not only out of the question that the captain should be appointed by a foreign government, but impolitic that he should be a foreigner. It is curious to notice a small ingenious policy to avoid offence to the haughty foreigners in the removal of the command from the Scots. The first captain of the Guard who was a native Frenchman,

* 'Origines des Dignitez et Magistrats de France,' p. 39.

was the Count of Montgomery, who, for his patrimonial name, which corresponded with that of an old Scots family, passed for a man of Scots descent. It was thought prudent that his son should succeed him; but the selection was not fortunate, for he was the same Montgomery who hit King Heury II. at the jousts in honour of his daughter Elizabeth's marriage to Philip II., and so made Mary Stewart Queen of France.

According to the old courtly creed of France, the privileges of the Scots Guard had an eminence that partook of sacredness. Twenty-four of them were told off as the special protectors of the royal person. They took charge of the keys of the chamber where the King slept, and the oratory where he paid his devotions. When, on a solemn progress, he entered a walled town, the keys were committed to the custody of the captain of the Guard. They guarded his boat as he crossed a ferry, and were essential to the support of his litter when he was carried. On ordinary occasions two of them stood behind him; but in affairs of great ceremony—the reception of embassies, the conferring high honours, the touching for the king's evil, and the like—six of them stood near the throne, three on either side. It was deemed a marked honour to them that the silk fringe with which their halberts were decorated was white—the royal colour of France.

There is something melancholy beyond description in contemplating the condition of a country, the vital treasures of which had to be confided to the fidelity and bravery of hireling strangers. If there was a fault in the affair, however, it was not with the Scots: they were true to their trust, and paid faith with faith.

On their side of the bargain, too, there is something touching in the picture of a hardy high-spirited race robbed of their proper field of exertion at home, and driven to a foreign land, there to bestow the enterprising energy that might have made their own illustrious; and serving a foreign master with the single-minded fidelity that had been nourished within them by the love of their own land and kindred. But it must be admitted that their hospitable patrons made their exile mighty comfortable. When the lank youth left behind him the house of his ancestors, standing up grey, cold, and bare, on the bleak moorland, it was not to pass into hard sordid exile, but rather to exult in the prospect of a land of promise or Eldorado: and faithfully was the promise kept; for the profuse hospitality and lavish generosity of France to her guests is a thing hardly to be elsewhere paralleled in history. It was but just that it should all be requited with sound fidelity and ardent devotion.

The trust which Louis XI. reposed in the Guard has been already referred to. It was not their blame that he took their assistance in grubbing up the roots of all the political institutions which checked or modified the supreme authority of the Crown. If we were to suppose, indeed, that they passed beyond the routine of duty to think of the political results of the affairs in which they were engaged, they would find a good many partisans in the present day, had they adopted the designs of their crafty master as their own, and backed them as the soundest policy for the future of France and of Europe at large; for Louis XI. is by no means championless.

In one of the most amusing of all the chronicles ever written—that of Comines—the Scots Guard figure frequently, and always creditably. Louis, who was reputed to trust no other creatures of human make, appears to have placed entire reliance on them. They saved him at a crisis of great peril in his renowned attack, along with the Duke of Burgundy, on the city of Liĕge. Both potentates were deeply plotting—the one to bring the Burgundian territories directly under the crown of France, the other to change his dukedom for a kingdom, which might in the end comprise France itself. Both were of one mind, for the time, in deadly malice and murderous projects against the industrious burghers of the city. By a concurrence of events which broke through the fine texture of his subtle policy, Louis found himself in the hands of his fierce rival; for he was within the lines of Burgundy's army, with no other resource or protection apparently but his Scots Guard. There was to be a storming of Liĕge, which was anticipated by the citizens breaking out and attacking the camp of the Duke. In the confusion of such an affair at such a juncture, it is easy to suppose that Louis could not know friends from enemies, and had reason to believe the enemies to be far the more prevalent of the two. Comines gives this distinct and homely narrative of what he saw of the affair, for he was present :—

"I, and two gentlemen more of his bed-chamber, lay that night in the Duke of Burgundy's chamber (which was very small), and above us there were twelve archers upon the guard, all of 'em in their clothes, and playing at dice. His main guard was at a good distance, and towards the gate of the town; in short, the master of the house where the Duke was quartered, having drawn out a good party of the *Lièegeois*, came so suddenly upon the Duke, we had scarce time to put on his back and breast plate and clap a steel cap upon his head. As soon as we had done it, we ran down the stairs into the street; but we found our archers engaged with the enemy, and much ado they had to defend the doors and the windows against 'em. In the street there was a terrible noise and uproar, some crying out, 'God bless the King!' others, 'God bless the Duke of Burgundy!' and others, 'God bless the King, and kill, kill!' It was some time before our archers and we could beat the enemy from the doors and get out of the house. We knew not in what condition the King was, nor whether he was for or against us, which put us into a great consternation. As soon as we were got into the street, by the help of two or three torches we discovered some few of our men, and could perceive people fighting round about us; but the action there lasted not long, for the soldiers from all parts came in thronging to the Duke's quarter. The Duke's landlord was the first man of the enemy's side that was killed (who died not presently, for I heard him speak), and with him his whole party (at least the greatest part of them) were cut in pieces.

"The King was also assaulted after the same manner by his landlord, who entered his house, but was slain by the *Scotch* Guard. These *Scotch* troops behaved themselves valiantly, maintained their ground, would not stir one step from the King, and were very nimble with their bows and arrows, with which, it is said, they wounded and killed more of the Burgundians than of the enemy. Those who were appointed made their sally at the gate, but they found a strong guard to oppose them, which gave 'em a warm reception and presently repulsed 'em, they not being so good soldiers as the others. As soon as these people were repulsed, the King and Duke met, and had a conference together. Seeing several lie dead about them, they were afraid their loss had been greater than really it proved to be; for upon examination they found they had not lost many men, though several were wounded; and without dispute, if they had not stopped at those two places, and especially at the barn (where they met with some small opposition), but had followed their guides, they had killed both the King and the Duke of Burgundy, and in probability would have defeated the rest of the army. Each of these princes retired to his quarters greatly astonished at the boldness of the attempt; and immediately a council of war was called to consult what measures were to be taken the next morning in relation to the assault, which had been resolved upon before. The King was in great perplexity, as fearing that if the Duke took not the town by storm, the inconvenience would fall upon him, and he should either be kept still in restraint, or made an absolute prisoner, for the Duke could not think himself secure against a war with France if he should suffer him to depart. By this mutual distrust of each other one may clearly observe the miserable condition of these two princes, who could not by any means confide in one another, though they had made a firm peace not a fortnight before, and had sworn solemnly to preserve it." *

French historians are tolerably unanimous in their testimony that the Guard were faithful fellows. As a small select body of men, highly endowed with rank and remuneration, they were naturally the prizeholders of a considerable body of their countrymen, who in the army of France strove to prove themselves worthy of reception into the chosen band. Thus the Scots in the French army carried the spirit of the service beyond the mere number selected as the

* 'Memoirs of Philip de Comines,' book ii. chap. 12.

Guard; and there was among them a fellow-feeling, mixed with a devotion to the crown of France, of a kind which there is no good term for in English, while it is but faintly expressed by the French *esprit de corps.* A few of the facts in the history of the Scots troops employed by France bring it closer home than any generalisation can; for instance, after other incidents of a like character, M. Michel quotes from D'Auton's Chronicle, how, in a contest with the Spaniards in Calabria, in 1503, the banner-bearer, William Turnbull, was found dead with the staff in his arms and the flag gripped in his teeth, with a little cluster of his countrymen round him, killed at their posts, "et si un Ecossais était mort d'un côté, un Espagnol ou deux l'étaient de l'autre." The moral drawn from this incident by the old chronicler is, that the expression long proverbial in France, "Fier comme un Ecossais," was because the Scots "aimaient mieux 'mourir pour honneur garder, que vivre en honte, reprochez de tache de lascheté.'"

When the two British kingdoms merged towards each other in the sixteenth century, the native element was gradually thinned out of the Scots Guard. When Scotland became part of an empire which called France the natural enemy, it seemed unreasonable that her sons should expect to retain a sort of supremacy in the French army. But there are no bounds to human unreasonableness when profitable offices are coming and going, and many of our countrymen during the seventeeth century were loud in their wrath and lamentation about the abstraction of their national privileges in France. Some Scotsmen, still in the Guard in the year 1611, had a quarrel with the French captain, De Montespan, and brought their complaint before King James. As French soldiers appealing to a foreign monarch, they were very naturally dismissed. Of course, they now complained at home still more loudly, and their cause was taken up by some great men. The French behaved in the matter with much courtesy. The men dismissed for a breach of discipline could not be replaced at the instigation of a foreign Court, but the Government would fill their places with other Scotsmen duly recommended. So lately as the year 1642, demands were made on the French Government to renew the ancient League and restore the "privileges" of the Scots in France, including the monopoly of the appointments in the Guard. But though made in the name of King Charles I. by the Scots Privy Council, these demands were, like many of the other transactions of the day, rather made in hostility to the King than in obedience to his commands. Louis XIV. gave a brief and effective answer to them. He said that he would renew the League only on the condition that the Scots should cease to act as the ally of England, either by giving obedience to the King of that country, "or under pretext of religion, without express permission from the King, their master"—a pretty accurate diplomatic description of the position of the Covenanting force.*

Down to the time when all the pomps and vanities of the French crown were swept away along with its substantial power, the Scots Guard existed as pageant of the Court of France. In that immense conglomerate of all kinds of useful and useless knowledge, the 'Dictionnaire de Trevoux,' it is set forth that "la première compagnie des gardes du corps de nos rois" is still called "La Garde Ecossaise," though there was not then (1730) a single Scotsman in it. Still there were preserved among the young Court lackeys, who kept up the part of the survivors of the Hundred Years' War, some of the old formalities. Among these, when the *Clerc du Guet* challenged the guard who had seen the palace gate closed, "il repond en Ecossois, I am hire—c'est à dire, me voilà;" and the lexicographer informs us that, in the mouths of the Frenchmen, totally unacquainted with the barbarous tongue in which the regimental orders had been originally devised, the answer always sounded, "Ai am hire."

In some luxurious libraries may be found a gorgeous volume in old morocco, heavily decorated with symbols of royalty, bearing on its engraved title-page that it is "Le Sacre de Louis XV., Roy de France et de Navarre, dans l'Eglise de Reims, le

---

* See 'Papers relative to the Royal Guard of Scottish Archers in France:' Maitland Club, 1835.

Dimanche, xxv. Octobre, MDCCXXII." After a poetical inauguration, giving assurance of the piety, the justice, the firmness, the devotion to his people, of the new King, and the orthodoxy, loyalty, and continued peace that were to be the lot of France, with many other predictions, wide of the truth that came to pass, there come a series of large pictures, representing the various stages of the coronation, and these are followed by full-dress and full-length portraits of the various high officers who figured on the solemn occasion. Among these we have the Capitain des Gardes Ecossois in full state uniform. This has anything but a military aspect; it is the single-breasted broad-flapped coat of the time, heavily embroidered, a short mantle, and a black cap, with a double white plume. The six guards are also represented in a draped portrait. It is far more picturesque than that of their captain, yet in its white satin, gold embroidery, and fictitious mail, it conveys much less of the character of the soldier than of the Court attendant, as will be seen by the inventorial description given below.* In the original engrav-

* "Un habit de satin blanc; par dessus une cotte d'armes en broderie d'or. Sur le corselet, les armes de France, surmontées d'un soleil, avec le devise: le tout brodé en cartisanne d'or sur un fond de trait d'argent, formant des mailles; les manches et basques de la cotte d'armes brodées en or, sur un fond blanc; un chapeau blanc, garni d'un bouquet de plumes blanches à deux rangs; la partuisanne à la main."

ing, by the way, the artist has thrown an air of absorbed devotedness into the very handsome countenance drawn by him, which is at variance, in some measure, with the tone of the attitude and costume, as pertaining to a mere figure in a state pageant.

Chapter II.

Personal Anecdotes of the Scots Immigrants—The Wolf of Badenoch's Son—The Albany and Darnley Stewarts—The Hamiltons and Douglases—Investment of the Scotch Duke of Touraine—Notices of Scotsmen settled in France, and the Families founded by them—The Settlement of the Scots compared with that of the Normans.

THE arrival of the Scots auxiliaries, the battles in which they were engaged, and the formation of the Scots Guard from the remnant, make an episode in history which I have thought it best to keep by itself. There were constant migrations, however, of Scotsmen to France, from the commencement of the Hundred Years' War downwards, and I now propose to give a few characteristics of the men who went thither, of the reception they met with, and of the destinies of their descendants.

King Robert III. had a younger brother Alexander, who was made lieutenant of the northern part of the kingdom. His royal birth and breeding were insufficient to control the temptation of using his opportunities to collect a Highland following, and setting them to their natural work, which was mischief. He became, of course, the terror of all the well-disposed within the district he was set to rule over, and they complimented him with the title of "The Wolf of Badenoch." He set his eye on some lands on the Spey belonging to the Bishop of Moray, and sent a few hundreds of his galley-glasses to take possession. The bishop had recourse to his own peculiar artillery, and excommunicated the Wolf. One would have thought this mattered little; but besides being the wolf beyond the Grampians, Alexander Stewart was prince and courtier at Holyrood, where the condition of excommunication carried with it many social inconveniences, not to speak of the insolence of the prelate, who dared to cast such a slur on a man of his condition. He therefore, to give the bishop a foretaste of what might follow, sent down a few handy lads to the plains of Moray, where they burnt the choir of the church of Forres and the house of the archdeacon. As this had not the desired effect, he collected a larger force of ruffians, and, descending on the Lowland like an avalanche, fell on the episcopal city of Elgin and burned its noble cathedral. This was going rather too far. The Wolf had not only to disgorge, but to propitiate the Church with gifts, and do penance until the Pope set him right by absolution. His ashes repose in the Cathedral of Dunkeld, where may be seen his recumbent effigy, with arms folded, in serene peace looking to another world, while, in a Gothic inscription, the forgiving Church records that here lies Alexander Stewart, Lord of Buchan and Badenoch, of good memory.

This worthy had a favourite illegitimate son, also called Alexander. He, as was natural, followed his father's footsteps, and collected a troop of bare-legged ruffians, who rieved and ravaged far and near. The Lindsays, Ogilvies, and other gentlemen of Angus, resolved to put a stop to this, and collected a body of men-at-arms and Lowland bowmen, a sort of force which held the Highland caterans in utter scorn as a set of rabble to be swept before them. The Wolf cub, however, alighted on the tactic which, in later times, made a Highland force terrible—a concentrated rush on the enemy. This the small body of Lowlanders caught on the rugged banks of the Isla, and they were at once swept away, mail-clad horsemen and all, before the horde of savages they had despised. A little incident in this battle is thus described by a bard who might have been present, and probably had it from an eyewitness. Sir David Lyndsay, trying to make head against the torrent as a mounted man-at-arms, had trodden several of the Highlanders down, and had one of them pinned to the earth with his long lance. Thereupon, in the words of old Wyntoun,

> "That man held fast his own sword
> Into his nieve, and up thrawing
> He pressed him, not again standing
> That he was pressed to the earth;
> And with a swake there of his sword,
> Through the stirrup-leather and the boot
> Three ply or four, above the foot,
> He struck the Lyndsay to the bone.
> That man no stroke gave but that one,
> For there he died." *

Nestling in a valley close to the mountain-range where the father and son held rather a roving commission than a right either of property or government, stood the Castle of Kildrummy. As its ruins still attest, it was not one of those grim, gaunt, starved-looking square towers which the impoverished nobility of Scotland were fain to hide themselves in, but a vast and beautiful Gothic fortress erected in the time of the great war of independence, probably by the English. This desirable residence the youth set his eye on; so with

---

* Scott could not but see the value of such an incident in heroic narrative, and accordingly, in the 'Lord of the Isles,' he brings it in at the death of Colonsay's fierce lord:—

> "Nailed to the earth, the mountaineer
> Yet wreathed him up against the spear,
> And swung his broadsword round;
> Stirrup, steel boot, and cuish gave way
> Beneath that blow's tremendous sway."

his Highland host he stormed and took it. It belonged to the widowed Countess of Mar. The country was not so absolutely without any nominal law that territory could be acquired in this way; at all events, it was prudent to have the military title of conquest fortified by some civil formalities to prevent future cavilling. The victor, therefore, married the widow, obtaining from her a conveyance of her property to himself and his heirs.

Some formalist having probably put him up to the notion that the transaction, as it stood, was still open to question, a second deed bears record how that the husband resigned the whole property back to the wife, and in token thereof approached the castle, and humbly placed the key in her hand, telling her to take possession of the castle, the furniture therein, and the title-deeds of the domain; whereupon she gave the whole back to be enjoyed by her husband and the heirs of the marriage. Still again the dread of the red-tapism of the day haunted the prudent marauder, and a scene occurred which must have been exceedingly amusing to all concerned. In presence of the Bishop of Ross and of the feudatories of the domain, assembled in general council in the fields beyond the walls of the Castle of Kildrummy, the Countess again executed an investiture of her husband in all her estates and properties, especially including those of which she was unjustly deprived, a gift which opened up indefinite fields of enterprise to so active a husband. The deed is so profuse in its attestations of the perfect freedom and absence of all restraint and intimidation wherewith the Countess acted, that one's suspicion would naturally be raised even without a knowledge of the antecedents.

Such was the career of one who afterwards made a brilliant figure at the Court of France. His reception there, or rather the position he took up, is recorded in his homely rhymes by the contemporary Wyntoun; and as M. Michel adopts his account, so may we. Here it is, with the spelling a little modernised, as in the preceding passage from the same rather wordy chronicle:—

"The Earl of Mar passed in France,
In his delight and his pleasance,
With a noble company
Well arrayed and daintily,
Knights and squires—great gentlemen,
Sixty or more full numbered there,
Men of council and of virtue,
Of his court and retinue.
In Paris he held a royal state
At the Syngne, knowen the Tynny Plate,*
All the time that he was there
Biding, twelve weeks full and mare,
Door and gate both gart he
Aye stand open, that men might se (so)
Enter all time at their pleasance
Til eat or drink, or sing or dance."

The Earl of Mar—for he was now firmly established in that dignified position—took part with some com-

* M. Michel calls it Plat d'Etain.

panions-at-arms of the best blood in Scotland, at the battle of Liège, fought on the 14th of September 1407 : it was one of the contests in which the Duke of Burgundy had to back the Prince-Bishop against the powerful corporation of that almost sovereign city. M. Michel cites an old French chronicler, a good pendant to Wyntoun, who, after Messieurs Guillaume Hay, and Jacques Scringour, and Helis de Guenemont, expands concerning the feats of other heroes, whose names, slightly disguised, will readily be recognised by their countrymen.

> "Sire Alexandre en son droit nom
> De Commech, qui ot cuer entier,
> Ce jour y fut fait chevalier,
> Et Messire Andrieu Stievart
> Fu chevalier de belle part.
> De Hay sire Guillebert
> Fut ce jour en armes appert,
> Com bon et hardi combattant.
> Sire Jehan de Sidrelant
> Doy bien en honneur mettre en compte,
> Car il est fiz d'un noble conte.
> Sire Alexandre d'Iervin,
> Qui le cuer ot humble et benin,
> En ce jour monstra hardie chiere;
> Et cil qui porta la baniere
> Du conte qui est tant prisiez
> Ce fu sire Jehan de Miniez."

Here are many familiar Scots names, some of them, it is true, a little disguised. Guenemont is Kinninmond, the name of a good old stock sometime decayed, and now, it is believed, unrepresented in Scotland, though it is supposed to be alive both in

Sweden and France. Sidrelant is Sutherland, and Miniez Menzies, the laird of that territory which bears the queer-sounding name of Pitfoddles. De Commech is puzzling, but M. Michel boldly transposes it into Keith. Alexandre d'Iervin, who represents the true knight of chivalry—a lamb at home, a lion in the field—is the same who gets like praise in the rude Scots ballad which details so accurately the great battle of Harlaw:—

> "Gude Sir Alexander Irvine,
> The much-renowned Laird of Drum,
> Nane in his days was better seen,
> When they were sembled all and some,
> To praise him we should not be dumb,
> For valour, wit, and worthyness,
> To end his days he there did come,
> Whose ransome is remeediless."

The same companions-at-arms, indeed, who fought with him in Flanders, followed Mar to victory in the great battle of Harlaw. The Continental campaign had therefore a great influence on British history. There, doubtless, the Scots knights obtained that consciousness of the prowess of trained, mail-clad men-at-arms, which prompted them with confidence and success to fight a host many times as large as their own. That critical day brought to an end what our common historians call the Rebellion of Donald of the Isles. The question it really decided was, whether the representative of the Norse race, which had founded an empire in the islands and western Highlands, should continue to be an independent monarch, ruling Scotland as far as the Forth,—and perhaps as far as the English border.

Here the roystering leader of ragamuffins, coming home with his foreign experience, became a mighty general and sage statesman; and like many others who pass from disreputable into creditable and profitable courses, he achieved the suppression of those who, while he was sowing his wild oats, were his companions and tools.*

Most conspicuous and illustrious among the emigrants to France were those who belonged to the royal race of Stewart: and here let me offer an explanatory protest for spelling the name in this unfashionable manner. It is the old Scots spelling, the other—namely, Stuart—having been gradually adopted in deference to the infirmity of the French language, which is deficient in that sinewy letter—a half-breed between vowel and consonant—which we call W. This innovation stands in the personal nomenclature of our day, a trivial but distinct relic of the influence of French manners and habits over our ancestors.

For all their illustrious birth, these Stewarts went

---

* It is curious to find the demure Fordun from his quiet cell, in dog Latin gently referring to the indiscretions of this hero's youth, as in contrast with the honoured decorum of his other years, thus—*In juventute erat multum indomitus et ductor catervanorum*—that is to say, of caterans or Highland thieves. But afterwards *in virum alterum mutatus placenter trans montes quasi totum aquilonem gubernabat.*

forth like the others, wandering unfortunates, with no hold upon the world but that which their heads and hands, and perhaps the lustre of their descent, gave them, and in the end they rooted themselves as landed Lords and Princes. John Stewart, Earl of Buchan, the High Constable, whose deeds and fate have been already recorded, was a son of the Regent Albany, and grandson of King Robert II. Alexander Stewart, Duke of Albany, a brother of James III., cuts a rather ugly figure in the history of his own country. He set up as king, calling himself Alexander IV., and agreed to do homage and acknowledge the old supremacy of England if Edward IV. would assist him, and make his nominal title a reality. After a rather adventurous life he went over to France. His antecedents did not in the least prejudice the tolerant heart of Louis XI. against him; on the contrary, he was a man very much after that monarch's own heart. He acquired great lordships in France, and thoroughly assimilated himself to the Continental system. He married Anne de la Tour, daughter of the Count of Auvergne and Boulogne, of a half-princely family, which became afterwards conspicuous by producing Marshal Turenne, and at a later period the eccentric grenadier, Latour d'Auvergne, who, in homage to republican principles, would not leave the subaltern ranks in Napoleon's army, and became more conspicuous by remaining there than many who escaped from that level to acquire wealth and power.

The sister of Anne de la Tour married Lorenzo de Medici, Duke of Urbino. From this connection Albany was the uncle of Catherine de Medici, the renowned Queen of France, and, in fact, was that nearest relation, who, as folks used to say in this country, "gave her away" to Henry II. On this occasion he got a cardinal's hat for Philip de la Chambre, his mother's son by a second marriage. He lived thoroughly in the midst of the Continental royalties of the day, and had the sort of repute among them that may be acquired by a man of great influence and connection, whose capacity has never been tried by any piece of critical business—a repute that comes to persons in a certain position by a sort of process of gravitation. Brave he seems to have been, like all his race, and he sometimes held even important commands. He accompanied his friend, Francis I., in his unfortunate raid into Italy in 1525, and was fortunately and honourably clear of that bad business, the battle of Pavia, by being then in command of a detachment sent against Naples. His son, a thorough Frenchman, became afterwards Regent of Scotland; but though he acted in the way of legitimate business, he was not, as we shall find, a much better friend to his country than his father had been. Well scolded as they have been through all legitimate history, it has been the fortune of M. Michel to show that to the Albanies Scotland owes a boon which would have gone far to retrieve their character a century ago—the use of and taste for French wines. This specialty as a national taste is not even yet dead; for every Englishman who gets at good tables in Scotland, remarks on the preference for the French wines over those of Spain and Portugal, although, until the other day, the duties, which in old Scotland had been greatly in their favour, were rather against the French. The following details about the commerce of the Scots in France seem interesting.

"During his residence in France, the Duke of Albany occupied himself actively, as it would appear, in favour of the Scotch merchants trading in our country, all the more that they were undoubtedly commissioned by the nobility. His efforts were crowned with success; and Francis I. gave at Amboise, in the month of May 1518, an order to free these foreigners from the dues to which foreign merchandise was subjected at Dieppe, the usual place of their disembarkation; which, however, did not prevent fresh demands on the part of Scotland some years after.

"What commodities could the Scotch bring to our country?

"Probably the same which they sent to Flanders, and of which we have a list in the great book of Andrew Halyburton, one of the first merchants of his time, who filled the high office of Conservator of the Privileges of the Scottish Nation in the Low Countries—or, as we should now say, Scottish Consul—at Middleburg. There was, in the first place, salmon, which came even to the inland towns, such as Reims, where a municipal order of 1380 regulated the sale of it; then herrings, cod, and other fish, for the common people; lastly, wool, leather, and skins.

"Afterwards this catalogue increased so much that a rhymer of the seventeenth century could say to a courtier—

'Tury, vous quittez donc la cour,
Pour vous jeter dans le negoce:
Ce n'est plus celui de l'amour,
Mais celui d'Espagne ou d'Escosse.'

Spain and Scotland, it seems, were the countries in which commerce was most lucrative, as there also seems reason to believe that the Spaniards and the Scotch were the foreigners best known in France, when we find another poet make an actor say—

'Je passe quand je veux, bien que je sois Français,
Tantôt pour Espagnol, tantôt pour Escossois.'

"In exchange for the goods which they brought us, the Scotch received from us the products of a more advanced civilisation, not only by regular commerce, but by diplomacy, the agents of which, as it seems, had the privilege of bringing in goods free of tax. On the 8th May 1586, Henry III. wrote to M. de Chateauneuf, his ambassador at the Court of Elizabeth: 'I beg of you also to mention to her the depredation which some of her subjects have committed near Dieppe on a Scotch vessel, which was returning to Scotland, in which there were, to the value of sixteen hundred crowns, wines, silken cloths, sugar, spices, and other things which the said Sire Esneval had caused to be purchased, and was having carried for his use into Scotland, by one of his people named Captain James. They had the cruelty to remove the sails of the said vessel, and to leave it and also another Scotch vessel at the mercy of the wind and sea; but God helped them so much that they were thrown up on the coast by the reflux of the tide there, where they were known and succoured.'

"The place occupied by wines in this enumeration of goods destined for Scotland shows the importance of the consumption of them by our allies in the sixteenth century. Even in the thirteenth, Henri d'Andeli describes the Scotch and some other Northern nations as drinking abundantly of the wines of La Rochelle; and in the following century Froissart shows us their ships coming into the port of Bordeaux to load with wine, at the risk of being captured in going out of the river, as happened under rather singular circumstances related by Cleirac, who supposes the master of a Scotch vessel, laden with wine for Calais, in connivance with Turkish pirates. A letter of James IV. to the first president of the parliament of Bordeaux—recommending to him the affair of his subject George Wallace, master of the ship Volant, seized for theft imputed to Robert Gardiner and Duncan Campbell—tells us that in

1518 the Scotch continued to come in quest of our wines, and did not always behave themselves in an exemplary manner.

"We know by President de Thou, that in his time, towards the end of the sixteenth century, Scotch wine-merchants came annually to Bordeaux; and we have a decree of the Council of State of the 3d June 1604, granting indemnification of 18,000 livres to John Anderson and John Williamson, Scotch merchants, from whom they had confiscated two hundred tons of wine at Havre." *

The Darnley branch of the Stewarts had a destiny in France which belongs to European history. Sir John Stewart of Darnley was one of Buchan's heroes, and fought at Baugé and Crevant, where he was wounded and taken. He was exchanged for the Earl of Suffolk's brother, Lord Pole. He was rewarded with the lands and lordships of Aubigny, Concressault, and Evereux, with the privilege of quartering the arms of France on his achievement. In 1427 he visited his own poor country in great state, with no less a function than that of ambassador from the Court of France. His mission was to negotiate a marriage between Louis the Dauphin and Margaret of Scotland. A year afterwards he and his brother were both killed in battle before Orleans, and were laid together in the cathedral of that memorable city. John Stewart's representa-

* Michel, i. 357-361.

tives merged all their other titles in that of Lennox, which his marriage brought to the family. The fifth in descent from him, Mathew Earl of Lennox, who succeeded to the title in 1526, served under the French banner in the Italian wars, and though he hardly reached historic fame, is recorded in the books of genealogy as that respectable personage "a distinguished officer." Coming to Scotland in all his foreign finery, he made love to Mary of Guise, the widow of James V., a pursuit in which, by the oddest of all coincidents, he was the rival of the father of that Bothwell who settled all questions of small family differences by blowing his son into the air. This Lennox achieved, as every one knows, a more fruitful alliance with royalty through a daughter of Margaret, the sister of Henry VIII.

Returning to Sir Alexander Stewart, we find that his second son, John, founded a great house in France. The titles of John's son and representative, Bernard, were, "Viceroy of Naples, Constable of Sicily and Jerusalem, Duke of Terra Nova, Marquis of Girace and Squillazo, Count of Beaumont, D'Arcy, and Venassac, Lord of Aubigny, and Governor of Melun." * He commanded the army of Charles VIII. which invaded Naples, and gained the victory of Séminara, an achievement which Sismondi thus describes :—

"D'Aubigny, who commanded in Calabria, re-

* Douglas's 'Peerage,' ii. 93.

solved to arrest the progress which King Ferdinand was making in his territories, seconded by Gonzalvo of Cordova; and although he could not collect more than 400 mounted men-at-arms, twice the number of light cavalry, and a small body of Swiss infantry, he crossed the river between Terra Nova and Séminara before the enemy, and attacked them on the opposite bank, although their number was at least three times as great as his. The Calabrians, who had forced Ferdinand and Gonzalvo to accept the battle, did not wait for the first attack, but fled as soon as they saw the French advance. Ferdinand would have been taken had not John of Altavilla given him his horse, at the sacrifice of his own life: he was killed shortly after. Gonzalvo, Hugh of Cordova, Emmanuel Bénavides, Peter de la Paz, Spanish captains who all, at a later period, became famous at the expense of the French, would have been taken prisoners the following night in Séminara, if D'Aubigny, who was enfeebled by the Calabrian fevers, and sick all the time during which he was fighting, had been able to attack that town immediately. The gates were opened to him the next day." *

Seven years later he was overpowered by numbers, and had to capitulate on the same spot; so that there is occasional confusion in history about the battle of Séminara, which is sometimes spoken of as a victory by, and sometimes as a defeat of, the

* Sismondi, 'Hist. des François,' ch. xxvi.

French. Between these two conflicts there were many gallant feats of which he was the hero; and he was as renowned for gentleness as for bravery. He was the companion of Bayard, and his rival in fame as a chivalrous soldier.* He died at Corstorphine, near Edinburgh. One of the recumbent stone figures in the picturesque little Gothic church of that village is reputed by tradition to represent the great Lord of Aubigny, Marischal of France; but heraldry does not confirm this.

Next to the royal family of Scotland in France were the houses of Hamilton and of Douglas, who at times almost rivalled them at home. The French dukedom of Chatelherault is a name almost as familiar in history as the home title of the Hamiltons. By the side of the Scottish Constable of France rode a countryman scarcely less powerful—the lord of the vast province of Touraine, which had been conferred on the gallant Douglas. It may interest some people to read an official contemporary account of the pomps and ceremonies, as also of the state of public feeling, which accompanied the investiture of the territory in its new lord. It is clear from this document that the people of Touraine took with signal equanimity the appointment of a foreigner from a distant land to rule over them.

"Four days after the date of the letters-patent,

---

* "Le Sire d'Aubigny dont la loyauté etoit célébrée dans tout le royaume de Naples."—Sismondi, ch. xxix.

the news of the change which they celebrated reached Tours. Several ecclesiastics, burghers, and inhabitants assembled in alarm in the presence of Jehan Simon, lieutenant of the Bailli of Touraine, William d'Avaugour, and charged Jehan Saintier, one of their representatives, and Jehan Garnier, King's Sergeant, to go to Bourges, to William de Lucé, Bishop of Maillezais, and to the Bailli, to learn whether the King intended to give and had actually given the Duchy of Touraine to the Earl of Douglas, of the country of Scotland; and, if it was true, to beg of them to advise the said churchmen, burgesses, and inhabitants, what course they ought to pursue, and what was to be done in the circumstances, for the honour and advantage of this town of Tours and country of Touraine.

"The which Jehan Saintier and Garnier brought back for answer, that the said nobles above mentioned said to them that it was true that the King has given the said Duchy of Touraine to the said Earl of Douglas, and that they should not be at all alarmed at it, and that the people of the said Tours and country of Touraine will be very gently and peaceably governed; and that before the said Earl of Douglas shall have, or shall go to take possession of the said Duchy, the King will send letters to the said churchmen, burgesses, and inhabitants, and each of his officers commissioned to make over to him the said possession, and that my Lord Chancellor and the said Bailli would in a short time be in the said town, the which would tell them at greater length what they had to do in the circumstances, and the causes by which the King had been moved to give him the said Duchy; and also the said Saintier and Garnier brought the copy of the letter of gift of the said Duchy to the said Earl.

"As soon as they knew at Tours that the King had given the Earl of Douglas the Duchy of Touraine, and that the new Duke was preparing to set out to take possession of it, they assembled at the Hôtel de Ville to consider whether they would go to meet this stranger, and whether they would make him the customary presents, which consisted of six pipes, that is twelve barrels, of wine, six measures of oats, fifty sheep, four fat oxen, and a hundred pounds of wax in torches.

"They deputed two churchmen and four of the most considerable citizens to go to Loches to compliment the Duke in name of the town, and they formed a company of mounted burghers to go to meet him. Having found him at a certain distance from the town, it accompanied him till his arrival at Tours, into which he made his entry on the 7th of May, by the gate of Notre Dame la Riche. There he was received by the four representatives of the town, and by all the burgesses, in arms. Martin d'Argouges, principal representative, spoke on presenting him the keys, and begged of him to maintain the inhabitants in their privileges, franchises, and liberties. The Duke promised, and the representatives took note of his consent, by three notaries, whom they had brought for the purpose. The Duke having then taken the keys, restored them immediately to the first representative. Then he entered the town, where he was received by the people with acclamation. The streets were hung with tapestry and strewed with flowers. He went straight to the cathedral, at the great door of which he found the archbishop and all the canons in canonicals. The dean presented to him a surplice, an amice, and a breviary. The Duke, having taken the oaths at his hands, was received as a canon, and installed in the choir in presence of Louis of Bourbon, Count of Vendome, grand chamberlain of France; of John of Bourbon, his brother, Prince of Carency; of Francis of Grigneux; and of several other noblemen. Next day he went to the church of St Martin, where he was similarly received as honorary canon. After these ceremonies he established his cousin, Adam Douglas, governor of the town and castle of Tours, according to his letters of the 27th May. The inhabitants, after deliberation by their representatives, made a present to the new governor of two pipes of wine and a measure of oats." *

So ends the history of the public inauguration of Douglas in his Duchy of Touraine, the extent of which one may see by looking at any old map of

---

* Extrait des Déliberations Municipales de la Ville de Tours—Michel, i. 139.

France in Provinces. Another ceremony, however, awaited him ere long. He paid for his honours with his gallant blood. He and the Constable Buchan were laid down together in one grave in the chancel of the cathedral church of Tours, the capital of his domain.

Passing from the great houses which were royal, or nearly so, the researches of M. Michel have brought out a vast number of Scotsmen of the more obscure families, whose condition was materially improved, to say the least of it, by migration to La Belle France. Conspicuous for his good fortune among those who had reason to lament the kindly King Charles VII., was Nicholas Chambers, écuyer d'ecurie du roi, who, in 1444, obtained the seigneury of Guerche, in Touraine, the district of the Douglases. Then follow certain Coninglants, Coigans, Coningans, Cogingands, and Conyghans, clustered together as variations on Cunningham ; to these are set down certain gallant achievements, escapes, and fatalities, but nothing very specific for the genealogist, until one of them is run to earth in acquiring the lands of Arcenay, in Burgundy, by union with the heiress, Martha of Louvois. After this the family is traced through many distinguished members to the first Revolution, when it disappears; but it reappeared, it seems, in 1814, and is supposed still to exist.

In tracing the alliances of the Lords of Arcenay, another Scots family of like origin turns up in the marriage of one of them to Marguerite de Humes, daughter of Jean de Humes, Seigneur de Chĕrisy. This Jean's mother was the daughter of a Guillaume Stuart, supposed to be of Scots origin; and his grandmother, before her marriage to his grandfather Humes, had been the widow of a George de Ramsay, "probablement Ecossais lui-même," as M. Michel says.

Next come the Quinemonts or Kinninmonds, also established in Burgundy and Touraine. Their estate in Touraine alone may stand as a sample of the lists, long to tediousness, of the domains attached to the names of Scots families by the French heralds. They were Seigneurs "de Saint-Senoch, de la Roche-Aymer, de Varennes, des Cantelleries, de Baugé, de la Guénerie, de la Houssière, de Vaugué-rin, de Paviers," &c.

Next in order comes La Famille Gohory. To them L'Hermite-Souliers dedicates a chapter of his 'History of the Nobility of Touraine,' wherein he derives them from the Gori of Florence; but M. Michel triumphantly restores them to their true distinction as Scots Gorrys or Gowries.* Among the noble houses of Touraine, follows that of Helye Preston de la Roche Preston, married to Dame

* Perhaps Gorsæus may be a variation of the same name, but this is merely a guess. Johannes Gorsæus, a celebrated physician in Paris, left a posthumous work, published at Frankfort in 1578, called 'Definitionum Medicarum Libri xxiiii.' It is in the form of a dictionary, the heads under which each matter is treated having the peculiarity of being

Eleanor Desquartes, eminent in its own province from its nobility, and illustrious as the stock of the great Descartes. It is questioned whether the husband was a son of Edward Preston, who took to wife Pregente d'Erian, or of Laurent Preston, married to another daughter of the same house. These Erians seem to have had a decided partiality for the bonny Scots, since the widow of Edward Preston married the Seigneur of Ponceau and La Menegauderie, who, having been an archer of the Scots Guard under the name of De Glais, is with reasonable probability supposed to have been a Douglas from Scotland; while another daughter is allied to the Seigneur de la Guenaudière, named Mauriçon, supposed to be a form of Morrison. There are still among other branches of the D'Erian race "plusieurs alliances avec des gentilshommes Ecossais de la garde du roi." One falls to Guillaume Dromont or Drummond, another to Guillaume le Vincton—the nearest approach which French spelling and pronunciation can make to Swinton, though one might think it more akin to Livingston. Another is destined to Henri de Crafort or Craufurd, Sieur de Longchamp et de la Voyerie.

Passing from the husbands of the D'Erians, the

---

in Greek. It professes to deal with all knowledge connected with medicine, but medicine at that time was discursive over all nature; and, in fact, the book—which is a bulky folio—may be considered one of the earliest scientific cyclopædias.

next Scot endowed by marriage is André Gray, a name that speaks for itself. There are two noble archers of the Guard called Bourtic—probably they were Bourties, the difference being a clerical error rather than a corruption; and these are followed by a group of distinguished Livingstons converted into Lévistons.

Passing into Champagne, we have the coats armorial and some genealogical particulars of the houses of Berey, D'Handresson, Locart, Tournebulle, and Montcrif—the origin of these is obvious. The last was probably an ancestor of that Moncriff who shines so brilliantly among the wits of the Grimm and Diderot school—one of the forty immortals of the Academy, and a popular dramatist. The next name does not so obviously belong to us—Val-Dampierre—and one can only take M. Michel's word for it. It may perhaps be resolved into its familiar original by a process such as that applied to its owner's neighbour as a great territorial lord in the land of vineyards—namely, the Sieur Devillençon. When we go back a step to Vullençon, and then to Villamson, something not unfamiliar dawns upon us, and at last we are landed in the homely surname of Williamson—very respectable in many instances, but distinguished among ourselves by no greater celebrity than that of poor Peter Williamson, who was kidnapped and sold as a slave in the plantations, whence he escaped to tell his adventures to the world.

It is quite delightful to see how this ordinary plant flourishes and blooms in Champagne. According to traditions of the family, collected by La Chenaye-Desbois, Thomas Williamson, second of the name, archer of the Guard in the reign of Charles VIII., was allied to the royal house of Stewart. This may be true, but it was a current *mot* among the French of old that every Scotsman was cousin to the king. Whatever they may have been, however, the Williamsons or D'Oillençons, with many territorial branches, clustered round "les terres de Saint-German-Langot, de Lonlai-le-Tesson, et de la Nocherie." They preserved their highly characteristic native motto, "Venture and win," which had, no doubt, been their guiding principle from generation to generation. Their blazon, too, is ambitious, and strange to behold: a double-headed eagle, like the Austrian, grasping in its claws something like a small beer-barrel; in scientific language—a spread eagle argent, membered and beaked, poised on a casquet of the same, hooped argent.

It would be easy to cull similar particulars about the house of Maxuel, Herisson, or Henryson, metamorphosing itself into D'Arson; Doddes or Dods; Estud from Stud, a name now scarcely known among us; the De Lisles, viscounts of Fussy, who are identified with our northern Leslies; Vaucoys, which is identified with Vauxe or Vans; Lawson, which turns itself into De Lauzun; D'Espences or Spences, who further decorate their simple native surnames with the territorial titles, De Nettancourt, de Bettancourt, de Vroil and de Villiers-le-Sec, de Launoy-Renault, de Pomblain, de Ville Franche, de St Sever, and many others. Surely the Spences, left behind in cloudy, sterile Scotland, ploughing sour moorlands, or drawing meagre profits from the retail counter behind the half-door of the burgh town, would have found it hard to recognise their foreign cousins fluttering thus among the brilliant noblesse of sunny France.

The changes, indeed, which our harsh, angular surnames undergo to suit them to the lazy liquid flow of the French utterance, are such as to give tough and tantalising work to the genealogical investigator; and it is difficult to appreciate the industry which M. Michel has bestowed in the excavation of separate families and names from the great mass of French genealogical history. We all know the lubricity of the French language at this day in the matter of names, and how difficult it is to recognise the syllables of one's own name even where it is read off from one's own visiting-card, if the reader be a Frenchman. Such a name as Halliday is easily reclaimable, even though its owner may flame in the territorial patronymic of Vicomte de Pontaudemer. Folcart and Le Clerk are resolvable into Flockhart and Clerk. In deriving D'Anglars from Inglis, however, as others have done, M. Michel acknowledges that the circuit is considerable, if not impracticable: "La distance nous paraît trop grande pour qu'un rapprochement soit possible." The name of William Stuyers, too, puts him at defiance, although in an old writ he is mentioned as an officer of the Guard, and designed a "natif du royaume d'Escosse." Sinson is, without much stretching, traced to Simpson. The name Blair appears in its native simplicity, only attaching itself to the titles Fayolles and L'Estrange, in preference to the territorial titles of Pittendriech or Balthayock enjoyed by the most eminent members of the house in Scotland. Wauchop transposes itself into Vaucop and Vulcob. Perhaps, however, the respectable but not dignified name of Monypenny owes the greatest obligation to change of climate. Even in its own original shape, when transferred to a country where it does not signify a large store of copper coinage, it floats down the mellifluous flood of the noblesse quite naturally in company with the territorial titles of Varennes and Concressant; but when altered into Menypeny, it might return home, as indeed it did, in the possession of a French ambassador, without risk of detection. The change is but slight, and shows how much may be accomplished by the mere alteration of a letter in removing vulgar and sordid associations.

Another remarkable type of the Scots emigrant families is that of Blackwood. It suffers little more by transference than the necessary remedy for the want of the w, in which it partakes with the royal house of Stewart. The French Blackwoods were of the later Scots emigrants fleeing from the Reformation, and their rewards in the country of their adoption were rather from offices than from lands. It would be difficult to find the distinction between the territorial aristocracy and the noblesse of the Robe better exemplified than in comparing the fortunes of the Blackwoods with those of the other families just spoken of. Adam Blackwood, the head of the house, held a judicial office which gave him the title of Conseiller au siège de Poitiers. His grandfather fell at Flodden. His father had been killed in the wars of Henry VIII., probably at Pinkie, when he was ten years old, and his mother died soon after, a widow broken-hearted. The boy, tended by relations whose religion gave them more influence in other countries than at home, was sent early abroad. He became a thorough Frenchman, studying at Paris, and spending his days at Poitiers. He was a champion of the old Church and the divine right of kings, and wrote with the controversial vehemence of the age against the opinions promulgated by Buchanan in his 'De Jure Regni apud Scotos.' But that for which he chiefly claims remembrance is his 'Martyre de la Royne d'Escosse, Douairiere de France,' &c., with an account of the "mensonges, calomnies, et faulses accusations dressées contre ceste tresvertueuse, trescatholique et tresillustre princesse." It is most easily to be found in the reprint of tracts on Queen Mary, by Jebb. Blackwood hit the key-note of that kind of chivalrous rejection of sublunary testimony, and deification of the accused, which have characterised the subsequent vindicators of Queen Mary's innocence; and there is in his resolute singleness of purpose, and energy of championship, the charm which, when one can forget the facts, pervades the writings of this class. Blackwood married Catherine Courtinier, daughter of the Procureur du Roi of Poitiers. She bore to him four sons and seven daughters—a progeny so abnormal in France, that it induces M. Michel to express admiration at his continuing the pursuit of letters, "malgré ses devoirs de magistrat, d'époux, et de père." He published a collection of pious meditations in prose and verse, of which M. Michel tells us that, paying a visit to London, where he was presented at court, King James showed him a copy of his 'Meditations' in the royal library. One of Blackwood's sons became a judge at Poitiers. His son-in-law, George Crichton, was professor of Greek "au collége de France." His brother Henry taught philosophy in the University of Paris; another brother, George, "fit un chemin assez brillant dans l'église de France."

This was a method of enrichment which could not give a territorial hold to a family; and whether it was from a distaste towards acquisitions which could not be made hereditary, or to difficulties in the way of a foreigner rising in the Church, it is observable that the ecclesiastical is the department in which the Scots took the least portion of the good things going in France. Yet some of them drew considerable temporal prizes in the profession which deals with our eternal destiny. A certain priest named John Kirkmichael, or Carmichael, seems to have had an eventful history, of which but the outline remains. As he is said to have escaped from the carnage of Verneuil, it is to be presumed that he fought there, and was not in orders. But he afterwards became Bishop of Orleans, and is known in French ecclesiastical history as Jean de St Michel. It is a question whether it is he who established in his cathedral church the *messe écossaise* for his countrymen slain at Verneuil. The great Cardinal Beaton, Bishop of Mirepaux, was an ecclesiastical prince in France, whence great portion of his lustre was reflected on his own poor country. His nephew James, a far worthier man, had a different career, spending his old age in peace among his French endowments, instead of coming home to fall in the wild contests of his native land. He was employed as Queen Mary's ambassador in France, and continued ever faithful to her cause. He saw, as the shadow of the change of rule and religion in his own country, a like change come over the fortunes of the Scot in France. His countrymen were now no longer adventurers seeking the region best fitted for pushing their fortunes, but poor refugees seeking bread or a place of hiding and refuge. Yet a gleam of patriotic feeling came over the old man when he heard from his retirement that the son of his old mistress—heretic though he was

—had succeeded to the broad empire of Britain; and he caused fire on the occasion certain *feux de joie* at St Jean de Lateran.

Several of the Kennedys, predominant among the hard-fighting clans near the Border, obtained distinctions in France, where the sharp contour of their name was smoothened into Cenedy. Thomas de Houston is pleased to accept from Louis XI. the seigneury of Torcy in Brie, in place of the châtellenie of Gournay, which he resigns. Robert Pittilloch, a Dundee man, seems to have first entered the service in the humblest rank, and to have worked his way up to be captain of the Guard, and to enjoy the nickname of Petit Roi de Gascogne, along with a more substantial reward in the lordships of Sauveterre. One could go on at great length with such an enumeration, but it is apt to be tiresome. This is not intended as a work of reference or a compendium of useful knowledge, and I must refer the reader who, either for historical or genealogical purposes, wishes to find all that is known about the settlements of the Scots families in France, to go to M. Michel's book.

The names and titles thus casually brought together, will serve to show how thoroughly reviving France was impregnated with good Scots blood. The thorough French aristocratic *ton* characterising the numerous territorial titles enjoyed by the adventurers, may strike one who meets the whole affair for the first time as mightily resembling the flimsy titles by which men of pretension beyond their caste try to pass themselves off for somebodies. But everything about these Scots was real and substantial, in as far as the fortunes they achieved were the fruit of their courage and counsel, their energy and learning. The terrible slaughter among the French aristocracy in the English battles made vacancies which came aptly to hand for the benefit of the enterprising strangers, and of course they could not do otherwise than adopt the custom of the country, with its complex system of territorial titles, in which men's proper names got swamped and buried, in so far that half-a-dozen Frenchmen, all brothers born of the same father and mother, will be commemorated under names totally distinct.

It was during the hundred years' war that this colony, as it might almost be termed, of Scots settled in France. The affair bears a striking resemblance to the influx of Northmen, or Normans, five hundred years earlier, with this grand distinction, that these came as enemies and depredators, seizing upon their prey, while the Scots came as friends and champions, to be thankfully rewarded. The great similarity of the two migrations is in the readiness with which both sets of men settled down, assimilating themselves with the people. The assimilation, however, was not that of slave or follower in the land of adoption—not even that of equal, but partook of leadership and guidance. Both were received as a sort of aristocracy by race and caste; and hence it came to be a common practice for those who were at a loss for a pedigree to find their way to some adventurous Scot, and stop there, just as both in France and England it was sufficient to say that one's ancestors came in with the Normans.

Colbert, who has left his mark on history as the most powerful of financiers, when he became great, got the genealogists to trace his family back to the Scots, as many a man in England, on rising to distinction, has spanned over intervening obscurities and attached his pedigree to a follower of the Norman. The inscription, indeed, on his Scottish ancestor's tomb will be found in Moreri—

> "En Escosse j'eus le berceau,
> Et Rheims m'a donné le tombeau."

Molière professed Scots descent, to cover, as the invidious maintained, the vulgarity of the sound of his paternal name of Poquelin. A mystery worth clearing up surrounds a suggestion sometimes made about the great Sully, that he professed relationship with the Beatons of Scotland to bring him rank. What makes such hints appear rather invidious is, that he claimed for his own family of Bethune a lustre which could get no aid from Scotland. He arrogated descent for it from the house of Austria, and specifically warned the public against the supposition that he meant the existing imperial house of Hapsburg, whose ancestors were but private gentlemen a century or two ago—*his* ancestors were of the old reigning house. There seems, however, to have been some hitch in his pedigree; for, in the notes to the common editions of his memoirs, allusion is made to a process "unjustly" disputing his right to bear the name of Bethune, in which a writer on his side mentions his connection with the Beatons of Scotland;* and M. Michel cites from a standard genealogical and heraldic authority the dictum that the Bethunes were of Scottish origin.† So little, by the way, did Sully know of the geographical relations of the archbishop, that he speaks of his diocese of Glasgow as a place in Ireland.

To return to the comparison with the Normans. Sir Francis Palgrave set all his learning to work with sedulous diligence to find out some of the antecedents, in their own northern land, of the illustrious houses

* Memoirs, book vi.

† "Bethun, originaire d'Ecosse, mais établi en France: écartelé, au 1 et 4 d'argent, à la fasce de gueules, accompagnée de trois macles de même; au 2 et 3 d'or, au chevron de sable, chargé en chef d'une hure de sanglier d'argent." From Saint Allais, 'Armorial Général des Familles Nobles de France.' (Michel, ii. 136). To the accomplished herald there will be much suggestive both in the identities and the marks of difference between this blazon and that of the head of the Scots family of Beaton: "Quarterly, 1 and 4 azure, a fesse between three mascles or; 2 and 3 argent, on a chevron sable an otter's head erased of the first." —Nisbet's 'Heraldry,' i. 210. The mascle, by the way, is supposed to be a peculiarly French symbol, being taken from a kind of flint found in Bretagne. Nisbet remarks that it had been sometimes mistaken for the lozenge.

of Normandy and England, but without success; all was utter darkness, as if one had passed from the unsetting sun into the arctic winter. The failure was more instructive than many a success. It showed emphatically how those brilliant adventurers, the Frenchest of the French, had cast their chrysalis when they spread their wings in the new land of their adoption. And somewhat similar it seems to have been with our Scots, who at once take their place with all proper national characteristics in the fastidious aristocracy of the most polished people in the world, preserving no traces of the influence of their native bogs and heaths and hard upbringing, and equally hard uncouth phraseology.

On one point, however, the Scots must have differed from their Scandinavian prototypes—they must have owned to pedigrees, whether fairly obtained or not. The specialty of the Northmen, on the other hand, at the commencement of their career, appears to have been to abjure pedigree with all its vanities, and start as a new race in competition with the old worn-out aristocratic Roman world. The old world professed to despise the rough barbarians of the new; but these gave scorn for scorn, and stood absolutely on their strength, their daring, and their marvellous capacity to govern men. It is among the most singular of social and historical caprices, that the highest source to which, in common estimation, a family can be traced, is that which is sure to come to a stop at no very distant date. Of families not Norman it may be difficult to trace any pedigree beyond the era of the Norman migrations; but of all Norman houses we know that the pedigree stops there absolutely and on principle. The illimitable superiority assumed over the rugged adventurers by the great families of the old world seems not to have rested so much on the specific pedigree of each, as on the fact that they were of the old world—that their roots were in the Roman empire—that they belonged to civilisation. But so utterly had the historical conditions here referred to been inverted in popular opinion, that it was usual to speak of the house of Hanover as in some way inferior to the Stewarts, who, in reality, were mere mushrooms beside the descendants of the Guelphs.

It would be too heavy a responsibility for the most patriotic among us to guarantee the unexceptionable respectability and good conduct of all those countrymen of ours who built up their fortunes under the auspices of our munificent ally. It would be especially perilous to guarantee that they all held that social position at home which they asserted and maintained abroad. All the world knows how difficult it is to adjust the equivalents of rank between nations, and to transfer any person from one social hierarchy into his exact place in another. There are specialties social, hereditary, and official, to be dealt with, some of them having nothing equivalent in the other hierarchy,—some with the same name, but a totally different meaning,—others fictitious or casual in the one, while they have a fixed, distinctive, even legal meaning in the other. To interpret, but far oftener to confuse, these difficult and distracting elements of identification, there are the variations in etiquette, in domestic usage, in costume, in physical condition and appearance, which would all teach towards a certain conclusion were men omniscient and infallible, but lead rather to distraction and blunder in the present state of our faculties. It was one of Hajji Baba's sage observations, that in England the great personages were stuck on the backs of the carriages, while their slaves or followers were shut inside to prevent their escape. How many people, supposing that, in a solemn, bearded, turbaned, and robed Oriental, they have had the honour of an interview with some one of princely rank, have been disgusted with the discovery that they have been doing the honours of society to a barber or a cook!

There are some Eastern titles of mysterious grandeur which are yet far from impressing the auditor with any sense of dignity in their mere sound—as, for instance, Baboo, Fudky, Maulvee, and the like. There is the great Sakibobo, too, of tropical Africa; how would his title sound at a presentation? and how can we translate it into English? To come to Europe, what notion of feudal greatness do we imbibe by hearing of the Captal of Buch, the Vidam of Amiens, the Ban of Croatia, and the Stavost of Olxstern? To come nearer home still, what can

Garter or Lion make of the Captain of Clanranald, the Knight of Kerry, The O'Grady, and The O'Donoghue? Is it not on record that a great Highland potentate, having in Paris presented a card bearing that he was Le Chef de Clandonochie, was put in communication with the chief of the culinary department of the hotel where he visited? Even some of the best established and most respectable titles have difficulty in franking themselves through all parts of the country. Has not an Archbishop of York been suspected of imposture on presenting his check on a Scotch bank with the signature of Eborac? and have not his countrymen had their revenge on the Scots Judges and their wives, when Mrs Home travelled in charge of Lord Kames, and Lord Auchinleck retired with Mrs Boswell? We may see, in the totally different uses of the same term, how subtle a thing titles are. The Sheriff of Mecca, the Sheriff of London, and the Sheriff of Lanarkshire, are three totally different sorts of personage, and would be troubled how to act if they were to change places with each other for a while. It is said to depend on niceties in its use whether the Persian Mirza expresses a Prince or a mere Mister. But, after all, where can we go for a greater social puzzle within the compass of three letters than in our own Sir, which is at once the distinctive form of addressing royalty, the exclusive title of knightship, the common term which every man gives another in distant polite communication, and an especial form of expressing haughty contempt, when communications are not intended to be polite?

There being thus, in fact, in titles of all sorts, considerable room to come and go upon, it is probable that the Scots adventurers made the best of the very considerable number of rather empty titles scattered over their barren acres. An instance of their assumption has been recorded as a flagrancy. A certain Monteith of obscure origin having got access to Richelieu, the Cardinal asked him which family of Monteiths he belonged to. As the story goes, remembering that his father was a fisherman on the Forth, he said he was "Monteith de Salmonnet;" and the anecdote is verified by the existence of a solid folio volume, first printed in French and afterwards translated into English, being a history of the civil wars of Britain in the seventeenth century, by Robert Monteith de Salmonet—a title as emphatic and distinct as that of the proudest De Chateau Rouge or De la Tremouille. But even this audacious case is not entirely beyond vindication. The right to a cast of a net was a feudal privilege or servitude inheritable by the head of the family, like any seignorial right; and, in a country where people spoke of the succession to the hereditary gardenership of the lordship of Monteith, it was not necessarily an act of flagrant imposition to make something dignified out of the piscatory privilege.

The history of almost every man's rise in the world consists of a succession of graspings and holdings—of positions taken up timidly and uncertainly, and made by degrees secure and durable. In the development of this tendency, it will be the policy of the immigrant to find, for any social title of a dubious or fugitive character which he may enjoy in his own country, some seeming equivalent, but of fixed character and established value, in the land of his adoption. Scotland, with its mixed and indefinite nomenclature of ranks, would thus afford good opportunities for the ingenuous youth transferring himself from his dubious home-rank into something more specific in the symmetrical and scientifically adjusted court precedency of France. The practice of the Lairds and Goodmen of presenting themselves by the territorial names of their estates, with or without their family patronymics, gave an opportunity for rendering the possession something equivalent to the French De and the German Von. The families that had lost their estates adhered to the old title with the mournful pride of deposed monarchs. If these had often the sympathy of their peculiar world with them, yet no one could, with a shadow of justice, blame the actual possessors of the solid acres for also claiming the honours attached to them. John Law of Lauriston, who ruled France for a few months with the capricious haughtiness of an Eastern despot, among the many strange chances which led to his giddy elevation, owed much to that which gave uniformity and consistency to the others—namely, that, although he was an Edinburgh tradesman, his possession of a small estate, happily named, in the neighbourhood of his business, enabled him to take rank in the *noblesse*. History affords one very flagrant case of the potent uses of the territorial *Of*. In Galloway there long existed a worshipful family called the Murrays of Broughton. They were not ennobled by a peerage, but belonged to the opulent and proud class of territorial aristocracy who often do not consider the peerage any distinction, and so they were thoroughly entitled to consider themselves within the category of noble in France and Germany. There happened also to be a small croft or paddock on the wayside between Noblehouse and Dumfries called Broughton, and its owner, some say its tenant only, being named Murray, took on himself very naturally and fairly the style and title of Murray of Broughton. Having found his uses in this title, he left it dedicated to perpetual infamy; for he it was who, having incited poor Prince Charles Edward to the Scottish expedition, and by his zeal obtained the office of "Secretary to his Royal Highness the Prince of Wales," afterwards used the information he had thus obtained to buy his own personal safety, by bringing his companions in rebellion to the block. So thoroughly had his notoriety impressed on the contemporary mind the notion of his representing the old Galwegian house of Murray of Broughton, that it is believed even by local antiquaries.

It will not do too rigidly to sift the pretensions by which men, young, poor, obscure, and struggling, have sought notice in early life, and found their way to honours and possessions which they have worthily and honourably enjoyed. Imagination is strong and criticism weak in matters of genealogy, and doubtless many of the adventurers who planned and built their fortunes in France, as fully believed themselves cadets of the noblest family bearing their name, as if they had carried with them the certificate of the Lion Office.

Whatever social position the Scottish adventurer might assume, there is little doubt that his claim to be somebody would be pretty substantially maintained by the proud reserve which naturally belongs to his race. We can, in fact, see at the present day the qualities which made the fortunes of these men. These qualities are now exercised in another sphere —in England, in the colonies, and especially in our Indian empire, where Scotsmen are continually rising from obscurity into eminence. On the brow of the industrious crofter on the slopes of the Grampians we may yet see the well-becoming pride and self-respecting gravity that, in the fifteenth century, took the honours and distinctions of France as a natural right. Whence comes his pride? He has no rank—he is poor—and he is no representative of an illustrious house. No, but he is founding a house. He rises up early, and late takes rest, that his son may go to college and be a gentleman; and when he reads contemporary history in the public press, he knows that the grandfather of the eminent law lord, or of the great party leader, or of the illustrious Eastern conqueror, whose name fills the ear of fame, laboured like himself in the fields close at hand.

It may be surely counted not without significance among ethnical phenomena, that though France has all along shown in her language the predominance of the Latin race, three infusions of northern blood had been successively poured into the country; first, the Franks—next, the Normans—and, lastly, the Scots. It seems not unreasonable that these helped to communicate to the vivacity and impetuosity of the original race those qualities of enterprise and endurance which were needed to make up the illustrious history of France. The more, however, that the standard of national character was raised by the new element, the more would it revolt at a continued accession of foreign blood. A country, the highest distinctions and offices of which were given by the despotic monarch to strangers, to enable him to keep down the native people, could not be sound at heart; and one hails it as the appearance of a healthy tone of nationality when murmurs arise against the aggrandising strangers.

It was not, indeed, in human nature, either that the French should not murmur at the distinctions and substantial rewards bestowed on the strangers, or that they themselves should not become domineering and exacting. M. Michel quotes some very suggestive murmurs of the time, in which it is questioned whether the slaughter of the Scots at Verneuil was not to be set down as a piece of good fortune to France in breaking the power of a set of masters likely to be more formidable even than the English.* But of some of the characteristic blemishes of a mercenary foreign force the Scots were free. They did not go to France to act the mendicant or marauder, but to be teachers and leaders; and the evil of their presence was not that their wretchedness made them a nuisance, but that their ambition and haughtiness made them a reproach to the native French. Hence there were occasional disagreeables and bickerings between the favoured foreigners and the natives, especially when these began to gain heart and recover from the abjectness they lay under during the great war. The following is a little incident connected with these affairs so very like the beginning of 'Quentin Dur-

* "Cet échec tourna à l'avantage de la France; car tels étaient et l'orgueil des Ecossais et le mépris dans lequel ils tenaient les Français, que s'ils fussent sortis vainqueurs de cette lutte, ils eussent comploté d'égorger toute la noblesse de l'Anjou, de la Touraine, du Berry, et des provinces voisines, pour s'emparer eux-mêmes de leurs maisons, de leurs femmes, de tous leurs biens les plus précieux; ce qui, certainement, ne leur eût pas été bien difficile, une fois vainqueurs des Anglais, comme ils l'avaient espéré."—Contemporary Chronicle in Meyer, 'Annales Rerum Belgicarum,' quoted in Michel, i. 149.

ward,' that it surely must have been running in Scott's mind when he framed the events of that romance :—

"Michael Hamilton, who had a share in the affair, relates that in Holy Week of the year 1429, he and several of his companions-in-arms were lodged in a village named Vallet, not far from Clisson, and threatened by the Bretons, who held the country in considerable number. A spy sent to report on the Scots having fallen into their hands, they made him inform them, and then hanged him. They then took to flight, but not without leaving some of their people in the power of the peasants. Amongst the prisoners was Hamilton, the weight of whose cuirass had prevented his flight; he was brought to Clisson and hanged by the very hand of the son of the spy, eager to avenge his father. From the moment that he had seen himself taken he had invoked St Catherine, and made a vow to go to thank her in her Chapel of Fierbois, if she would preserve him from death. He was successful; for, he having been hanged, on the following night the curate of the town heard a voice which told him to go and save Hamilton.

"He paid little attention to it, and it was only on a reiterated order that he made up his mind to bid one of his parishioners go to the gibbet and look whether the wretch was dead or not. After having turned him again and again, the messenger, to assure himself fully, bared the right foot of the culprit, and pricked the little toe in such a manner as to make a large wound, from whence blood sprang. Feeling himself wounded, Hamilton drew up his leg and moved. At this sight terror took possession of the messenger; he fled, and in all haste bore to the curate an account of what had passed. He perceiving in the whole affair an interposition from on high, related the facts to the people who were present; then having arrayed himself and his clergy in sacerdotal vestments, they went in procession to the place of execution, and cut down Hamilton. All this passed in the presence of him who had hanged him: furious at seeing that his victim was on the point of escaping him, he struck him on the ear with a sword, and gave him a great wound—an act of barbarity which is not to be commended.

"Then Hamilton is laid upon a horse and taken to a house and given into care; soon after the Abbess of the Regrippière, having heard of what had taken place, sent in quest of our Scot to have him treated in her convent: he is taken there; and as he was ignorant of French, the charitable lady gives him a fellow-countryman for his sick-nurse. He had just related his adventures to him when a voice reminded him that he had a vow to fulfil. Unable then to walk, he waited a fortnight, then set off for Fierbois, but not without finding by the way companions, with whom he remained some days to recover his strength. In this history, as in another of the year 1423, in which we find Scots in Berry hanging eight poor peasants to revenge themselves for having been robbed not far from there, and as also in the history of Captain Boyce Glauny, I see the faithful picture of the miseries which, during the Hundred Years' War, desolated our central provinces, become the prey of undisciplined hordes; but I find also that the Scots figure there in great numbers." *

* Michel, i. 163-5.

Chapter III.

The other side of the Reciprocity—Contrast between the Scot in France and Le Français en Ecosse—An Ambassador snubbed—French Chevaliers treated to a Border Raid—The Admiral Vienne's Expedition, and how it fared with him and his followers—The Gladiatorial Spectacle on the Inch of Perth—Ferdinand of Spain's Dealings with Scotland—Rule of Albany, and its results—A Story of Ecclesiastical Patronage—The foreign Friar of Tongueland—The Slaughter of La Bastie.

BEFORE coming to the later history of the League, let us take a glance at the reciprocity from the other side, and having seen what a good thing our wandering Scots made of it in France, see how the French got on in Scotland. We must prepare for differences which are not unlike some that we now see in ordinary social life. Suppose the common case of two friends, each having an independent position, and each useful to the other, but, from specialties in his private affairs, the one keeps a dinner-giving house, the other does not. It need not necessary follow that the one is the other's inferior or dependant—he who goes to dinner perhaps thinks he is giving more favour and honour than he receives; but the conditions on which the friends will meet each other in their respective dwelling-houses will take a decided colour from the distinction. In the one house all will be joviality and social enjoyment—in the other, hard business, not perhaps altogether of the most agreeable kind. For centuries the French could expect no enjoyment in Scotland. The country was, on the whole, not poorer than their own—perhaps not quite so poor—but there was no luxurious class in it; all was rough, hard, and ungenial. Some of them had to come over on embassies and warlike expeditions, but they would as soon have sought Kamtschatka or Iceland, as a place wherein to pitch their tabernacle and pursue their fortune.

Many a Scot had sought his fortune in France; and names familiar to us now on shop-signs and in street-directories had been found among the dead at Poitiers, before we have authentic account of any Frenchmen having ventured across the sea to visit the sterile territory of their allies. Froissart makes a story out of the failure of the first attempt to send a French ambassador here. The person selected for the duty was the Lord of Bournezel or Bournaseau, whose genealogy is disentangled by M. Michel in a learned note. He was accredited by Charles V. in the year 1379, and was commanded to keep such state as might become the representative of his august master.

Bournezel set off to embark at Sluys, and there had to wait fifteen days for a favourable wind. The ambassador thought there was no better way of beguiling the time than a recitation among the Plat Deutsch of the splendours which he was bound in the way of public duty to exhibit in the sphere of his mission. Accordingly, "during this time he lived magnificently; and gold and silver plate were in such profusion in his apartments as if he had been a prince. He had also music to announce his dinner, and caused to be carried before him a sword in a scabbard richly blazoned with his arms in gold and silver. His servants paid well for everything. Many of the townspeople were much astonished at the great state this knight lived in at home, which he also maintained when he went abroad."

This premature display of his diplomatic glories brought him into a difficulty highly characteristic of one of the political specialties of France at that period. It was the time already spoken of when the nobles of the blood-royal were arrogating to themselves alone certain prerogatives and ceremonials distinguishing them from the rest of the territorial aristocracy, however high these might be.

The Duke of Bretagne and the Count of Flanders, who were near at hand, took umbrage at the grand doings of Bournezel, and sent for him through the bailiff of Sluys. That officer, after the manner of executive functionaries who find themselves sufficiently backed, made his mission as offensive as possible, and, tapping Bournezel on the shoulder, intimated that he was wanted.

The great men had intended only to rebuke him for playing a part above his commission, but the indiscretion of their messenger gave Bournezel a hold which he kept and used sagaciously. When he found the princes who had sent for him lounging at a window looking into the gardens, he fell on his knees and acknowledged himself the prisoner of the Count of Flanders. To take prisoner an ambassador, and the ambassador of a crowned king, the feudal lord of the captor, was one of the heaviest of offences, both against the law of nations and the spirit of chivalry. The Earl was not the less enraged that he felt himself caught; and after retorting with, "How, rascal, do you dare to call yourself my prisoner, when I have only sent to speak with you?" he composed himself to the delivery of the rebuke he had been preparing in this fashion: "It is by such talkers and jesters of the Parliament of Paris and of the King's chamber as you, that the kingdom is governed; and you manage the King as you please, to do good or evil according to your wills: there is not a prince of the blood, however great he may be, if he incur your hatred, who will be listened to; but such fellows shall yet be hanged until the gibbets be full of them." Bournezel carried this pleasant announcement and the whole transaction to the throne, and the King took his part, saying to those around, "He has kept his ground well: I would not for twenty thousand francs it had not so happened."

The embassy to Scotland was thus for the time frustrated. It was said that there were English cruisers at hand to intercept the ambassador, and that he himself had no great heart for a sojourn in the wild unknown northern land. Possibly the fifteen days' lording it at Sluys may have broken in rather inconveniently on his outfit; but the most likely cause of the defeat of the first French embassy to our shores was, the necessity felt by Bournezel to right himself at once at court, and turn the flank of his formidable enemies; and Froissart says, the Earl of Flanders lay under the royal displeasure for having, in his vain vaunting, defeated so important a project as the mission to the Scots.

A few years afterwards our country received a visit, less august, it is true, than the intended embassy, but far more interesting. In 1384, negotiations were exchanged near the town of Boulogne for a permanent peace between England and France. The French demanded concessions of territory which could not be yielded, and a permanent peace, founded on a final settlement of pending claims, was impossible. A truce even was at that time, however, a very important conclusion to conflict; it sometimes lasted for years, being in reality a peace under protest that each party reserved certain claims to be kept in view when war should again break out. Such a truce was adjusted between England on the one side and France on the other—conditional on the accession of her allies Spain and Scotland. France kept faith magnanimously, in ever refusing to negotiate a separate peace or truce for herself; but, as the way is with the more powerful of two partners, she was apt to take for granted that Scotland would go with her, and that the affair was virtually finished by her own accession to terms.

It happened that in this instance the Duke of Burgundy took it on him to deal with Scotland. He had, however, just at that moment, a rather important piece of business, deeply interesting to himself, on hand. By the death of the Earl of Flanders he succeeded to that fair domain—an event which vastly influenced the subsequent fate of Europe. So busy was he in adjusting the affairs of his succession, that it was said he entirely overlooked the small matter of the notification of the truce to Scotland. Meanwhile, there was a body of men-at-arms in the French service at Sluys thrown out of employment by the truce with England, and, like other workmen in a like position, desirous of a job. They knew that the truce had not yet penetrated to Scotland, and thought a journey thither, long and dangerous as it was, might be a promising speculation. There were about thirty of them, and Froissart gives a head-roll of those whose names he remembered, beginning with Sir Geoffry de Charny, Sir John de Plaissy, Sir Hugh de Boulon, and so on. They dared not attempt, in face of the English war-ships, to land at a southern harbour, but reached the small seaport called by Froissart Monstres, and not unaptly supposed by certain sage commentators to be Montrose, since the adventurers rode on to Dundee and thence to Perth.

They were received with a deal of rough hospitality, and much commended for the knightly spirit that induced them to cross the wide ocean to try their lances against the common enemy, England. Two of them were selected to pass on to Edinburgh, and explain their purpose at the Court of Holyrood. Here they met two of their countrymen on a mission which boded no good to their enterprise. These were ambassadors from France, come at last to notify the truce. It was at once accepted by the peaceable King Robert, but the Scots lords around him were grieved in heart at the prospect that these fine fellows should come so far and return without having any sport of that highly flavoured kind which the Border wars afforded. The truce they held had been adjusted not by Scotland but by France; and here, as if to contradict its sanction, were Frenchmen themselves offering to treat it as naught.

There was, however, a far stronger reason for overlooking it. Just before it was completed, but when it was known to be inevitable, the Earls of Northumberland and Nottingham suddenly and secretly drew together two thousand men-at-arms and six thousand bowmen, with which they broke into Scotland, and swept the country as far as Edinburgh with more than the usual ferocity of a Border raid; for they made it to the Scots as if the devil had come among them, having great wrath, for he knew that his time was short. It was said even, that the French ambassadors, sent to Scotland to announce the truce, had been detained in London to allow time for this raid coming off effectively. "To say the truth," says Froissart, mildly censorious, "the lords of England who had been at the conference at Bolinghen, had not acted very honourably when they had consented to order their men to march to Scotland and burn the country, knowing that the truce would speedily be concluded: and the best excuse they could make was, that it was the French and not they who were to signify such truce to the Scots."

Smarting from this inroad, the Scots lords, and especially the Douglases and others on the border, were in no humour to coincide with their peaceful King. They desired to talk the matter over with the representatives of the adventurers in some quiet place; and, for reasons which were doubtless sufficient to themselves, they selected for this purpose the Church of St Giles in Edinburgh. The conference was highly satisfactory to the adventurers, who spurred back to Perth to impart the secret intelligence, that though the King had accepted the truce, the lords were no party to it, but would immediately prepare an expedition to avenge Nottingham's and Northumberland's raid. This was joyful intelligence, though in its character rather surprising to followers of the French Court. A force was rapidly collected, and in a very few days the adventurers were called to join it in the Douglases' lands.

So far Froissart. This affair is not, so far as I remember, mentioned in detail by any of our own annalists writing before the publication of his Chronicles. Everything, however, is there set forth so minutely, and with so distinct and accurate a reference to actual conditions in all the details, that few things in history can be less open to doubt. We come to a statement inviting question, when he says that the force collected so suddenly by the Scots lords contained fifteen thousand mounted men; nor can we be quite reconciled to the statement though their steeds were the small mountain horses called hackneys. The force, however, was sufficient for its work. It found the English border trusting to the truce, and as little prepared for invasion as Nottingham and Northumberland had found Scotland.

The first object was the land of the Percies, which the Scots, in the laconic language of the chronicler, "pillaged and burnt." And so they went onwards; and where peasants had been peacefully tilling the land or tending their cattle amid the comforts of rude industry, there the desolating host passed—the crops were trampled down—their owners left dead in the ashes of their smoking huts — and a few widows and children, fleeing for safety and food, was all of animal life left upon the scene.

The part taken in it by his countrymen was exactly after Froissart's own heart, since they were not carrying out any of the political movements of the day, nor were they even actuated by an ambition of conquest, but were led by the sheer fun of the thing and the knightly spirit of adventure to partake in this wild raid. To the Scots it was a substantial affair, for they came back heavy-handed, with droves and flocks driven before them—possibly some of them recovered their own.

The King had nothing to say in his vindication touching this little affair, save that it had occurred without his permission, or even knowledge. The Scots lords, in fact, were not the only persons who had broken that truce. It included the Duke of Burgundy and his enemies, the Low Country towns; yet his feudatory, the Lord Destournay, taking advantage of the defenceless condition of Oudenarde during peace, took it by a clever stratagem. The Duke of Burgundy, when appealed to, advised Destournay to abandon his capture; but Destournay was wilful: he had conquered the city, and the city was his—so there was no help for it, since the communities were not strong enough to enforce their rights, and Burgundy would only demand them on paper. What occasioned the raid of the Scots and French to be passed over, however, was that the Duke of Lancaster, John of Gaunt, who had the chief authority over the English councils, as well as the command over the available force, was taken up with his own schemes on the crown of Castile, and not inclined to find work for the military force of the country elsewhere. The truce, therefore, was cordially ratified; bygones were counted bygones; and the French adventurers bade a kindly farewell to their brethren-in-arms, and crossed the seas homewards.

Driven from their course, and landing at the Brille, they narrowly escaped hanging at the hands of the boorish cultivators of the swamp; and after adventures which would make good raw materials for several novels, they reached Paris.

There they explained to their own Court how they found that the great enemy of France had, at the opposite extremity of his dominions, a nest of fighting fiends, who wanted only their help in munitions of war to enable them to rush on the vital parts of his dominions with all the fell ferocity of men falling on their bitterest feudal enemy. Thus could France, having under consideration the cost and peril of galleying an invading army across the Straits, by money and management, do far more damage to the enemy than any French invading expedition was likely to accomplish.

In an hour which did not prove propitious to France, a resolution was adopted to invade England at both ends. Even before the truce was at an end, the forges of Henault and Picardy were hard at work making battle-axes; and all along the coast, from Harfleur to Sluys, there was busy baking of biscuits and purveyance of provender. Early in spring an expedition of a thousand men-at-arms, with their followers, put to sea under John of Vienne, the Admiral of France, and arrived at Leith, making a voyage which must have been signally prosperous, if we may judge by the insignificance of the chief casualty on record concerning it. In those days, as in the present, it appears that adventurous young gentlemen on shipboard were apt to attempt feats for which their land training did not adapt them—in nautical phrase, "to swing on all top-ropes." A hopeful youth chose to perform such a feat in his armour, and with the most natural of all results. "The knight was young and active, and, to show his agility, he mounted aloft by the ropes of his ship, completely armed; but his feet slipping he fell into the sea, and the weight of his armour, which sank him instantly, deprived him of any assistance, for the ship was soon at a distance from the place where he had fallen."

The expedition soon found itself to be a mistake. In fact, to send fighting men to Scotland was just to supply the country with that commodity in which it superabounded. The great problem was how to find food for the stalwart sons of the soil, and arms to put in their hands when fighting was necessary. A percentage of the cost and labour of the expedition, had it been spent in sending money or munitions of war, would have done better service. The scene before the adventurers was in lamentable contrast to all that custom had made familiar to them. There were none of the comfortable chateaux, the abundant markets, the carpets, down beds, and rich hangings which gladdened their expeditions to the Low Countries, whether they went as friends or foes. Nor was the same place for *them* in Scotland, which the Scots so readily found in France, where a docile submissive peasantry only wanted vigorous and adventurous masters.

"The lords and their men," says Froissart, "lodged themselves as well as they could in Edinburgh, and those who could not lodge there were quartered in the different villages thereabout. Edinburgh, notwithstanding that it is the residence of the King, and is the Paris of Scotland, is not such a town as Tournay and Valenciennes, for there are not in the whole town four thousand houses. Several of the French lords were therefore obliged to take up their lodgings in the neighbouring villages, and at Dunfermline, Kelso, Dunbar, Dalkeith, and in other towns." When they had exhausted the provender brought with them, these children of luxury had to endure the miseries of sordid living, and even the pinch of hunger. They tried to console themselves with the reflection that they had, at all events, an opportunity of experiencing a phase of life which their parents had endeavoured theoretically to impress upon them, in precepts to be thankful to the Deity for the good things they enjoyed, but which might not always be theirs in a transitory world. They had been warned by the first little band of adventurers that Scotland was not rich; yet the intense poverty of the country whence so many daring adventurers had gone over to ruffle it with the flower of European chivalry, astonished and appalled them. Of the extreme and special nature of the poverty of Scotland, the great war against the English invaders was the cause. It has been estimated, indeed, by those devoted to such questions, that Scotland did not recover fully from the ruin caused by that conflict until the Union made her secure against her ambitious neighbour. It was the crisis referred to in that pathetic ditty, the earliest specimen of our lyrical poetry, when

> "Away was sonse of ale and bread,
> Of wine and wax, of gaming and glee;
> Our gold was changed into lead;
> Cryst borne into virginity.
> Succour poor Scotland and remede,
> That stad is in perplexity."

The alliance between the two powers was not so unequal in the fourteenth as it became in the sixteenth century. On the map of Europe the absolute dominions to which the house of Valois succeeded occupied but a small space in comparison with the kingdom of Francis I. Scotland, on the other hand, had a respectable position among the European powers. It was larger than many of them; and although the contest with England was bringing it to beggary, it had still the repute of recent wealth and prosperity. Not a long period had passed since Berwick-upon-Tweed, the capital, took rank with Ghent, Rotterdam, and the other great cities of the Low Countries, and was almost the rival of London in mercantile enterprise. Stately edifices, baronial and ecclesiastical, still stood, testifying to a people equal in wealth to the English when they were built, though they were doomed to fall into decay and be succeeded by sordid hovels, when the weight of a long war against a powerful and oppressive empire had impoverished the people. Before the French came over and made acquaintance with their allies at home, that poverty had set its desolating mark all over the land, and the French saw and felt it.

The poverty of the Scots proceeded from a cause of which they need not have been ashamed; yet, with the reserve and pride ever peculiar to them, they hated that it should be seen by their allies, and when these showed any indications of contempt or derision, the natives were stung to madness. Froissart renders very picturesquely the common talk about the strangers, thus:—"What devil has brought them here? or, who has sent for them? Cannot we carry on our wars with England without their assistance? We shall never do any good as long as they are with us. Let them be told to go back again, for we are sufficient in Scotland to fight our own battles, and need not their aid. We neither understand their language nor they ours, so that we cannot converse together. They will very soon cut up and destroy all we have in this country, and will do more harm if we allow them to remain among us than the English could in battle. If the English do burn our houses, what great matter is it to us? We can rebuild them at little cost, for we require only three days to do so, so that we but have five or six poles, with boughs to cover them."

The French knights, accustomed to abject submission among their own peasantry, were unable to comprehend the fierce independence of the Scots common people, and were ever irritating them into bloody reprisals. A short sentence of Froissart's conveys a world of meaning on this specialty: "Besides, whenever their servants went out to forage, they were indeed permitted to load their horses with as much as they could pack up and carry, but they were waylaid on their return, and villanously beaten, robbed, and sometimes slain, insomuch that no varlet dare go out foraging for fear of death. In one month the French lost upwards of a hundred varlets; for when three or four went out foraging, not one returned, in such a hideous manner were they treated." As we have seen, a not unusual incident of purveying in France was, that the husbandman was hung up by the heels and roasted before his own fire until he disgorged his property. The Scots peasantry had a decided prejudice against such a process, and, being accustomed to defend themselves from all oppression, resisted even that of their allies, to the extreme astonishment and wrath of those magnificent gentlemen.

There is a sweet unconsciousness in Froissart's indignant denunciation of the robbing of the purveyors, which meant the pillaged peasantry recovering their own goods. But the chronicler was of a thorough knightly nature, and deemed the peasantry of a country good for nothing but to be used up. Hence, in his wrath, he says: "In Scotland you will never find a man of worth; they are like savages, who wish not to be acquainted with any one, and are too envious of the good fortune of others, and suspicious of losing anything themselves, for their country is very poor. When the English make inroads thither, as they have very frequently done, they order their provisions, if they wish to live, to follow close at their backs; for nothing is to be had in that country without great difficulty. There is neither iron to shoe horses, nor leather to make harness, saddles, or bridles; all these things come ready-made from Flanders by sea; and should these fail, there is none to be had in the country." What a magnificent contrast to such a picture is the present relative condition of Scotland and the Low

Countries! and yet these have not suffered any awful reverse of fortune—they have merely abided in stagnant respectability.

It must be remembered, in estimating the chronicler's pungent remarks upon our poor ancestors, that he was not only a worshipper of rank and wealth, but thoroughly English in his partialities, magnifying the feats in arms of the great enemies of his own country. The records of the Scots Parliament of 1395 curiously confirm the inference from his narrative, that the French were oppressive purveyors, and otherwise unobservant of the people's rights. An indenture, as it is termed—the terms of a sort of compact with the strangers—appears among the records, conspicuous among their other Latin and vernacular contents as being set forth in French, in courtesy, of course, to the strangers. It expressly lays down that no goods of any kind shall be taken by force, under pain of death, and none shall be received without being duly paid for—the dealers having free access to come and go. There are regulations, too, for suppressing broils by competent authority, and especially for settling questions between persons of unequal degrees; a remedy for the practice of the French, who left the settlement entirely with the superior.

This document is one of many showing that, in Scotland, there were arrangements for protecting the personal freedom of the humbler classes, and their rights of property, the fulness of which is little known, because the like did not exist in other countries, and those who have written philosophical treatises on the feudal system, or on the progress of Europe from barbarism to civilisation, have generally lumped all the countries of Europe together. The sense of personal freedom seems to have been rather stronger in Scotland than in England; it was such as evidently to astound the French knights. At the end of the affair, Froissart expresses this surprise in his usual simple and expressive way. After a second or third complaint of the unreasonable condition that his countrymen should pay for the victuals they consumed, he goes on, "The Scots said the French had done them more mischief than the English;" and when asked in what manner, they replied, "By riding through the corn, oats, and barley on their march, which they trod under foot, not condescending to follow the roads, for which damage they would have a recompense before they left Scotland, and they should neither find vessel nor mariner who would dare to put to sea without their permission."

Of the military events in the short war following the arrival of the French, an outline will be found in the ordinary histories; but it was attended by some conditions which curiously bring out the specialties of the two nations so oddly allied. One propitiatory gift the strangers had brought with them, which was far more highly appreciated than their own presence; this was a thousand stand of accoutrements for men-at-arms. They were of the highest excellence, being selected out of the store kept in the Castle of Beauté for the use of the Parisians. When these were distributed among the Scots knights, who were but poorly equipped, the chronicler, as if he had been speaking of the prizes at a Christmas-tree, tells how those who were successful and got them were greatly delighted.

The Scots did their part in their own way: they brought together thirty thousand men, a force that drained the country of its available manhood. But England had at that time nothing to divert her arms elsewhere, and the policy adopted was to send northwards a force sufficient to crush Scotland for ever. It consisted of seven thousand mounted men-at-arms, and sixty thousand bow and bill men—a force three or four times as large as the armies that gained the memorable English victories in France. Of these, Agincourt was still to come off, but Crecy and Poitiers were over, along with many other affairs that might have taught the French a lesson. The Scots, too, had suffered two great defeats—Neville's Cross and Halidon Hill—since their great national triumph. The impression made on each country by their experiences brought out their distinct national characteristics. The French knights were all ardour and impatience; they clamoured to be at the enemy without ascertaining the amount or character of his force. The wretched internal wars of their own country had taught them to look on the battle-field as the arena of distinction in personal conflict, rather than the great tribunal in which the fate of nations was to be decided, and communities come forth freed or enslaved.

To the Scots, on the other hand, the affair was one of national life or death, and they would run no risks for distinction's sake. Picturesque accounts have often been repeated of a scene where Douglas, or some other Scots leader, brought the Admiral to an elevated spot whence he could see and estimate the mighty host of England; but the most picturesque of all the accounts is the original by Froissart, of which the others are parodies. The point in national tactics brought out by this incident is the singular recklessness with which the French must have been accustomed to do battle. In total ignorance of the force he was to oppose, and not seeking to know aught concerning it, the Frenchman's voice was still for war. When made to see with his own eyes what he had to encounter, he was as reluctant as his companions to risk the issue of a battle, but not so fertile in expedients for carrying on the war effectively without one.

The policy adopted was to clear the country before the English army as it advanced, and carry everything portable and valuable within the recesses of the mountain-ranges, whither the inhabitants not fit for military service had gone with their effects. A desert being thus opened for the progress of the invaders, they were left to wander in it unmolested, while the Scots army went in the opposite direction, and crossed the Border southwards. Thus the English army found Scotland empty—the Scots army found England full. The one wore itself out in a fruitless march, part of it straggling, it was said, as far as Aberdeen, and returned thinned and starving, while the other was only embarrassed by the burden of its plunder. Much destruction there was, doubtless, on both sides, but it fell heaviest where there was most to destroy, and gratified at last in some measure the French, who "said among themselves they had burned in the bishoprics of Durham and Carlisle more than the value of all the towns in the kingdom of Scotland."

But havoc does not make wealth, and whether or not the Scots knew better from experience how to profit by such opportunities, the French, when they returned northward were starving. Their object now was to get out of the country as fast as they could. Froissart, with a touch of dry humour, explains that their allies had no objection to speed the exit of the poorer knights, but resolved to hold the richer and more respectable in a sort of pawn for the damage which the expedition had inflicted on the common people. The Admiral asked his good friends the Lords Douglas and Moray to put a stop to those demands; but these good knights were unable to accommodate their brethren in this little matter, and the Admiral was obliged to give effectual pledges from his Government for the payment of the creditors.

There is something in all this that seems utterly unchivalrous and even ungenerous; but it had been well for France had Froissart been able to tell a like story of her peasantry. It merely shows us that our countrymen of that day were of those who "know their rights, and, knowing, dared maintain them;" and was but a demonstration on a humbler, and, if you will, more sordid shape, of the same spirit that had swept away the Anglo-Norman invaders. The very first act which their chronicler records concerning his knightly friends, after he has exhausted his wrath against the hard and mercenary Scot, is thoroughly suggestive. Some of the knights tried other fields of adventure, "but the greater number returned to France, and were so poor they knew not how to remount themselves, especially those from Burgundy, Champagne, Bar, and Lorraine, *who seized the labouring horses wherever they found them in the fields*," so impatient were they to regain their freedom of action.

So ended this affair, with the aspect of evil auspices for the alliance. The adventurers returned "cursing Scotland, and the hour they had set foot there. They said they had never suffered so much in any expedition, and wished the King of France would make a truce with the English for two or three years, and then march to Scotland and utterly destroy it; for never had they seen such wicked people, nor such ignorant hypocrites and traitors." But the impulsive denunciation of the disappointed adventurers was signally obliterated in the history of the next half-century. Ere many more years had passed over them, that day of awful trial was coming when France had to lean on the strong arm of her early ally; and, in fact, some of the denouncers lived to see adventurers from the sordid land of their contempt and hatred commanding the armies of France, and owning her broad lordships. It was just after the return of Vienne's expedition that the remarkable absorption of Scotsmen into the aristocracy of France, already spoken of, began to set in.

This episode of the French expedition to Scotland, small though its place is in the annals of Europe, yet merits the consideration of the thoughtful historian, as affording a significant example of the real causes of the misery and degradation of France at that time, and the wonderful victories of the English kings. Chivalry, courage, the love of enterprise, high spirit in all forms, abounded to superfluity among the knightly orders, but received no solid support from below. The mounted steel-clad knights of the period, in the highest physical condition, afraid of nothing on the earth or beyond it, and burning for triumph and fame, could perform miraculous feats of strength and daring; but all passed off in wasted effort and vain rivalry, when there was wanting the bold peasantry, who, with their buff jerkins, and their bills and bows, or short Scottish spears, were the real force by which realms were held or gained.

An affair occurred in Scotland in the year 1396, which is not naturally associated with the French alliance. It has usually been spoken of, indeed, as a phenomenon of pure Scottish barbarism. But M. Michel, in looking at it from the French side, suggests some considerations which may possibly give help in the solution of a mystery. The affair referred to is that great battle or tournament on the North Inch of Perth, where opposite Highland factions, called the Clan Quhele and Clan Chattan, were pitted against each other, thirty to thirty—an affair, the darker colours of which are lighted up by the eccentric movements of the Gow Chrom, or bandy-legged smith of Perth, who took the place of a defaulter in one of the ranks, to prevent the spectacle of the day from being spoilt. That such a contest should have been organised to take place in the presence of the king and court, under solemnities and regulations like some important ordeal, has driven historical speculators to discover what deep policy for the pacification or subjugation of the Highlands lay behind it. The feature that gives it a place in M. Michel's book is the briefest possible notification, taken from one of the chroniclers, that a large number of Frenchmen and other strangers were present at the spectacle.

This draws us back from the mysterious arcana

of political intrigue to find a mere showy pageant, got up to enliven the hours of idle mirth—an act, in short, of royal hospitality—a show cunningly adapted to the tastes of the age, yet having withal the freshness of originality, being a renaissance kind of combination of the gladiatorial conflict of the Roman circus with the tournament of chivalry. The Highlanders were, in fact, the human raw material which a king of Scots could in that day employ, so far as their nature suited, for the use or the amusement of his guests. Them, and them only among his subjects, could he use as the Empire used the Transalpine barbarian—"butchered to make a Roman holiday." The treatment of the Celt is the blot on that period of our history. Never in later times has the Red Indian or Australian native been more the hunted wild beast to the emigrant settler than the Highlander was to his neighbour the Lowlander. True, he was not easily got at, and, when reached, he was found to have tusks. They were a people never permitted to be at rest from external assault; yet such was their nature that, instead of being pressed by a common cause into compact union, they were divided into communities that hated each other almost more bitterly than they did the common enemy.

This internal animosity has suggested that the king wanted two factions to exterminate each other as it were symbolically, and accept the result of a combat between two bodies of chosen champions, as if there had been an actual stricken field, with all the able-bodied men on both sides engaged in it. It was quite safe to calculate that when the representatives of the two contending factions were set face to face on the greensward, they would fly at each other's throats, and afford in an abundant manner to the spectators whatever delectation might arise from an intensely bloody struggle. But, on the other hand, to expect the Highlanders to be fools enough to accept this sort of symbolical extinction of their quarrel was too preposterous a conclusion for any practical statesman to adopt. They had no notion of leaving important issues to the event of single combat, or any of the other capricious rules of chivalry, but slew their enemies where they could, and preferred doing so secretly, and without risk to themselves, when that was practicable.

Meanwhile, as the centuries followed each other, changes came over the condition of the European nations and their position towards each other, as over all human things. Scotland was gradually recovering from prostration, and England was shaken by the wars of the Roses, to the dire calamities of which it was some offset that they enfeebled the crown of England for mischief, whether against its neighbours or its own people. In the balance of Europe in the reign of Henry VII. England was counted with Spain and Scotland with France. Both the British countries were in some measure subsidiary and protected states, Scotland being nearly as powerful as her neighbour. Her hold on France, indeed, was something like an incorporation, while the relation of Spain to England was suspicious and fidgety. The sagacious and grasping Ferdinand looked with respect and sympathy to a prince so like himself as Henry VII.; but he would have fain had a more securely-seated father-in-law for his daughter. He had an ambassador in Scotland who had two alternative jobs on hand—either to get the influence of Scotland over France to operate in his favour, or to detach these sworn friends and make a powerful European alliance, including Spain, England, and Scotland. Ferdinand, indeed, was not very sure whether, if he could not unite with both, Scotland might not be the more valuable friend. The intrigues, as historians term it, at the Court of James IV., are highly amusing, and have a special liveliness imparted to them by both monarchs playing the card they called "Him of York," being the Perkin Warbeck, who professed to be, and made many people believe him to be, the younger of the princes reputed to have been murdered in the Tower. Ferdinand regretted that he had not a daughter to give to James, and instructed his ambassador to try whether it would be practicable to pass off one of his natural children as a legitimate daughter of the house of Castile; but he was told that such a trick would be a very dangerous one, for the Scots were a proud people and fierce in their resentment of slights and injuries.*

To watch in history the action and counteraction of opposing forces which have developed some grand result, yet by a slight and not improbable impulse the other way might have borne towards an opposite conclusion equally momentous, is an interesting task, with something in it of the excitement of the chase. In pursuing the traces which brought Scotland back to her English kindred, and saved her from a permanent annexation to France, the arrival of John Duke of Albany in Scotland, in 1515, is a critical turning-point. Already had the seed of the union with England been planted when James IV. got for a wife the daughter of Henry VII. It would serve pleasantly to lighten up and relieve a hard and selfish reputation, if one could figure this King, in the depths of his own heart, assuring himself of having entered in the books of fate a stroke of policy that at some date, however distant, was destined to appease the long bloody contest of two rival nations, and unite them into a compact and mighty empire. The prospects of such a consum-

* There is an immense deal of new light thrown on the relations of Spain, England, France, and Scotland during the reign of Henry VII. in the 'Calendar of Letters, Despatches, and State Papers,' printed by Mr Bergwroth, from the archives of Simancas, for the series of papers and chronicles issued under the auspices of the Master of the Rolls.

mation were at first anything but encouraging. The old love broke in, counteracting prudential policy; and, indeed, never did besotted lover abandon himself to wilder folly than James IV., when, at the bidding of Anne of France as the lady of his chivalrous worship, he resolved to be her true knight, and take three steps into English ground. When a chivalrous freak, backed by a few political irritations scarce less important, strewed the moor of Flodden with the flower of the land, it was time for Scotland to think over the rationality of this distant alliance, which deepened and perpetuated her feud with her close neighbour of kindred blood. Well for him, the good, easy, frank, chivalrous monarch, that he was buried in the ruin he had made, and saw not the misery of a desolated nation. Of the totally alien object for which all the mischief had been done, there was immediate evidence in various shapes. One curious little item of it is brought out by certain researches of M. Michel, which have also a significant bearing on the conflict between the secular and the papal power in the disposal of benefices.

The Pope, Julius II., was anxious to gain over to his interest Mathew Lang, bishop of Gorz, and secretary to the Emperor Maximilian. The bishop was consequently called to Rome and blessed by the vision of a cardinal's hat, and the papal influence towards the first high promotion that might open. The archbishopric of Bourges became vacant. The chapter elected one of our old friends of the Scots emigrant families, Guillaume de Monypeny, brother of the Lord of Concressault; but the King, Louis XII., at first stood out for Brillac, bishop of Orleans, resisted by the chapter. The bishop of Gorz then came forward with a force sufficient to sweep away both candidates. He was favoured of the Pope: his own master, Maximilian, desired for his secretary this foreign benefice, which would cost himself nothing; and Louis found somehow that the bishop was as much his own humble servant as the Emperor's.

No effect of causes sufficient seemed in this world more assured than that Mathew Lang, bishop of Gorz, should also be archbishop of Bourges; but the fortune of war rendered it before his collation less important to have the bishop of Gorz in the archiepiscopate than another person. The King laid his hand again on the chapter, and required them to postulate one whose name and condition must have seemed somewhat strange to them—Andrew Forman, bishop of Moray, in the north of Scotland. There are reasons for all things. Forman was ambassador from Scotland to France, and thus had opportunities of private communication with James IV. and Louis XII. This latter, in a letter to the chapter of Bourges, explains his signal obligations to Forman for having seconded the allurements of the Queen, and instigated the King of Scots to make war against England, explaining how *iceluy Roy d'Escosse s'est ouvertement declaré vouloir tenir nostre party et faire la guerre actuellement contre le Roy d'Angleterre.* Lest the chapter should doubt the accuracy of this statement of the services performed to France by Forman, the King sent them *le double des lectres que le dict Roy d'Escosse nous a escriptes, et aussy de la defiance qu'il a faite au dict Roy d'Angleterre.*

The King pleaded hard with the chapter to postulate Forman, representing that they could not find a better means of securing his own countenance and protection. The Scotsman backed this royal appeal by a persuasive letter, which he signed *André, Arcevesque de Bourges et Evesque de Morray.* Influence was brought to bear on the Pope himself, and he declared his leaning in favour of Forman. The members of the chapter, who had been knocked about past endurance in the affair of the archbishopric from first to last, threatened resistance and martyrdom; but the pressure of the powers combined against them brought them to reason, and Forman entered Bourges in archiepiscopal triumph.

But the ups and downs of the affair were as yet by no means at an end. That great pontiff, who never forgot that the head of the Church was a temporal prince, Leo X., had just ascended the throne, and found that it would be convenient to have this archbishopric of Bourges for his nephew, Cardinal Abo. By good luck the see of St Andrews, the primacy of Scotland, was then vacant, and was given as an equivalent for the French dignity. Such a promotion was a symbolically appropriate reward for the services of Forman; his predecessor fell at Flodden, and thus, in his services to the King of France, he had made a vacancy for himself. He kept for some time in his pocket, afraid to show it, the Pope's bull appointing him Archbishop of St Andrews and Primate of Scotland.

This was a direct act of interference contrary to law and custom, since the function of the Pope was only to collate or confirm, as ecclesiastical superior, the choice made by the local authorities. These had their favourite for the appointment, Prior Hepburn, who showed his earnestness in his own cause by taking and holding the Castle of St Andrews. A contest of mingled ecclesiastical and civil elements, too complex to be disentangled, followed; but in the end Forman triumphed, having on his side the efforts of the King of France and his servant Albany, with the Pope's sense of justice. The rewards of this highly endowed divine were the measure alike of his services to France and of his injuries to Scotland. He held, by the way, *in commendam*, a benefice in England; and as he had a good deal of diplomatic business with Henry VIII., it may not uncharitably be supposed that he sought to feather his hat with English as well as French plumage. It was in the midst of these affairs, which were bringing out the dangerous and disastrous elements in the French alliance, that Albany arrived.

We have seen how Albany's father, the younger brother of James III., lived in France, getting lordships there, and how the son became a thorough naturalised Frenchman. There are men who, when they shift their place and function, can assimilate themselves to the changed elements around them—who can find themselves surrounded by unwonted customs and ways, and yet accept the condition that the men who follow these are pursuing the normal character of their being, and must be left to do so in peace, otherwise harm will come of it; and in this faculty consists the instinct which enables men to govern populations trained in a different school from their own. Albany did not possess this faculty. He appears to have been ignorant of the language of Scotland, and to have thought or rather felt that, wherever he was, all should be the same as in the midst of Italian and French courtiers; and if it were not so, something was wrong, and should be put right. It was then the commencement of a very luxurious age in France—an age of rich and showy costumes, of curls, perfumes, cosmetics, and pet spaniels—and Albany was the leader of fashion in all such things. It is needless to say how powerfully all this contrasted with rough Scotland—what a shocking set of barbarians he found himself thrown among—how contemptible to the rugged Scots nobles was the effeminate Oriental luxury of the little court he imported from Paris, shifted northwards as some wealthy luxurious sportsman takes a detachment from his stable, kennel, and servants' hall, to a bothy in the Highlands.

He arrived, however, in a sort of sunshine. At that calamitous moment the nearest relation of the infant king, a practised statesman, was heartily welcome. He brought a small rather brilliant fleet with him, which was dignified by his high office as Admiral of France; he brought also some money and valuable trifles, which were not unacceptable. Wood, in his 'Peerage,' tells us that "The peers and chiefs crowded to his presence: his exotic elegance of manners, his condescension, affability, and courtesy of demeanour, won all hearts." If so, these were not long retained. He came, indeed, just before some tangible object was wanted against which to direct the first sulky feelings of the country towards France; and he served the purpose exactly, for his own handiwork was the cause of that feeling. In a new treaty between France and England, in which he bore a great if not the chief part, Scotland was for the first time treated as a needy and troublesome hanger-on of France. Instead of the old courtesy, which made Scotland, nominally at least, an independent party to the treaty, it was made directly by France, but Scotland was comprehended in it, with a warning that if there were any of the old raids across the Border, giving trouble as they had so often done, the Scots should forfeit their part in the treaty. This patronage during good behaviour roused the old pride, and was one of many symptoms that Albany had come to them less as the representative of their own independent line of kings, than as the administrator of a distant province of the French empire. The humiliation was all the more bitter from the deep resentments that burned in the people's hearts after the defeat of Flodden; and it was with difficulty that the Estates brought themselves to say that, though Scotland believed herself able single-handed to avenge her losses, yet, out of respect for the old friendship of France, the country would consent to peace with England.

Setting to work after the manner of one possessed of the same supreme authority as the King of France, Albany began his government with an air of rigour, insomuch that the common historians speak of him as having resolved to suppress the turbulent spirit of the age, and assert the supremacy of law and order. He thus incurred the reputation of a grasping tyrant. The infant brother of the king died suddenly; his mother said Albany had poisoned the child, and people shuddered for his brother, now standing alone between the Regent and the throne, and talked ominously of the manner in which Richard III. of England was popularly believed to have achieved the crown by murdering his nephews. It is from this period that we may date the rise of a really English party in Scotland—a party who feared the designs of the French, and who thought that, after having for two hundred years maintained her independence, Scotland might with fair honour be combined with the country nearest to her and likest in blood, should the succession to both fall to one prince, and that it would be judicious to adjust the royal alliances in such a manner as to bring that to pass.

Such thoughts were in the mean time somewhat counteracted by the light-headed doings of her who was the nation's present tie to England—the Queen-Dowager. Her grotesque and flagrant love-affairs are an amusing episode, especially to those who love the flavour of ancient scandal. But more serious agencies came in force, and any gracious thoughts that had turned themselves towards England were met in the teeth by the insults and injuries which her savage brother, Henry VIII., continued to pile upon the country.

Up to this point I have not observed any instances of offices of emolument in Scotland given to Frenchmen, and the fuss made about one instance of the kind leads to the supposition that they must have been rare. Dunbar the poet, who was in priest's orders, was exceedingly clamorous, in prose and in verse—in the serious and in the comic vein—for preferment. Perhaps he was the kind of person whom it is as difficult to prefer in the Church as it was to make either Swift or Sydney Smith a bishop. His indignation was greatly roused by the appointment of a foreigner whom he deemed beset by his own special failings, but in far greater intensity, to the abbacy of Tongueland; and he committed his griefs to a satirical poem, called 'The fenyet Freir of Tungland.' The object of this poem has been set down by historians as an Italian, but M. Michel indicates him as a countryman of his own, by the name of Jean Damien. He is called a charlatan, quack, and mountebank, and might, perhaps, with equal accuracy, be called a devotee of natural science, who speculated ingeniously and experimented boldly. He was in search of the philosopher's stone, and believed himself to be so close on its discovery that he ventured to embark the money of King James IV., and such other persons as participated in his own faith, in the adventure to realise the discovery, and saturate all the partners with riches indefinite.

It might be a fair question whether the stranger's science is so obsolete as the social tone of the literature in which he is attacked, since Dunbar's satirical poem, among other hints that the precedents of the adventurer unfitted him for the higher offices in the Christian ministry, insinuates that he had committed several murders; and although the charge is made in a sort of rough jocularity, the force of it does not by any means rest on its absurdity and incredibility. He was accused of a mad project for extracting gold from the Wanlockhead Hills, in Dumfriesshire, which cannot be utterly scorned in the present day, since gold has actually been extracted from them, though the process has not returned twenty shillings to the pound. This curious creature completed his absurdities by the construction of a pair of wings, with which he was to take a delightful aerial excursion to his native country. He proved his sincerity by starting in full feather from Stirling Castle. In such affairs it is, as Madame du Deffand said about that walk taken by St Denis round Paris with his own head for a burden, *le premier pas qui coute.* The poor adventurer tumbled at once, and was picked up with a broken thigh-bone. Such is the only Frenchman who became conspicuous before Albany's time as holding rank and office in Scotland.

Albany had not long rubbed on with the Scots Estates when he found that he really must go to Paris; and as there seems to have been no business concerning Scotland that he could transact there, an uncontrollable yearning to be once more in his own gay world is the only motive one can find for his trip. The Estates of Scotland were in a surly humour, and not much inclined to allow him his holidays. They appointed a council of regency to act for him. He, however, as if he knew nothing about the constitutional arrangements in Scotland, appointed a sort of representative, who cannot have known more about the condition and constitution of Scotland than his constituent, though he had been one of the illustrious guests present at the marriage of James IV.

He is named, in the chronicle called Pitscottie's, "Monsieur Tilliebattie," but his full name was Antoine d'Arces de la Bastie, and he had been nicknamed or distinguished, as the case might be, as the Chevalier Blanc, or White Knight, like the celebrated Joannes Corvinus, the knight of Wallachia, whose son became king of Hungary. M. Michel calls him the "*chevalresque et brillant La Bastie, chez qui le guerrier et l'homme d'état etaient encore supérieurs au champion des tournois.*" He was a sort of fanatic for the old principle of chivalry, then beginning to disappear before the breath of free inquiry, and the active useful pursuits it was inspiring. M. Michel quotes from a contemporary writer, who describes him as perambulating Spain, Portugal, England, and France, and proclaiming himself ready to meet all comers of sufficient rank, not merely to break a lance in chivalrous courtesy, but *à combattre à l'outrance*—an affair which even at that time was too important to be entered on as a frolic, or to pass an idle hour, but really required some serious justification. No one, it is said, accepted the challenge but the cousin of James IV. of Scotland, who is said to have been conquered, but not killed, as from the nature of the challenge he should have been; but this story seems to be a mistake by the contemporary, and M. Michel merely quotes it without committing himself.

Such was the person left by the Regent as his representative, though apparently with no specific office or powers acknowledged by the constitution of Scotland. Research may perhaps afford new light to clear up the affair; but at present the only acknowledgment of his existence bearing anything like an official character, are entries in the Scots treasurer's accounts referred to by M. Michel, one of them authorising a payment of fifteen shillings to a messenger to the warden of the middle march, "with my lord governor's letters delivered by Monsr. Labawte;" another payment to his servant for summoning certain barons and gentlemen to repair to Edinburgh; and a payment of twenty shillings for a service of more import, thus entered—"Item, deliverit be Monsieur Lawbatez to Johne Langlandis, letters of our sovereign lords to summon and warn all the thieves and broken men out of Tweeddale and Eskdale in their own country—quhilk letters were proclaimed at market-cross of Roxburgh, Selkirk, and Jedwood."

This proclamation seems to have been the deadly insult which sealed his fate. The borders had hardly yet lost their character of an independent district, which might have merged into something like a German margravate. There had been always some family holding a preponderating and almost regal power there. At this time it was the Homes or Humes, a rough set, with their hands deeply dipped in blood, who little dreamed that their name would be known all over Europe by the fame of a fat philosopher sitting writing in a peaceful library with a goosequill, and totally innocent of the death of a fellow-being. It was one of Albany's rigorous measures to get the leaders of this clan brought to justice, or, in other words, executed. This was a thing to be avenged; and since La Bastie was taking on himself the responsibilities of Albany, it was thought as well that he should not evade this portion of them.

To lure him within their reach, a sort of mock fight was got up by the borderers in the shape of the siege of one of their peel towers. Away went La Bastie in all his bravery, dreaming, simple soul, as if he were in Picardy or Touraine, that the mere name of royalty would at once secure peace and submission. His eye, practised in scenes of danger, at once saw murder in the gaze of those he had ventured among, and he set spurs to his good horse, hoping to reach his headquarters in the strong castle of Dunbar. The poor fellow, however, ignorant of the country, and entirely unaided, was overtaken in a bog. It is said that he tried cajoling, threats, and appeals to honour and chivalrous feeling. As well speak to a herd of hungry wolves as to those grim ministers of vengeance! The Laird of Wedderburn, a Home, enjoyed the distinction of riding with the Frenchman's head, tied by its perfumed tresses at his saddle-bow, into the town of Dunse, where the trophy was nailed to the market-cross. As old Pitscottie has it, "his enemies came upon him, and slew and murdered him very unhonestly, and cutted off his head, and carried it with them; and it was said that he had long hair platt over his neck, whilk David Home of Wedderburn twust to his saddle-bow, and keeped it."

This affair brought Scotland into difficulties both with England and France. Henry VIII. professed himself displeased that a French adventurer should have been set up as ruler in his nephew's kingdom; and Francis I., who had just mounted the throne of France, demanded vengeance on the murderers of his distinguished subject, with whose chivalrous spirit he had a congenial sympathy. There is an exceedingly curious and suggestive correspondence between France and Scotland at the commencement of M. Teulet's volumes.* It closely resembles the papers that might be returned to Parliament by our Indian Government on the negotiations with some wily Affghan or Scinde chief, in which reparation is demanded for outrages on a British subject. There is much fussy desire to comply with the demands of the great power, but ever a difficulty, real or pretended, in getting anything done.

Proclamations and other denunciatory documents were issued in the loudest and angriest terms against the traitors and foul murderers of the representative of the illustrious ally of Scotland.

---

* 'Relations Politiques de la France et de l'Espagne avec l'Écosse au xv. Siècle: papiers d'état, pièces, et documents inédits ou peu connus tirés des bibliotheques et des archives de France,' publié par Alexandre Teulet, archiviste aux archives de l'empire, i. 9-16.

Francis was told that a great army was organised to march to the borders, and utterly annihilate the criminals and their faction; and to give the expedition all the more thorough an aspect of serious business, it was accompanied by actual artillery—a new device in the art of war but little known up to that time in Scotland. But when this powerful host arrived at the country of the Homes, the lords had fled to England. What more could be done? The correspondence concludes with a suggestion close on sarcasm, if not intended for it, that Francis had better demand the criminals from Henry VIII. It is not necessary, however, to suppose that there was absolute perfidy in all this. It may have been then in Scotland as probably it often is in the East, that the difficulty in punishing a set of powerful culprits has a better foundation in their capacity for self-defence than the government is inclined to acknowledge.

But Francis was not in a condition to press the matter so far as to risk a quarrel with an old friend. Evil days, indeed, were coming to both kingdoms, and they were knit together again by the ties of a common adversity. Albany gave great provocation to Henry VIII. by joining in, if he did not organise, a project by which France, the northern powers, and Scotland were to unite for the restoration of the house of York in England through its representative, Reginald de la Pole. The wrath of Henry fell heavily on the land, and appeal after appeal was made to Francis for assistance. But his hands were full. He had to keep up three great armies—one in Italy, another in Picardy, and a third in Guienne—and was in great alarm for the safety of his own frontiers. He sent first M. Le Charron, and then M. De Langeac, as his ambassadors, with supremely kind and sympathising messages, recommending Scotland to keep up heart until better days should come, but he could give no material assistance. Driven to extremes, the Scots represented that they had been offered peace with England on the condition of abandoning the French alliance. They had sternly refused this humiliating condition; but they now put it to France, whether, being quite unable to give them assistance, she would resign, for a time at least, her claims to the exclusive friendship of the Scots, and let them make peace with England. But Francis was in the climax of his adversity. The great battle of Pavia had just been fought. The Scots were asked if it was a time to desert steady old friends when their king was defeated and a captive in the enemy's hands? The chivalry which ruled the diplomacy of that day prevailed, and the request was withdrawn. The two nations, in externals, became faster friends than ever.*

In 1537 there was a gallant wedding, when

* Teulet, 'Relations Politiques,' i. 43-55.

James V. went to bring home Madeleine of France. He received special royal honours, not known before to have been conferred on foreigners. According to the documents given by M. Teulet, the officers charged with the traditions of state precedents grumbled about this prince of a northern island, who knew no civilised language, receiving honours which had heretofore been deemed sacred to the royal blood of France, the Parliament being specially aggrieved by having to walk in procession in their scarlet robes, carrying their mantles and velvet caps. The national policy that held by this marriage would have had but a frail tenure, for poor Madeleine soon drooped and died. She had said, as a girl, that she wanted to be a queen, be the realm she ruled what it might; and so she had a brief experience—this word seems preferable to enjoyment—of the throne of cold uncomfortable Scotland. There was speedily another wedding, bearing in the direction of the French alliance,—for that was still uppermost with the governing powers, whatever it might be with the English and Protestant party, daily acquiring strength among the district leaders, nobles or lairds. It may have seemed to these, that when the queen was no longer a daughter of France, but a young lady, the child of one feudatory and the widow of another, with no better claim to share the throne than her beautiful face, there was no further danger from France. But the young queen was a Guise—one of that wonderful race who seemed advancing onwards to a destiny of which it was not easy to fix the probable limits. Scotland, by her royal alliances, might now be said to have hold of England with one hand and France with the other. The question came to be, which would pull hardest?

Chapter IV.

The Birth of Queen Mary—French Writers on her Life and Character—Her Influence on the Fate of Europe—Catherine of Medici—Their Strife—Mary's Bequest to Philip—The apparent Supremacy of the Old League—The Underworkings that were destroying it—French Government in Scotland—Reaction—Recent Revelations—The Reformation in Scotland, and how it came about—The Winding-up.

ON the 7th of December in the year 1542 was born the infant afterwards renowned over the world as Mary Queen of Scots. The heir to the throne of England was a boy five years older — Edward, the son of her grand-uncle, Henry VIII. They were in the degree of what is called first and second cousins. Nothing seemed so rational as that these two should be united, and so heal the wounds of two bleeding countries. It was indeed so extremely reasonable, that Henry VIII., to prevent any possibility of its falling through, resolved to effect it at once by force—the most dangerous of all means for accomplishing any object with the Scots. He demanded the personal custody of the royal child; and when this was refused, he restored the old claims of superiority, and sent an army to fetch her. Here again history is overloaded with the cruel feats of one exterminating army following on the heels of another, and all set to their bloody work because their passionate tyrant had resolved to cut the child out of the very heart of her people. He had almost accomplished his object, and Scotland seemed but a step from annexation, when, on the 16th of June 1548, strange sails were seen in the Firth of Forth, and, to the joy of high and low, the Sieur d'Essé, a tried soldier, landed with a small army in the pay of France, accompanied by a field-train of unusual strength for the times. These men were of all nations—soldiers by trade, and ready to fight for any paymaster. They were well accustomed, of course, to all sort of scenes of ruffianism; but they had yet to know, and they did so with some twinges of revulsion, the ferocity imparted to those who fight for their homes against the invader. When the mercenaries took prisoners from the English, they were of course ready to sell them, by way of ransom, to the highest bidder—friend or enemy. The highest bidders were in many instances the Scots, who thus invested their scant supply of money that they might have the gratification of putting the hated invaders to death. These were symptoms of a spirit that snapped at once all the ties of diplomacy and royal alliances. The great object now was how to render Henry's object impossible. This was done by spiriting the royal infant off to France—a feat skilfully and gallantly accomplished with the assistance of the French vessels.

We now approach the time when the destinies of Europe depended on the character and actions of three women—a sort of three Fates who spun and cut the threads of nations. These were Catherine of Medici, Queen Elizabeth, and Mary of Scotland. It is with the last that we have chiefly to do here. The story of the alliance between France and Scotland had reached its climax when both had the same queen. Her influence on the two nations is not alone historical: it has affected the tenor of French literature, and the eye with which it has regarded Scotland; and in this respect the position of the two countries towards each other can be exemplified among the people of our own generation.

French authors have indeed lately thrown themselves, with their natural impetuosity, on the great problems of Mary's character and actions.* And

* Besides Mignet's—beyond any question the best Life of Queen Mary—and also, besides, the works of Teulet and Michel, a considerable portion of which applies to her, we have,—

'Etudes sur W. Shakspeare, Marie Stuart, et L'Arêtin—

though we claim credit for more coolness and historical impartiality than our neighbours, yet it may be that those qualities which we count defects in them, enable them to take a more genial and natural view

---

Le Drame, le Mœur, et la Religion au xvi. Siècle,' par M. Chasles-Philarète, 1854.

'Marie Stuart et Catherine de Medicis, étude historique sur les Relations de la France et de l'Ecosse,' 1858.

'Histoire de Marie Stuart,' par J. M. Dargaud.

'Les Crimes Célèbres,' par Alexandre Dumas—Marie Stuart.

'The Life of Mary Stuart,' by Marie Louis Alphonse Prat de Lamartine.

'Marie Stuart et le Comte de Bothwell,' par L. Wiesener, Professeur d'Histoire à Lycée Louis-le-Grande, 1863.

'Lettres de Marie Stuart, publiées avec summaires, traductions, notes, et fac-simile,' par Jean Baptiste Alexandre Theodore Teulet.

The last is intended as a supplement to the collection by Prince Labanoff, with which my reader either is or is not acquainted. This venerable member of the select circle of Russian grandees, claiming descent from the pristine Rurik, stands conspicuous as a living illustration of the fascinations of our northern Cleopatra. It is related among the triumphs of Ninon de l'Enclos, that she had lovers among the contemporaries of her grandchildren, one of them, according to a questionable legend, turning out to be an actual descendant in that degree. But the fascinations of Mary present to us a far more potent testimony in a living lover, who loves and must love on, as some of the sentimental songs say, down into the third century after that in which the object of his passion breathed the breath of life. The Prince has spent a great portion of a long life in the functions of a knight-errant, vindicating the spotless honour of the lady of his love. If it has not been his lot to put the spear in rest against the caitiff maligners, or to knock on

of such a nature as hers. With nothing but our plain black and white to paint with, we are unable to impart to our picture the rich blending of hues which harmonises the light with the shade, and im-

---

the shield hung outside the gate of the castle where the object of his vows lies captive, he has performed the drearier, if less dangerous, task of ransacking every library in the world for evidence of the innocence of his peerless lady, and has published the result of his labours in seven dense octavo volumes. They are a curious and valuable collection, but rather dryish on the whole; and though the price of the volumes is considerable, I have little doubt that they have been paid for by many more people than they have been read by. The Prince's labours were not directed to the end of discovering the truth—that was already fixed and indubitable as divine truth; he sought in his humble devotion only to collect and record the documents calculated to illustrate it, and bring it home in its full lustre to careless or obdurate hearts. Accordingly, he rejected from his collection as spurious, and in a manner blasphemous, those documents which, in the view of the impartial, throw doubt on the purity of his bright particular star. M. Teulet observes, with a sort of dry sarcasm, "C'est là sans doute une conviction aussi sincère que respectable; malheureusement tout le monde ne la partage pas;" and he remarks very justly, that to those acquainted with the Prince Labanoff it is quite unnecessary to explain that he is a complete stranger to the volume issued to the world for the purpose of completing his collection.

There is, in fact, a sort of Quixotism in M. Teulet himself, and one cannot help being amused by the enthusiasm for historical accuracy, which has set the one collector and editor to dog the steps, as it were, of the other, and supply his rejections and omissions, in order that the world may know the real truths. There is no getting off with a fond hallucination, or a well-pleaded one-sided theory, while

parts a general richness to the tone of the composition throughout. It will require a hardish course of reading in the Causes Célèbres, the Mémoires, and the recent school of French novels, to give a native of this country a conception of the assimilation of French people's thoughts to such a topic—to let one see how thoroughly, and almost devoutly, they would relish the story of her beauty, her wit, her lively vitality, her marvellous capacity for fathoming the human heart, her equally marvellous power of allurement, and her perfect good sense, good taste, and good-humour. And indeed these qualities were rather enhanced than blotted by the one prevailing weakness—a submission to the empire of the master passion so entire, that under its relentless rule no duty to God or man was powerful enough in restraint; and if such a thing as the life of a wretched poltroon calling himself husband stood in the way,—why, let it go. When we convince ourselves, as in the story

---

there are archæological detectives to track our steps in this fashion. The two editors are not only honest, but disinterested, each in his own peculiar way. To the affluent and distinguished Prince, the cost of printing seven volumes for an unappreciating public would be a trifling addition to the sacrifices made by him in his laborious search over the world for their contents. It is questionable whether his sacrifice is nearly so great as that of the distinguished archæologist; since any man, master of the abilities and industry embarked on the supplemental volume, might surely, had he desired it, have found a more profitable and a more distinguished method of employing them.

of Chatelar, that the resources of the syren's fascinations are drawn upon to awaken wild hopeless love in a poor youth until he is driven frantic, and rushes into such scrapes that he must be killed out of the way, we get angry and use hard words, instead of looking at the affair in a purely artistic aspect.* Hence one set of our writers will have it that she was a meek and injured angel, the other that she was a remorseless and cruel demon.

Unless Mr Froude is to be counted an exception,

---

* There is something, too, in the intense silliness of Chatelar's conduct which our insular natures cannot away with, and so scarce any one has raised a voice against his cruel death. It is a pity that the process against him has been lost, were it only to remove curious doubts as to the portion of the royal premises in which he was hidden. If we adopt a very plain-spoken statement in a letter from Randolph to Cecil, the poor youth's account of the place he went to, and his reason for going to it, is so gross an outrage at once on the dignity of history and the ideal purity of romance, that one cannot wonder at both having passed it by in ignominious silence (see Von Raumer's 'Contributions to Modern History,' p. 22). It is, by the way, a misapprehension to suppose that Chatelar's position was so humble as to make his aspirations, had he conducted himself decorously, an utter misconception and a symptom of insanity. He was a youth of birth and condition—otherwise Brantome would not have spoken of him as he does—and related to the chivalrous Bayard. No doubt, an alliance with one in whom the destinies of Europe were so heavily involved, would have been a mightily presumptuous expectation for him to form. But he was in the position in which a lift in the world by marriage with a supernumerary daughter of some secondary royal family might not have seemed utterly preposterous.

our writers have made coarse work of this delicate historical morsel. We cannot enter into the spirit of that long, patient, noble *supplice*—we have not a word for it in our own language—which dignifies guilt. Once believing in what we call the guilt, we cast the unclean thing away, and will give it no place in our heart. It is very difficult for us, indeed, to understand how lightly murder would lie on a conscience trained under the shadow of Catherine of Medici, and how consistently a laxness about it might coexist with beauty, gentleness, and kindness. The ethics, indeed, which ruled that court were deeper and more devilish than anything of native-born French origin. They were Italian—the views which the Borgias practised, and Machiavelli taught. Among the small states of their native growth they might be used for the slaughtering of half a village, or the poisoning-off of a family: imported to the mighty kingdom of France, their fruit expanded into the great battue of St Bartholomew's Day. The Florentine's precepts were intended for the private use of the Medici family; and there was something so self-contradictory in their publication to the world, that he was supposed to be in jest, like Swift with his advice to servants; for it is the ruling spirit of all such policy that it is personal to the owner, hidden within the dark recesses of his own breast, and concealed for use against the scrutiny of the keenest adversary. There was no better place of concealment for it than behind youth, beauty, genial courtesy, and gaiety of heart.

In addition to a more genial appreciation of the nature of the heroine, the French were placed in a better position to see the whole expanse of the stage on which she acted. Our own historians, dealing with but a corner of the world, are not prepared duly to estimate the expansive scene which Mary's peculiar position opened up. I propose, in a few words, before winding up the "Ancient League," to sketch the chief conditions of which she was in the several steps of her career the centre.*

* Along with their tact in appreciating the spirit of their heroine, the more ambitious of these French authors are sometimes amusingly inaccurate in minute matters of fact. M. Chasles opens thus—"Il y a un nom qui semble destiné à servir d'anneau brillant et douloureux entre la civilisation du Midi et le rude esprit du Nord pendant le xvie siècle. Ce nom éclatant et voilé de pleurs est le plus tragique des temps modernes; tragique surtout par l'obscurité équivoque et le bruit confus de ses fautes, de ses talents, et de ses angoisses! Jamais on ne pourra rêver de roman plus pathétique que le sien: c'est une femme voluptueuse, gaie comme le soleil de France, passionnée comme le ciel d'Italie; faible et forte; entourée d'hommes sauvages, qui poignardent son ministre dans ses bras. Captive dans un donjon humide et malsain, elle, habituée à toutes les recherches; elle brave du fond de ce cachot Élisabeth vieillie dans le despotisme; enfin elle tend au bourreau sa tête royale et catholique, qui n'a pas plié devant sa rivale."

This is no doubt well turned, but the turning-point about the death of Rizzio is inaccurate. He was not stabbed in her arms—he was not killed in her presence; she did not

It was not alone her queenly rank, her extraordinary beauty, and her mental gifts, even accompanied as these were by the more potent gift of an irresistible seductiveness, that gave her the influence she held over her age, as the manner in

---

know of his death till some time after the deed. In fact, her conduct during the interval between his removal and her knowledge of his fate furnishes some of the most significant conjectures about her concern in the tragedy next to come off.

The mistakes in the book of another Frenchman, M. Dargaud, are the more amusing from his almost chivalrous efforts to be quite accurate. He tells us that he explored the collections, the museums, the ancient portraits, the rare engravings, the traditions, the ballads, the lakes, the sea and its shores, the mountains and plains, the fields of battle, the palaces, the prisons, all the ruins, all the sites, and all the innumerable traces of the past—the enumeration is the author's own, not a travesty of it. He then explains how lifeless all history is without topography; and thus, with much simplicity, sets the reader on the watch to find whether his own topography is quite accurate. We begin with Mary, a happy child in the island of Inch Mahome, in the Lake of Menteith. That she enjoyed the national ballads and legends, and listened with delight to the pibroch, "sorte de mélodie guerrière exécutée sur le cornemuse," is a statement which it would be difficult to disprove were it worth while; but the author, when he describes her bounding over the rocks at early dawn, is at once contradicted by the fact that the island is a bit of meadow as flat as a carpet. There is no doubt a great contrast, especially in these days of tile-draining, between the fruitful plains of the lowlands and the highland Grampians. But the author's vivid picture of Queen Mary's enjoyment of the contrast in the northern tour ending in the battle of Corrichie is utterly thrown away, since in the course of that

which these fine court cards were played. They happened to be in the hand, or rather in the several hands, of a house which counted within its own family circle a group of the most accomplished, daring, and successful political gamesters of the day.

---

journey the country she passed over is an almost continuous tract of bleak, low, uniform acclivities.

This author tells us of peculiarities in the habits of John Knox which, had they been known to his biographer, Dr M'Crie, would have changed the tone of his book, and, indeed, have slightly perplexed that grave and earnest biographer. It seems that the great preacher frequented the Pentland Mountains, where "tous les soirs très tard, il s'endormait au bruit d'une cascade de la montagne. La chute harmonieuse et monotone de cette grande nappe d'eau pouvait seule calmer l'agitation formidable de ses pensées"—(p. 193). There is something exceedingly comical in the idea of Knox thus posed. If the practice could be established, it might add to the renown of the only waterfall on the Pentlands—the much-infested Habbie's Howe. But there is evidently some confusion in the author's mind between our great Reformer and Brian, the Celtic seer in the 'Lady of the Lake:'

> "Couched on a shelve beneath its brink,
> Close where the thundering torrents sink,
> Rocking beneath their headlong sway,
> And drizzled by the ceaseless spray,
> Midst groan of rock and roar of stream,
> The wizard waits prophetic dream."

M. Dargaud derived some valuable ideas from the "statuette du docteur" which he saw in the High Street—a well-known piece of rude carving by some ambitious mason, who intended to symbolise Moses. A picture in Holyrood is pronounced to be the veritable "docteur imperieux et terrible de l'idée nouvelle;" and doubtless, among the rubbish of odds and ends collected in Holyrood, there is a

The fortune which made Mary the daughter of a Guise, put a character on the events of the time. Had she been the daughter of her father's first wife, poor gentle Madeleine of Valois, whatever destinies might have awaited her, it is not likely that they

---

picture which it is the rule of the house to call a portrait of Knox, though every observing onlooker, seeing the compasses in the hand, pronounces it to be the portrait of an architect or a geometrist.

But M. Dargaud met with wonders in Edinburgh denied to the eyes and ears of the common herd even of tourists. He gives a succinct account of the manner in which Darnley was put to death before the house of the Kirk-o'-Field was blown up to conceal the deed. This account is carefully culled from the traditions which he collected "au pied de l'église expiatoire bâtie sur ce funèbre lieu." This statement suggests uneasy suspicions as to the stories that may be palmed off by guides upon confiding tourists. Monstrous falsehoods are told by the whole class; and it is a signal exemplification of their resolution utterly to abandon their sense and discretion along with their work, that holiday tourists should take instructions in the most abstruse portions of archæology from the most ignorant of the human race. The "rises" which this class of public instructors take out of their victims are in the general case extravagant enough. Yet the guide who so far fathomed the French historian's appetite and discretion as to show him the expiatory church on the scene of the death of Darnley, must have been an honour to his profession. M. Dargaud is an inveterate hunter after traditions, and finds them in the most unpromising ground. Thus, he found among the cottars of the counties of York, Derby, Northampton, and Stafford a well-preserved description of Queen Mary riding along, surrounded by her maids of honour, and followed by the ferocious dragoons of Elizabeth. He might about as well go to the coast of Kent and gather an account of the

would have been so high. It was not the greatness of her mother's family, but its characteristic of being a pushing rising family, that gave her name its wide influence. During that period and for some time later—so late, indeed, as the construction of the

---

appearance and costume of Julius Cæsar on the occasion of his celebrated landing in Britain.

On matters of historical opinion every man is free. M. Dargaud looked with mysterious awe in Hamilton Palace on the identical hackbut with which Bothwellhaugh shot the Regent Murray. Having also seen this weapon, I take it, notwithstanding an inscription on it engraved in brass by some eminent maker of door-plates, to have been constructed by some Brummagem rifle-manufacturer about the period of the American War, or perhaps a little later. There is a curious harmony between this author's notions about the assailant's weapon and the defence of the assailed. The Regent Murray, it seems, would not have been pierced by Bothwellhaugh's bullet, if he had had the precaution to put on the "souple et impénétrable cotte de mailles," the work of Henry Wynd, the celebrated armourer of Perth. This coat of mail must be about as imaginary an article as a sermon by the celebrated hypocrite Tartuffe, or a cameo from the collection of the Count of Monte Christo. If we are to have history founded on such materials, it were well to put the right tradition in the right place. So when we have Queen Mary at Hamilton with her followers, after her escape from Loch Leven, displeased with their inactivity, she resolves to rouse them by one of those "symboles familiers au génie des peuples du Nord." Accordingly, she sets before the assembled barons a dish prepared by her own royal hands. The cover is lifted, and behold—a pair of spurs! Universal applause and enthusiasm follow—the war-cry is sounded, and all leap to the saddle to conquer or die for their Queen. Everybody is familiar with this, as a Border legend of the method which the goodwife

Prussian kingdom — the regal duchies which fell into the hands of clever ambitious families had a way of expanding into kingdoms and empires. The King of France represented but a Duke of Paris, and the Czar a Duke of Muscovia. It seemed clear to contemporaries that the Guises of Lorraine were to aggrandise themselves into a royal house. They fell by their too eagerly grasping at a great crown, and the ambition that o'erleaps its sell. Their aim was to rule over France, if not farther; and how near they were to accomplishing that object we can

---

took to remind her husband of an empty larder. There is a certain licence, perhaps, to be permitted to an author of rhetorical and popular tendencies, who is speaking of a foreign country, and is apt to get inveigled between the real and the ideal. There are other little inaccuracies which some of the author's friends will no doubt consider ornaments, in as far as they exemplify a sort of scorn of minute accuracy in the matters of foreign countries, which, in French literature, is something like the inability of great people to remember the personal histories and genealogical connections of their inferiors. Hence French literature seems to cultivate a sort of imbecility in foreign nomenclature—be it applicable to institutions, persons, or places. There is a rather preposterous instance of this assumptive inaptness in M. Dargaud, when he gives us his brilliant description of the marriage of Mary and Darnley, where the Queen is served by "les Comtes Atholl, Sewer, Morton, Caver, et Crawford." One might attribute the appearance of the Earls Sewer and Caver to extremely careless correction of the press; but there is something about the tone of the passage tending to leave it doubtful whether its author had so read his authorities as to be aware that on that occasion Atholl performed the part of sewer, and Mor-

only now judge by looking back on that age by the light of the present, in which the experiment which was then made, but failed, has been successful.

What the Buonaparte dynasty has done for itself, was in fact pretty nearly anticipated by the dynasty of Guise. It is extremely interesting to compare, at the two extremes of such a stretch of time, conditions so unlike in their mere external and incidental characteristics, yet possessing so much unity in their real essence. There was the same restlessness and fickleness among all classes of the French people,

---

ton of carver. There are surely not many British readers of French books who would suppose that a *maître d'hôtel* is a personage like the Master of Ravenswood, or that a *chef de cuisine* indicates the chief of some Gallic clan. It will not disturb this author's equanimity, that he has made mistakes of this kind, should they come to his knowledge. But there are other points coming in contact with French literature, on which even so ambitious a writer as M. Dargaud might be expected to take the trouble of being precise. Doubtless the pretty lines beginning—

> "Adieu, plaisant pays de France,
> O ma patrie
> La plus chérie,"

were long attributed to Queen Mary, and cited as critical evidence of the impossibility of her having written other things so far lower both in morality and genius. But a French writer ought to have known that the piece was written by Meunier de Querlon, a clever miscellaneous author of the middle of the last century.

I feel some regret in yielding to a malicious temptation, in noticing these trifling inaccuracies in a book which has much interest, and also a deal of historical truth, as distinct from mere accuracy in detail.

the same vibration between anarchy and abject submission, the same insane determination to drive the one principle uppermost for the time to its most relentless conclusions ; and, what is more to the point, the same thirsting for a leader brave, strong, relentless, and successful. Since the tide turned against Francis I.—since the date of the battle of Pavia, we may say—the French were losing conceit of the house of Valois. They did not satisfy the national craving for brilliancy and success, for the satisfaction of which Frenchmen will at once cheerfully abandon their liberties. France, indeed, was waning in the eyes of Europe before the rising influence of Spain and England, the great representatives of the two contending forces of the age. She thus continued in imminent peril of revolution, until Henry IV. gave the crown the lustre of heroism. Immediately afterwards Richelieu handed over a well-drilled territory to Louis XIV., by whose brilliant career of victories and unjust aggrandisements the lease was effectually renewed, and the Revolution postponed.

Le Balafré, or the Scarred, the head of the Guises, had in the period of weakness and despondency performed the one redeeming achievement which was glorious to his countrymen, in the capture of Calais from the English. He was the most popular man of his day, and he knew how by a subtle diplomacy to make that as well as every other element of his strength tell. There can be no doubt that he was the supreme guiding spirit in that bold movement by which the precious infant was spirited out of Scotland, and carried far beyond the reach of Henry VIII., and the influence of his plans for uniting England and Scotland under his son and her. The next great step was her marriage with the Dauphin. Fortune favoured them mightily at one stroke, when Montgomery poked out the eye of Henry II. in the tilt-yard. A member of the house of Guise was now Queen of France. It does not seem probable that then they looked to sovereignty in France. They were but increasing their power by every feasible means that offered, and the displacement of their niece's husband was not to be so defined. Indeed, it is not likely that the Balafré himself ever thought of the throne of France. It was on his more unscrupulous and restless son that that consummation of their power seems to have dawned.

To the world in general it seemed as if all this fabric of power had toppled down at once with the death of the poor feeble King of France. Queen of France and Queen of Scotland—the two things were as far apart in power and brilliancy as the palace from the cottage, and the latter now only remained. To these restless and ambitious spirits, however, the game was by no means up. The court card was still in their hands to be played again; and though they lost the fortune that seemed secured, there were others even greater within the range of possibilities. No time was lost before their busy brains were at work devising a new alliance. The several available monarchs and heirs to thrones were scrutinised. Denmark and some of the smaller German states were lightly passed over by an eye that looked ever upwards, and at last rested on the supreme pinnacle of European power—the Spanish empire. It was there that whatever France lost had been gained. It was the empire whose monarch boasted that the sun never set on his dominions. As his ambassador Don Ferdinand de Mandosa put it, "God was supreme in heaven, but the King of Spain was supreme on earth." He had brought under his feet the independent states of Spain, snatched Portugal, ruled the greater part of Italy; and though the Dutch were then working out their independence, they were, in the eye of Spain and the greater part of Europe, merely a handful of rebels struggling in a swamp, and earning for themselves condign punishment. He crushed the Moors, and in the conflict afterwards crowned at Lepanto he had proved himself the champion and protector of Christendom against the domineering Turk.

To preserve a full impression of the mighty position of Spain under Philip II., it is necessary to remember that the revival of the Empire was the aim of every great Continental power. Spain seemed marching on to this high destiny. France was thrown out in the misfortunes of Francis I. Germany, though nominally in possession of the Cæsarship, had not throughout her scattered states concentrated power to give it vitality. The greatness of England was of another kind—a fresh growth, totally apart from the remains of the imperial system, and supported by the separate vitality of its energetic, free, industrious people. Thus the Spanish monarch had no effective rival in the ambitious course which he was slowly, but cunningly and resolutely, pursuing; and when he finally succeeded, his would be a greater empire than ever Roman eagle soared above: for had there not been found a new world on the other side of the Atlantic—the yet undeveloped empire called "the Indies"?

What a position, then, for these ambitious princes of Lorraine, could they get their niece, with her possession of Scotland and her claims to the succession of England, made Queen of Spain! With such sources of influence in their hands, it would go hard but that the head of the house of Lorraine ruled in France, be it as Mayor of the Palace, as deputy of the Emperor of Europe, or as actual King. And then there was the Empire itself to look forward to.

It is significant of the reach of their ambition that the great Duke, when, as head of the League, he was more powerful than any contemporary monarch except the King of Spain, had it spoken of that he was a descendant of Charlemagne. The pedigree was not very accurate, but it was as good as that which served the turn of the Lorraine Hapsburgs. The spirit of his policy is reflected in the 'Argenis' of Barclay, who was a keen observer, and designed to leave behind him in his book a closer view of the inner intricacies of the statecraft of the age than the common histories afforded. He wanted to do the difficult duty of speaking to posterity without letting his own generation hear what he said, and so he wove his revelations into a ponderous allegory. In his Lycogenes, however, the great Duke was at once recognised. His talk is exactly that of his position and views. He is not himself a king, but is at the head of a kingly family. So, when a relation, in the course of some flattering talk, rails against monarchs, Lycogenes rebukes him: None should govern but those of kingly race; but they should not be absolutely hereditary; there should be a choice, and the best man among them should get each vacant throne—precisely the doctrine to suit his position and views.* It has often been maintained that he was not sincere in the Popish fanaticism which he professed. He knew, however, that the Pontificate and the Empire were necessary to each other, as the two orbs of one

* "Timerat Lycogenes invidiam, quod ab suo nepote oppugnaretur jus regium. Nam et hoc inutile suis cœptis facinus erat, qui non delere sed habere sibi regnum optaert. Aliud commodius visum: quandoquidem ille sermo inciderat arguere gentium ritum, quæ uni se stirpi in hereditatem permiserant, cæterasque extollere post singulorum obitum regum in comitia et suffragia euntes."—'Argenis,' lib. i. ch. 15.

system—Pope and Emperor being as natural a conjunction as Church and King.

Accordingly a marriage was projected, and all but concluded, with Don Carlos, the heir to the Spanish crown. The project suited admirably with the ambitious notions of Philip II. In fact, like the Guises on the death of King Francis, he had just lost by death the hold he had on England through his marriage with Henry VIII.'s daughter, Mary; and here was another available in its place; for with all the Roman Catholics there was no doubt that Queen Mary of Scotland was the true heiress of the throne of England, and that the overthrow of Elizabeth the usurper was to be brought about by Providence in its own good time, with such judicious aid from the sword as Philip was able and very willing to supply.

There was a dark and subtle spirit, however, which in close quarters might come to be more powerful than the Guises or the King of Spain either, dead against the match. This was our friend Catherine of Medici, the mother-in-law of Mary. The motives of this terrible woman have been an enigma to historians. And yet there is a view of them simple enough, which tallies pretty well with the facts of history: it is, that she had no scruples of any kind, and let nothing stand between her and her object. If lies could accomplish her object, tell them; if life were in the way, out with it, by bullet, steel, or poison, as may be most convenient, considering time and purpose. Her policy was an engine to be kept going, though nothing but human blood should be available for working it; and as to the nature of her policy, it was not that of despotism or of liberty, of the Church of Rome or of freedom of conscience, but the enjoyment of self-centred power. It seems to add a new shade to one of the darkest pictures of human wickedness, to say that the author of the Massacre of St Bartholomew had no fanaticism or religious zeal in her; but so it was. As to Philip, he was a thorough bigot, who consoled himself on his death-bed by reflecting on the numbers he had put to death, and the quantity of human agony he had inflicted for the sake of the Church; but as to his rival in bloodshed and cruelty, she would have become a Huguenot or a Mohammedan could it have served her purpose. At a celebrated conference at Bayonne, on the frontier, whither she went professedly to meet her daughter, she met also with the Duke of Alva and other historic personages. It was a general opinion that there, in dark conclave, a league was formed for the extirpation of the Protestants, of which Catherine honestly observed her part on St Bartholomew's Day. But in their recently published state papers the French Government have given the world a full and particular account of the sayings and doings at this conference, and represent to us Catherine cool and politic, sarcastic almost, at the fiery enthusiasm of

Spain, and absolutely charged with a secret partiality towards the Huguenots.*

She had no love for Mary Stewart. The day on which she, the mother of the king, had to give precedence to the young beauty who had become reigning queen, stamped its mark on her black heart. Mary stung the dowager occasionally with her sarcastic tongue; for few were better adepts at that dangerous accomplishment which torments and makes enemies. For all its illustrious history, the house of Medici was an anomaly among the feudalities, from having founded its wealth and power on commerce instead of rapine, and it lay open to sneers as not legitimately regal; hence Mary called her mother-in-law the *fille de Marchand*—a sneer which Catherine committed to her dangerous and retentive memory. She was pretty freely accused, indeed, of having shortened her son's life, because she thought she would have more power were he out of the way; and no doubt she was quite capable of the deed. The only thing in which she showed any of the confiding weakness of mankind was in being a devotee of astrology and divination; but these, if they were supernatural, yet were agencies put in the power of man which she might turn to her own immediate purpose, and which were therefore far more to be respected than the religion which belonged to another world, in which she could not command obedience.

* 'Papiers d'Etat du Cardinal de Granville,' ix. 319.

Well, Catherine was against the Spanish match, for the obvious reason that it would render the power of the Lorraine Guises preponderant over that of herself and her sons. She was indefatigable in carrying her point. M. Chéruel has published some of her letters on the affair to the Bishop of Limoges, the French ambassador in Spain. Strange documents they are, subtle almost to unintelligibility, full of ingenious suggestion and eager pleading, with a shadowy half-hidden under-current of menace. It was difficult to bring very powerful arguments to bear against an arrangement so advantageous to both the parties concerned. She tried to make out that it would be extremely detrimental to the Catholic cause, because, if her hand were weakened by the aggrandisement of the Guises, it would be the Huguenot King of Navarre, and not she, who would really obtain the chief influence in France. She endeavoured to work through King Philip's confessor and several of his confidential advisers. Her daughter was Philip's third wife—to her the most plausible arguments were addressed.

It was proposed that Don Carlos, instead of having Mary, should be married to the younger sister of his stepmother, the Queen of Spain. Thus that Queen would have a sister with her, and her position would be strengthened by an alliance with the heir to the throne, on whom her own personal claim as his stepmother would be but small. Catherine even endeavoured to move Queen Elizabeth to her ends by presenting to her a prospect, no doubt sufficiently alarming, both for the cause of Protestantism and her own personal interest. But how Elizabeth could have acted in the matter save through the influence of Murray, afterwards the Regent, on his sister, is not very clear. The match, however, was defeated. People so unscrupulous as Catherine are very successful in accomplishing their ends. She had in her employment a countryman of her own, one Bianci, or Blanc, as the French annalists call him, an expert confectioner, who got the title of Queen Catherine's poisoner—that being the function by which he was reputed to gain his living. A powerful effect would be produced on the mind by such a thought passing over it as—"Well, if I push her to the wall, that woman will poison me." From whatever cause, however, she had her way on this occasion, and one of the most brilliant of the dreams of ambition was dispersed.

So ends the first act; but the tragedy in which the King of Spain, the Lorraine Guises, and Queen Mary, continue to be the chief characters, is not yet acted out. The first casualty is among the Guises. Mary has not long endured her dreary banishment to her own kingdom, when a despatch arrives telling her how the brave Balafré has been murdered by the fanatic Poltrot. The blow is a severe one. The uncle and niece had an abundant fund of common sympathies. Both were princely, not alone by descent and conventional rank, but by the original stamp of the Deity, which had given them majesty and beauty in externals, balanced by bravery, wit, geniality, and high spirit as their intellectual and moral inheritance. She was proud of the great warrior and the wise statesman who had guided her youthful steps to greatness, and he was proud to be the parent and instructor of the most fascinating princess of her age.

It was just after his death that the dark days of Mary came upon her. Her maternal house still kept up a close intercourse with her, but personally their relation had widened. They were cousins now, not uncle and niece, and their intercourse was rather diplomatic than affectionate.

Upwards of twenty years have passed, and preparation is made for the chamber of execution at Fotheringay, yet still the chief persons in the drama are the same. A whisper arises and passes over Europe, Is a King of France, a descendant of St Louis, a grandson of the great Francis, going to permit his sister-in-law, who wore the crown, and yet bears the title of a Dowager Queen of France, to be put to death like a felon? Certainly not. There is a certain Monsieur Belliévre accredited to the Court of Elizabeth, for the purpose of bringing her to reason, and stopping any attempt at violence. He seems to have acted in some degree like the consul who quoted Bynkershook and Puffendorf and Grotius, and proved from Vatel, &c.; and in the text of the inviolability of princes, he quoted Cicero, and referred to Mark Antony, Mutius Scævola, and Porsenna with such apt diplomatic scholarship, that De Thou thought his speeches to Elizabeth, as reported by the speaker, worthy of being incorporated in full in his great History. But in reality Belliévre had a wondrously difficult part to perform, and his big classic talk was all intended to blazon over and hide his real helplessness.

Had the King of France determined to act?—that was the critical question. He had come to no such determination; or rather he had determined, if such a term is appropriate, *not* to act, and Elizabeth knew it. His object in the embassy was to hide his real abandonment of his sister-in-law from the eye of Europe. The ambassador, however, had personally too much chivalry for such a task. When he was done with his classical citations, at a long personal interview he at last distinctly threatened Elizabeth, should she persist, with the vengeance of the French Government. The virago fired up at this; she put it sharply to Belliévre, had he the authority of the King her brother to hold such language to her? Yes, he had, expressly. Well, she must have a copy of this, under the ambassador's own hand. If Belliévre gave her the genuine instructions communicated to him, they would be found but faintly to warrant his brave words of defiance; for after some rather unchivalric proposals for adjusting the affair without the necessity of a beheading, they contain a vague sort of threat of resentment if they be not adopted.*

Elizabeth, after the tragedy was over, wrote a jeering letter to King Henry about this threat, showing how lightly she esteemed it—if not, indeed, showing that there was a common understanding between them on the point. After the execution, which was supposed to take everybody by surprise, the next question was, whether the King of France would avenge it. M. Chéruel, who has the inner history of the French part of the affair ready to his hand, says the country was filled with cries of vengeance. He selects as the key-note of this sentiment the words in which it was echoed by l'Ecossais Blackwood :—"Le Roi, parent et beau-frère de cette dame, laissera-t-il son meurtre impuni? il ne souffrira jamais que cette tache déshonore son très illustre nom, ni que telle infamie tombe sur le royaume de France." †

But he was just going, with his own hands, to drop a darker blot on his illustrious name. M. Chéruel notices the significant little fact, that when Renaud de Beaurne, Archbishop of Bourges, preached a funeral sermon on Queen Mary, in which he called her relations, the Guises, *foudres de guerre*, or thunder-

* "Si la Reine d'Angleterre ne les met en aucune consideration, mais veut faire procéder à l'éxécution de si rigoureux et si extraordinaire jugement, il ne se pourra qu'il ne s'en ressente comme de chose qui l'offense fort particulièrement."—Chéruel, 165.

† Quoted, Chéruel, p. 171.

bolts of war, he was required to suppress this expression when he published the sermon. The question between the Guises and the house of Valois was coming to an issue; within a few months after the execution of Mary, the first war of barricades was fought on the streets of Paris; a month or two later the Duke of Guise was murdered in the King's audience-chamber, and the family broken. Henry's lukewarmness to Queen Mary had its practical explanation—he was not going to commit himself against a powerful monarch like Elizabeth, either to frustrate or to avenge the fate of a member of the detested family doomed by him to destruction.

The drama is not yet entirely played out. A great scene remains before the curtain drops, in which Spain has to play a part; it has been dictated by the departed enchantress, and is the last, as it is the grandest, instance of her power. The history of this affair, as now pretty well filled up by the documents printed by the Frenchmen, is extremely curious, both for the minuteness of the particulars, and the vastness of the historical events on which they bear. It will be remembered that, in her latter days, Queen Mary rested her hopes on the King of Spain, feeling that, unless her cousins the Guises were successful, she need expect nothing from France, and conscious, at the same time, that countenance and help from Spain would be the most powerful means of accomplishing their success. Accordingly, with marvellous perseverance and adroitness, she kept up a close correspondence during her imprisonment with Philip II., and every new document discovered renders it clearer than ever that it was at her instigation chiefly that Philip undertook the invasion of England.

Mary left behind her a last will, which Ritson the antiquary said he saw, blotted with her tears, in the Scottish College at Paris. It was, like her ostensible acts, a monument of kindness and generosity, performed with a mournful dignity becoming her rank and her misfortunes. All who had been kind and faithful to her, high and low, were gratified by bequests, which were precious relics, more dear than the riches she could no longer bestow. She had, however, issued another will of a more important character, which, with her other papers, was seized at Chartley. This will contained such strange and ominous matter that it was deemed wise at once to burn it; and lest there should be any doubt that it was effectually destroyed, or any suspicion that its purport had gone abroad, Elizabeth burnt it with her own hands. It gave its warning—it showed the enemy—it should go no further on its mischievous path; so thought Cecil and his mistress. But they had to deal with one not easily baffled in the accomplishment of her fixed designs. She confided her testamentary bequests verbally to two different persons, on whose fidelity she could rely.

Her executor was the King of Spain. The nature of these bequests had not been entirely concealed. James himself, in his lubberly schoolboy-like complaints about his mother, showed that he knew about them. They now make their appearance in the shape of a statement of the reception which the King of Spain gave to the testamentary injunctions. If we are to suppose—which we are at liberty to do—that they were utter falsehoods, invented by the persons who pretended to be accredited to the King of Spain, there is, at all events, this much of fact in the whole affair, that the King of Spain believed them to be genuine, and acted on them fully and emphatically. It is the record of his so acting that we now possess.

Gorion, Queen Mary's French physician, was one of the recipients of this deposit. He was commissioned to convey to the King of Spain her desire that he would pay certain debts and legacies, and distribute pensions and other rewards among her more faithful adherents. As to the debts and the smaller recompenses of services, the Queen appealed to his religious feeling, on the ground that to leave the world without the prospect of these things being paid, pressed heavily on her conscience. The sums of money absolutely named in these requests were considerable ; and in asking that the pensions of the English Catholics, including the Earl of Westmoreland, Lord Paget, Charles Arundel, Charles Paget, Throckmorton, and Morgan, might be continued, she evidently drew upon a liberal hand. Philip appears not only to have unhesitatingly met the larger and ostensible demands thus made on him, but with a religious zeal to have sought out the more obscure objects of Mary's goodwill, that he might rigidly perform her injunctions to the utmost farthing.

One great injunction still remained—it was that, notwithstanding her death, he would not abandon his enterprise on England—an enterprise devised in the cause of God, and worthy of a true Catholic king. This bequest also, as all the world knows, the King of Spain did his best to carry into effect. There were some little subsidiary services to be performed by him when he had accomplished it. Mary's account with the world had a debtor as well as a creditor side. If the King of Spain could reward friends, it was also hoped that he would be in a position to punish enemies : her last request, therefore, was, that when once master of England, he would not forget how she had been treated by Cecil, Leicester, Secretary Walsingham, Lord Huntington, Sir Amyas Paulet, and Wade, the clever Secretary of the Council, who had discovered the designs of Spain by putting the fragments of a torn letter together

While the French physician bore to the King of Spain what might be termed the burdens and obligations of the testament, it was commissioned to other messengers—being the Queen's two faithful attendants, Elizabeth Curle and Jane Kennedy—to intimate what may be called the beneficial portion, which was no less than the bequeathing to the King of Spain the crowns of Scotland and England, in the event of her son James continuing obstinate in his heresy. It is with almost ludicrous gravity that M. Teulet says, "Philippe II. accepta sans hésiter les charges d'une succession qui lui offrait des éventualités si avantageuses." Advantageous eventualities indeed—but, as they proved to the executor, calamitous realities.

Within eighteen months after the death of Mary, the Armada was in the Channel. It was the last grand explosion of the ancient crusading chivalry,—an expedition to restore the Catholic Church to its supremacy, and at the same time to carry out the dying wish and avenge the wrongs of an injured woman and a holy martyr. The great actual drama is now completed, and it is wonderful with what a close contiguity in time its long-suspended issues complete themselves. Early in the year 1587 Queen Mary is executed; in the summer of the ensuing year the Armada comes forth and is destroyed. That winter the Duke of Guise is murdered and his family crushed; and again, before another year passes, the perfidious perpetrator of the deed, Henry III., is murdered by a Popish fanatic, who thus clears the throne for the tolerant monarch who did more than any other for the real greatness of France.

From this great epoch history starts afresh with new actors, who are to bring out a new development of events. The mighty empire of Spain from that period collapses like the bankrupt estate of an over-sanguine trader, who has risked all his capital on some great adventure ending in shipwreck. A powerful little colony of industrious Protestants rises up where her yoke has been thrown off in Holland. France is no longer in the hand of the Guise or of the Medici, but is ruled by one who, if he dare not be Protestant, will at all events be tolerant, and in the balance of the European powers, Protestantism, if not predominant, is at least made secure. In the great recasting of the position of the European powers, Scotland's relations to France and England respectively have undergone a revolution. Let us take a glance backwards, then, and sketch the events which bring our own special story—that of the Ancient League—to its natural conclusion.

The firm footing of Protestantism in the north of Europe, and the fusion of England and Scotland, must have seemed among the most unlikely of human events, on that 10th of July 1559, when Henry II. died of the wound he got in a tournament, and his son Francis succeeded him, with Mary of Scotland for queen. Elizabeth had not been quite eight months on the throne of England. She had kept her leaning towards Protestantism—it was little more than a leaning—so close, that foreign nations seem for some time to have known nothing of it. Philip II., the widower of her Popish sister Mary, had no conception of the change that was coming. He could see nothing in the general state of Europe, except the symptoms that things were righting themselves again, after the partial storm of the Reformation, and settling quietly under the wings of the Popedom. He looked on England, next to his own dear Spain and the Netherlands, as the most Catholic kingdom in Europe. He wished the English crown to have been entailed on him in case of his surviving his wife. He thought it strange and rather unreasonable that this should not have been done; but he took the personal disappointment with magnanimity, intimating that he would still take a paternal interest in his late wife's dominions. He was prepared, if duty required him, to marry Elizabeth on a dispensation from the Pope, and was astonished beyond measure when he heard that a hint of the possible distinction in store for her had not been received by the eccentric young Queen with the grateful deference which it should have commanded. But it was long before he could permit himself to doubt that her kingdom would stand by him for the Popedom, against the lax notions which the monarchs of France had allowed to arise in the Gallican Church. In the calculations of the Continental powers, the prospect of England continuing at the command of Philip and the Court of Rome was a thing so probable, that, in the negotiations for the great treaty of Chateau Cambresis, France, when called on to give back Calais to England, had the face to plead as a reason for declining, at least deferring this sacrifice, the probability that this fortress might thus be put at the command of the King of Spain, and help him to invade France from his Flemish dominions.

Some of the most picturesque movements of the diplomacy of the day wind round the affair of Calais. France, having got it, was determined to keep it. Elizabeth and her advisers were determined to get it back by any means short of capture, but that was just short of the only means by which it was to be had. Elizabeth pleaded, rather ludicrously, that the English people considered it so essential a possession of the English crown that they would not submit to its loss. It was maintained rather more reasonably on the other hand, that, as part of the soil of France, it would be a dangerous offence to the French people to give it up. The argument more to the point on the present occasion, however, was one that carried keen alarm to Elizabeth's Court. It was thus briefly put by the French to the English commissioners at Chateau Cambresis: "Put the case that Calais was to be re-delivered, and that we did owe such debts to the crown of England, to whom shall we deliver Calais? to whom shall we pay the debts? Is not the Queen of Scots true Queen of England? Shall we deliver Calais and those debts to another, and thereby prejudice the rights of the Queen of Scotland and the Dauphin, her husband?" *

When such words could be spoken while the

* Stevenson, 'Calendar of State Papers (Foreign), 2d March 1559.'

young couple were waiting for the death of a man in the prime of life to succeed to the throne of France, it was to be expected, when the succession suddenly opened to them, that there would be more audacious pretensions still. The affair was no empty bravado, such as the pretensions of the Tudors to the throne of France had come to be. With Roman Catholics, at home as well as abroad, Mary was the heiress to the throne of England. A large portion of England was still Romanist, and it was not yet known what effect Elizabeth's Reformation tendencies might have on the popular mind. The pretensions of the young couple to the throne of England were not the less ominous that they were made in coinage and heraldry, in a very quiet way, and as a matter of course. The English ambassador observed it all, reporting home in angry letters to his angrier mistress. It came to the climax of insult when he had either to abstain from the good things at state banquets, or eat off platters on which the arms of England were quartered with those of France and Scotland.*

* The quartering was noticed by Throckmorton on a memorable occasion—the tournament in which Henry II. received his fatal wound. "When the Dauphin's band began the jousts, two heralds which came before the band were Scots, fair, set out with the King and Queen Dauphin's arms, with a scutcheon of England, set forth to the show, as all the world might easily perceive; the same being embroidered with purple velvet, and set out with armoury upon their breasts, backs, and sleeves.

"The 29th, the bands of the Prince of Condé, of the Dukes of Longueville and Buillon, ran against the challengers, at

Few things in the uncertain future of the destinies of nations had ever approached nearer to a certainty than the steadfastness at that juncture of the Old League between Scotland and France; and yet within it elements of political decomposition were at work, which might bring it down with a crash, as a fair building consumed by dry rot is in a condition to fall to pieces, and is most likely to do so when it is most relied on and put to most trying use. Two hundred years had changed the France which received Buchan's detachment as the rescuers and guardians of the land. By the acquisition of Burgundy, Brittany, Maine, Anjou, Guienne, and other fiefs, the territories absolutely ruled by the house of Valois had increased some fourfold. Scotland had improved in wealth, yet the relative proportions of

---

which triumph were the Pope's Nuncio, the Ambassador of Venice, and the writer, in a place appointed by the constable. The Ambassador of Portugal was there, not in their company, but stood in a house right over against them, which was of his own provision.

"The 30th, the Prince of Nevers, called Count d'Eu, came to the tilt with his band; no other ambassador besides himself was there to see them run. Whereat it happened that the King, after running a good many courses well and fair, meeting with young M. de Lorges, Captain of the Scottish Guard, received at his hand such a counterbuff as, first lighting on the King's head and taking away the pannage (whereupon there was a great plume of feathers), which was fastened to his headpiece with iron, did break his staff; and with the rest of the staff hitting the King's face, gave him such a counterbuff as he drove a splinter right over his eye on the right side, the force of which stroke was so vehe-

the two countries had vastly altered. Their diplomatic relations had changed, at least on the French side, in the assumption of a protecting and patronising nomenclature. There was offence to Scotland even in the marshalling of arms that had enraged England, since the lion occupied the subsidiary quarterings on the royal shield, as indicating a territorial possession, instead of being charged on a pale or some honourable ordinary, as a merely personal difference derived from a matrimonial alliance.

But the mere assumption of superiority was not all,—in fact, the assumption was concealed as well as such a thing could be, under decorous externals, beneath which there were designs to accomplish something far more effective than a magnanimous protectorship.

---

ment, and the pain so great, that he was much astonished, and had great ado to keep himself on horseback, and his horse also did somewhat yield. Whereupon, with all expedition, he was unarmed in the field, even against the place where Throckmorton stood, as he could discern. The hurt seemed not to be great, whereby he judges that he is but in little danger. Marry, he saw a splint taken out of a good bigness. Nothing else was done to him upon the field, but he noted him to be very weak, and to have the sense of all his limbs almost benumbed; for being carried away as he lay along, nothing covered but his face, he moved neither hand nor foot, but lay as one amazed. Whether there were any more splints entered in (as in such cases it happens), it was not known. There was marvellous great lamentation and weeping, both of men and women, for him. Thus God makes himself known, that in the very midst of these triumphs suffers this heaviness to happen."

The papers revealed to the world by M. Teulet show that from the time when the heiress to the crown of Scotland came into the possession of her ambitious kinsfolk, they were laying plans for governing Scotland in Paris, and annexing the country to the throne of France. Dated in the year 1552 is a "Declaration" or Memorandum of the Parliament of Paris on the adjustment of the government of Scotland.* In this document one can see, under official formalities, the symptoms of an almost irritable impatience to get the nominal government vested in the young Queen, in order that the real government might be administered by her kinsfolk. She had then entered on her twelfth year. That she ought to take the sovereignty into her own hands is a proposition reached by two steps, which may be defined as a long and a short. The long step reaches the position, that when twelve years old she would be entitled to govern—a proposition fortified by a curiously tortuous application of precedents from the sovereignty of France, to which male heirs only could succeed. A Roman maxim which imports that a day begun is to be counted in law as completed, is then brought up, and it is shown that in proper logical consistency the maxim should apply to a year. Along with the technical argument came two of a wider and more statesman-

* 'Déclaration du Parlement de Paris sur le Gouvernement de l'Écosse,' Teulet, 8vo ed., i. 274.

like character, which are, however, signally open to the charge of being inconsistent with each other. The one was, that the Deity, in consideration of the heavy responsibilities devolved on them, had endowed young royal personages with precocious capacities; the other was, that, however youthful a sovereign may be, there are always at hand wise and clever persons to govern the realm—and this, in fact, pointed to the real object. The document was no doubt drawn up by the persons who were ready to take the responsibility of governing Scotland on themselves.*

A plan was, however, found for accomplishing the desired end more simple and practical than the devices of the civilians and feudalists. The Governor of Scotland was the head of the house of Hamilton, who held that office as next in hereditary succession to the crown if the young Queen should die. This office was taken from him, and he was compensated for the loss by the Dukedom of Chatelherault. Mary of Guise became Regent of Scotland, under the direction of her brothers, the great Duke and the great Cardinal.

The Scots lords now saw sights calculated, as the

---

* "Il y a donc grande différence entre la tutelle d'un privé et le gouvernement d'un royaulme; mesmement que les rois, en quelque aage qu'ilz soient, sont accompagnés de princes, grands seigneurs, et gens de grand sçavoir et expérience, par le conseil desquelz ilz ont administré les royaulmes."—Teulet, 8vo ed., i. 277.

Persians say, to open the eyes of astonishment. A clever French statesman, M. d'Osel, was sent over as the adviser of the Regent, to be her Prime Minister, and enable her to rule Scotland after the model of France. A step was taken to get at the high office of Chancellor by appointing Monsieur de Rubay to be Vice-Chancellor, with possession of the Great Seal. The office of Comptroller of the Treasury was dealt with more boldly, and put into the hands of M. Villemore. At Eyemouth, near the east border, a great fortress was erected, on the new plans of fortification, to confront the English fortress of Berwick, and a Frenchman was appointed its Governor. The Regent cast an eye on the strongholds of the great lords, determining to fill them with garrisons more obedient to the crown than their existing occupants. When she began with Tantallon, which, by its situation and strength, would be a desirable acquisition, the Earl of Angus, with epigrammatic point worthy of her own nation, said his house was at her service, but assuredly he should remain governor, for no other could hold it so well.

Suspicious surveys and inventories were made of property, and it was declared, almost more to the amazement than to the indignation of the country, that a tax was to be levied for the support of a standing army. Now, the feudal array, which by old custom could be called by the sovereign, each freeholder contributing to it so many men-at-arms for a short period, was the only military force known in Scotland, and any attempt to create a royal army in any other shape was always received with the most nervous jealousy. On this occasion three hundred of the chief persons interested assembled in the church of Holyrood and declared resistance.

There were ugly stories afloat about attempts, on the occasion of the Queen's marriage, to juggle with the official nomenclature which represented the independence of Scotland as a sovereignty. It was requested that the crown and other "honours," as they were termed, might be sent to Paris; but there was suspicion about the use these might be put to—such as crowning the Dauphin, perhaps—and the request was refused. It was said that Mary had been required to sign a deed importing her husband's absolute right to the crown on survivorship; and, whether true or not, belief in such a story had its influence. It is certain that an expression which afterwards gave a deal of trouble was then used in conferring on the Dauphin the "crown matrimonial." It was stated by the Lords of the Congregation in Scotland to have been an invention of the Guises, who had some hidden meaning in it.* When the question of its meaning afterwards came up in the refusal of the crown matrimonial to Darnley, it was explained that it would pervert

* Teulet, ii. 10: "Honoris causa diademate matrimoniali ornare: ad rem, quæ exemplum apud historicos scripteres nusquam habet, novato usu vocabili quo nobis oculos perstringerent."

the line of succession—that the crown matrimonial meant the sovereignty in the survivor and the survivor's heirs, whether descendants of Queen Mary or of another wife. In this sense, the arrangement was equivalent to the kind of entail which Philip thought it so unreasonable that he did not get of the crown of England.

The state papers of France at that time speak of Scotland as of a highly-favoured dependency. An act of the French Government, which externally was one of grace and free-hearted generosity, did not mend matters. There had been many acts of naturalisation in favour of Scotsmen, and now, by one sweep of hospitality, the whole nation was naturalised. The privilege was a large one, for France, by her *droit d'aubaine*, was conspicuously inhospitable to unprivileged foreigners; but the phraseology of the document made its object too plain, and some comments referring to the practice of the Roman empire in admitting the inhabitants of distant provinces to a limited citizenship did not improve its effect.*

When the eight commissioners sent from Scotland to assist at the marriage were on their way home, a special epidemic seemed to break out among them, which killed four out of the eight at Dieppe,

---

* The letters were addressed "à tous les habitans du dit royaume d'Éscosse subjectz de nostre filz Roy-Dauphin et nostre fille son espouse."

and their death was as naturally attributed to poison as the disappearance of watches in a London mob is attributed to pocket-picking; it was maintained that they knew some facts about the affairs of the marriage which it was desirable that they should not have an opportunity of communicating to the Scots Estates.

These facts fitting in with the method of the Regent's government in Scotland, resistance and war came at last. The Regent, finding at the commencement that she might have the worst of it, accepted in a very frank manner of a treaty, which she broke on the first opportunity, and with a rapidity which had in it a sort of deliberateness, since it showed that she did not yield reluctantly to sore temptation, but acted on deliberate design. This united those who were otherwise shy of each other, and a war, the events of which are well known in history, broke forth against Popery and French influence.

The great turning-point in the destinies of the British empire had now come, and to bring it on with the tide depended on the skill of the English Government. The wounds of Henry's tyrannous invasions were still fresh. How narrowly England escaped the wrong tack is shown in the later revelations from the State Paper Office, which set forth a plan for declaring and enforcing the old feudal claim of superiority over Scotland. So was that poor country pulled on the other side. But, fortunately, the new Queen of England had advisers about her who could read the tenor of old experience, and see that force was not the way to make good the precious opportunity. Indeed, it behoved them to be rid of their own fears before they bullied others. England was in imminent danger. France had grand designs of annexation and empire; Spain was relaxing her friendly grasp; and if these two Popish powers, with Scotland at their service, fell on England, where would Elizabeth's throne be? The instructions to the English commissioners at the great treaty of Chateau Cambresis might have given comfort to the Scots, had they known the anxiety of their powerful enemy for peace with them. "We think the peace with Scotland of as great moment for us as that with France, and rather of greater; so, as to be plain with you, if either there should not be a peace there fully concluded betwixt us and Scotland, we see not but it were as good to leave the matter in suspense with the French as to conclude with them, and to have no other assurance of the French but a bare comprehension of Scotland." The French, it seems, were ready in their haughty manner to stipulate for Scotland, but Cecil knew the temper of his neighbours too well to be content with such an assurance. The instructions come back to the topic, and press it on the commissioners: "And for our satisfaction beside the matter of Calais, nothing in all this conclusion with the French may in surety satisfy us, if we have not peace with

Scotland: and so we will that ye shall plainly inform our said good brother's commissioners, and that with speed."*

The Queen reminds her trusty counsellors that they, "not ignorant of the state of our realm having been much weakened of late with sickness, death, and loss by wars, can very well consider how unmeet it is for us to continue in these manner of wars, if we may be otherwise provided of a peace like to continue; and how fit it is and necessary to have peace." The commissioners are directed at great length to bully powerfully for the restoration of Calais. But the real dangers visible, and the acute hungering for peace, squeeze out a brief and agonising permission to sacrifice everything for peace: "We do give you authority at the very last end, being as loath thereunto as may be desired, rather than continue these wars, to make the peace as you best and most honourably may, and as the difficulty of the time may serve, so that we may have certainly peace with Scotland, with reservation of our claims as well to Calais as to all other our titles, pensions, and arrearages heretofore due by France."†

The negotiation of the treaty was attended by some incidents, ludicrous in themselves, and far beneath the dignity of history, yet curious as indi-

---

* 'Calendar of State Papers, Foreign, 1858-59,' p. 151.

† Ibid., p. 139.

cative of that stubborn pride which bore up the Scots in all their difficulties and calamities. Where was the treaty to be negotiated? Of course, England, the greater power, was not to go to Scotland; but, on the other hand, Scotland refused so far to acknowledge a superiority as to step over the border into England. On the 12th of May 1559, Bishop Tunstall writes to say, that they had extreme difficulty in being absolutely certain of neutral ground, and "our first meeting was in the midst of the river between us both; for the Scots do regard their honour as much as any other king doth;" and he rather naturally adds, that he will not fail to be at the next meeting, "God granting him health."*

In some inexplicable manner the Scots seem to have pulled too strong in the matter of the meeting-place for their diplomatic opponents, for on the 5th of January the Earl of Northumberland makes this ludicrous complaint to Cecil: "They were ready to meet the Scottish commissioners on the first day, on the bounders that are in the midstream; but they claimed customs, and caused the messengers to go to and fro so often, that they forced the English commissioners to come over the water into Scottish ground, or else would not have met at all."†

Peace being established, the next step was the

* Calendar, p. 251. † Ibid., p. 300.

dissolution of the old French League and a fusion of interests with England. We have now, thanks to the documents published by Mr Stevenson, a minute insight into the difficult and perilous course of hints and promises and bargains which constitute the diplomacy of this revolution. The gradual unfolding of the mysteries is exceedingly curious, and so exciting as to carry a reader with ease over the six hundred pages already issued, and make him long for the rest. The general picture left in the mind is a vision of the cluster of sagacious men who surrounded the young Queen's throne, discovering in the condition of Scotland a tower of strength which had only to be honestly occupied in that hour of peril, but baffled and paralysed by the perfidy and caprices of their mistress. She wanted them to do everything, but to do it on their own responsibility without any authority from her; and, indeed, with the certainty that at any moment, when it suited her policy or caprice, she would assert that they acted the part of rebels and traitors, and "untop" them, to use a favourite expression of hers, without remorse. Cecil was provoked almost beyond endurance and proper respect to his royal mistress, when he found that a few thousand pounds would do the business, yet could not get them.*

* "The man is poor and cannot travail in these matters without charges, wherein he must be relieved by the Queen if these proceedings go forwards—and so must as many as be principal doers have relief. They be all poor, and ne-

Hints, indeed, were thrown out that it would be good service in her advisers to invest some of their own cash in the adventure; but their patriotism was not strong enough to induce them to part with what under no circumstances would be repaid, while it suspended over their heads a charge of treason.

There was one feature, indeed, in the affair, which the Queen intensely disliked. It had a very ugly resemblance to the backing of subjects in rebellion against their sovereign—a kind of proceeding against which she had fundamentally rooted objections. She tried in vain to get the matter put into the shape of a war of succession, in which she could

---

cessity will force them to leave off when all they have is spent, and you know in all practices money must be one part."—P. 401.

Knox, who knew very well how to wield the arm of the flesh, writes to Crofts on 30th July 1559: "Not only must the Queen and her council have respect that soldiers must be laid in garrison among us, and that men and ships must be in constant readiness if we be assailed, but also that some respect must be had to some of the nobility, who are not able to sustain such households as now in the beginnings of these troubles are requisite. For the practice of the Queen Regent is to stir up enemies against every nobleman particularly, even in the parts where he remaineth."—P. 431. On the 29th of September Sadler and Crofts write to Cecil that certain leaders cannot keep their men together unless they get pecuniary relief, and how "four or five thousand pounds would be well spent in their cause, and save the Queen men; for how near it would touch England if the French had the upper hand of Scotland they refer to her wisdom."

advocate the cause which she might acknowledge as the rightful sovereign's. The heir of the house of Hamilton, who, as the descendant of James II., was next heir to the crown, had many allurements thrown in his way to start as king; but he was unequal to the occasion. Murray—afterwards the Regent—was spoken to, and it is pretty clear that that sagacious and cautious statesman, had he chosen to run risks before his sister's return, might have had a chance of gaining a crown about equivalent to his chance of retaining a head to wear it on.

Among the somewhat clumsy projects for giving unacknowledged assistance to the Protestant and English party in Scotland was to get a body of English soldiers induced to cross the Border, and then to proclaim them rebels for breaking the peace with France and Scotland—rebels who must needs fight where they were, since they could not return to England. One cheap and rather effective method of stirring up the Scots was to ply them with news of the bloody intentions of France; and, so far as intentions went, they could not well be too highly coloured.*

---

* Throckmorton writes from France to Cecil: "The news touching Scotland are come to the Court, whereupon it is said that the King minds forthwith, under colour to suppress the Protestant preachers, to send thither a number of men. . . . It is discoursed here that all sects of religion, as they call it, shall be utterly subverted, and that the French King minds to use all extremity against the Protestants immediately after the triumph. It will not be amiss

Kirkaldy of Grange, who afterwards cut some figure in politics, is revealed in these papers as one of the most active and ingenious agents in the national revolution. His hand appears before the conclusion of the treaty of Chateau Cambresis. The Earl of Northumberland wrote, on 11th February 1559, to Queen Elizabeth, that "one William Kirkaldy, a Scotchman, came to his brother to Norham and entered into communication for abstinence of wars, to the intent that peace might follow." Three months afterwards, when matters had practically advanced a step or two, we find him writing to Sir Henry Percy that the Protestant gentry, after the Queen Regent, Mary of Guise, had played them false, "have gathered themselves together, and have pulled down all the friaries within their bounds." "Herefore," he continues, "I pray you let me understand what will be your mistress's part, if we desire to be joined in friendship with her; for I assure you there was never a better time to get our friendship nor at this time; therefore make labours, and lose no time when it is offered."* Two months afterwards, when the rising against French influence was in still better shape, he wrote to Cecil intelligence thus rendered: "At present they dare not

to do the Protestants in Scotland to understand that there is meant utter destruction to their houses, that they may provide for the worst, and make themselves strong."—P. 301.

* Calendar, p. 278.

make the matter known to many, for fear of sudden disclosing the secrecy of their purpose; for the Queen Regent already suspects that there is some intelligence with England in this case, insomuch that she has spoken openly that there is a servant sent from the Earl of Northumberland to the Earl of Argyle and the Prior. Also some of their number are poor, and corruption by money is feared, but in the end they fear them not. If these latter were removed from their council, they would not be much weaker, as the hearts of the whole barons and commonalty are so bent to this action, and so influenced against France, that if any of the nobility would decline—of which they see no appearance—they could not withdraw their friends nor servants from the professing of Christ and the maintaining of the liberty of their country." *

Co-operating with Kirkaldy was a more potent spirit—the great John Knox, who had just returned from tasting the tender mercies of France as a galley-slave. In July, while Cecil had still no others but Kirkaldy and Knox committed to him, he wrote an extremely cautious letter to Sir Henry Percy, observing that it was misliked that no better personages had opened themselves than these two, being private persons; though Knox had got to himself a position of no small credit. Of him it is said, "He desireth, in his letter to me, to have licence to come hitherward,

* Calendar, p. 385.

wherein it is ordered that he should thus use it. . . . For his coming hitherward, it may be permitted to him, so as it be used with secrecy and his name altered; for otherwise the sequel will be fruitless, yea, very hurtful. Ye may appoint him to come to my house, called Burley, near Stamford (where I mean to be about the 24th or 25th inst.) If he come, changing his name, he may be directed not to come through Stamford, but on the back side. If his chance should be to come before my coming thither, he may have this paper included, whereby he shall be there used to his contentation." *

It would have been of questionable safety to himself and his friends had Knox ventured upwards of three hundred miles into England to negotiate, having to return again to Scotland. The first embassy, however, was conducted by him. We have his powers in eleven articles of a very distinct and practical kind, without too much admixture of religion. In the most comprehensive and emphatic of them he is authorised to say for his countrymen—"That they and their posterity will bind themselves to be enemies to the enemies and friends to the friends of the English, if they thoroughly agree in this league; and that they will never contract with France without the consent of the English, so as to be united with them in one body, so that neither can make war nor peace without the consent of the other." †

* Calendar, p. 371. † Ibid., p. 431.

With credentials of this momentous import in his pocket, Knox touched English ground by taking boat to Holy Island, where Crofts picked him up, taking him for secret conference to Berwick, whence his entertainer wrote to Cecil, giving as much of the matter as he could trust to a despatch, and observing that it could not be carried out "without charges—and, peradventure, *cum sudore et sanguine;* therefore the matter requires good deliberation, and what aid to be given, and what charges, and when to spend and when to spare." *

It confers a touch of humour on these grave and momentous proceedings, that Queen Elizabeth at that time hated Knox personally in her own hearty manner. He had written his 'First Blast of the Trumpet against the Monstrous Regiment of Women;' and though he professed to let fly his shafts at Popish women only, yet, as

> "Many an arch at random sent
> Finds mark the archer never meant,"

some of his left their barbs sticking deep in the most sensitive parts of the Protestant Queen's public and private character. Her wise men had much ado to get her to receive his advances with patience; but his power was great, and he must be put up with. When his name comes up in their secret correspondence, Throckmorton says to Cecil—"Though Knokes the preacher did heretofore unadvisedly and

* Calendar, p. 446.

fondly put his hand to the book, yet, since he is now, in Scotland, in as great credit as ever man was there with such as may be able to serve the Queen's turn, it were well done not to use him otherwise than for the advancement of her service." *

It will be worth while even to be domestically civil, and so Throckmorton again writes to the purport that "the wife of Knokes the preacher and her mother are at Paris, who shortly depart into England. They have made means to apply to him for letters in their favour, which he has promised to send by them to Mr Secretary. The Queen should consider what Knokes is able to do in Scotland, which is very much—all the turmoil there being by him stirred up as it is. His former faults should be forgotten, and no means used to annoy him for the same, but that his wife should perceive, before she depart into Scotland, that there is no stomach borne to her husband therefore, but that he may have good hope rather to look for favour and friendship at her hands than otherwise, which may work somewhat to good purpose." † A humble follower of Knox, called Sandy Whylowe or Whitlaw, taking credentials from Throckmorton to Cecil, is represented as one "who has done and may do good service to the Queen;" and the sealed document he carried with him contained this double admonition:—"This bearer is very religious, and therefore

* Calendar, p. 306. † Ibid., p. 310.

you must let him see as little sin in England as you may. He seemeth to me very willing to work what he can that Scotland may forsake utterly the French amity and be united to England. Sir, in these services and occasions, to preserve you from farther inconveniences, the Queen's purse must be open, for fair words will not serve." *

It was on the 4th of July that, in an extremely cautious and yet somewhat decided tone, English assistance was promised, Cecil telling Percy that he may assure Kirkaldy "that, rather than that Scotland should be oppressed with a foreign nation, and deprived of the ancient liberties, and the nobility thereof (and especially such as seek to maintain the truth of the Christian religion) be expelled, the authority of England would adventure with power to aid that realm against any such foreign invasion—wherein upon farther certainty 'understand' thence, there may be showed in plain manner more particularly of this offer." †

The almost simultaneous arrival of an English and a French force in Scotland, and the contest that followed, are well known in history. Two treaties,—one called the treaty of Berwick, between the Scots Protestants and Elizabeth—the other the treaty of Edinburgh, between France and England,—ended all. Queen Mary's friends considered that she had been betrayed in this pacification, because

* Calendar, p. 340. † Ibid., p. 359.

her claim to the English throne was abandoned, and Elizabeth made secure; but there were others who thought it well that a mere personal claim, pregnant with endless strife and bloodshed, should be expunged.

The 24th of August 1560 was a wonderful day for Scotland. It dawned on the Romish hierarchy, still nominally and legally entire, with all its dignities and wealth. Ere eve the whole had been cast down, and to adhere to that Church was a crime. The Acts of Parliament making "the Reformation" passed on that day in an "Act for abolishing the Pope and his usurped authority." They had to pass through the necessary routine, and were not therefore quite unexpected. Still there is a suddenness in the carrying of the Reformation in Scotland which arises from this, that it was a declaration of triumph over enemies, and these not domestic but foreign—the French, with whom the Scots had been in close and devoted alliance for more than two hundred years. It is a common mistake to say that while in other countries the Reformation was partly a secular and partly a religious movement, in Scotland it was wholly religious. On the contrary, it was probably in no other country so thoroughly secular and political in the hearts and objects of those who carried it, though no doubt they subsidised religious influences to aid them. Since the reconstruction of the Popedom in its old completeness had become the great mission of the Guises,

Popery became irretrievably mixed up with arbitrary power and the annexing designs of France. The great prelates were becoming French courtiers. Increasing in wealth and power, they imported from their allies practices of tyranny and cruelty at which the Scots nature revolted. The Church, a vast, compact corporation, ever getting and never giving up, was eating away the territorial wealth of the temporal barons to enrich the haughty prelates. From the same cause there crept in a social degradation humiliating to the landed gentry in this shape, that the poorer among them were content to let their daughters become companions to the affluent dignitaries; and although an attempt was made to give a kind of established character to the connection, especially in the rank allowed to the offspring, yet it could not be made the same as honest wedlock.

When, therefore, there was seen arising in the land a set of divines who maintained that these haughty prelates were wolves who had broken into the fold, and should be immediately deprived of their ill-gotten spoil, the barons immediately said, "That's the religion for us!" Among the Protestant clergy there was, no doubt, a deep fund of religious zeal, supported by austere purity of life, and it might be possible to pick out one or two of their lay allies participating in some measure in these qualities; but, generally speaking, a set of men wilder and rougher, and more devoted to immediate gross and secular objects, than the "Lords of the Congregation," is not easily to be found in history. When the affair was finished, and Knox and his brethren, having waited in meek expectation for some time, reminded their active coadjutors that what had been taken from the false church belonged to the true, the Lords of the Congregation laughed in their faces, and told them they were under the hallucination of "fond imaginations."

Knox could only scold them, and that he did with his own peculiar heartiness and emphasis. So, when his celebrated 'Book of Discipline' did not go down with them, he came out with—"Others, perceiving their carnal liberty and worldly commodity somewhat to be impaired, thereby grudged, insomuch that the name of the 'Book of Discipline' became odious unto them. Everything that impugned to their corrupt affections was called, in their mockage, 'devote imaginations.' The cause we have before declared. Some were licentious; some had greedily gripped to the possessions of the Kirk; and others thought that they would not lack their part of Christ's coat—yea, and that before that ever he was hanged, as by the preachers they were oft rebuked. . . . Assuredly some of us have wondered how men that profess godlyness could, of so long continuance, hear the threatenings of God against thieves and against their houses, and knowing themselves guilty in such things as were openly rebuked, and that they never had remorse of conscience, neither yet intended to restore any things of that which long they had stolen and reft." *

Queen Mary always evaded any acknowledgment of the treaty which left Elizabeth's title undisputed, and of the Reformation Statute. Her policy about the Statute, indeed, developed a quiet profundity of duplicity, which makes a beautiful antithesis to the noisy brazen mendacity of the other Queen. Mary solemnly engaged not to interfere with the religion established by law. Almost every one knew what she meant, and that when the time suited she would hold that an Act of Parliament which had not the royal assent was no law. Yet it would have been impolitic to push the point by requiring her assent to the Act, since an ultimate refusal might make it more unsatisfactory than it was. Her policy, however, afterwards cut both ways; for the treaty and the Act were productive of highly important political effects, being brought up as precedents to the effect that the Estates of Parliament could enter on treaties and pass laws without the consent of the Crown. When Murray came into power, he thought it judicious to fortify the Act by another.

To us who look back upon the time with the advantage of having seen the plot worked out, it becomes clear at this juncture that the French alliance is gone for ever, and England and Scotland are to be

* History, ii. 128, 129.

one. But between the return of Queen Mary and the death of Elizabeth there was a deal of hard critical work to be gone through in Scotland, and much of it was connected with the efforts of France to renew the old friendship.

Of the labours of Queen Elizabeth's emissaries in Scotland—Throckmorton, Walsingham, Sadler, and Randolph—we have full accounts, which have been well ransacked and instructively commented on. But the no less interesting negotiations of the French emissaries in Scotland have hitherto been little studied; nor, indeed, could they easily have been so until they were gradually brought forth from their hiding-places in foreign libraries and public offices by the zeal of the archæologists of France. They are not less interesting from the glimpses which they afford of the designs of France, than from the picturesque descriptions which they contain of events which it is profitable to see from as many sides as possible, and which certainly often acquire a new shape and character when seen through the eyes of the accomplished and acute foreigner employed to report on them to the Guises or Catherine of Medici.

The most remarkable in accomplishments and wisdom of these French ambassadors, Michel de Castelnau de Mauvissière, was alike conscious of the importance of the Scottish alliance and of the almost hopelessness of recovering it. After a lively description of the miseries of the country when tortured in the terrible wars and plunderings of Morton, he says, "Je suis et serais toujours d'opinion qu'il n'y a nulle alliance au monde que la France doive avoir plus chěre que celle de ce petit pays d'Ecosse." *

Castelnau was one of the really great men whose eminent labours, wasted on tough and hopeless materials, can only be estimated by close inspection. As M. Chéruel well observes, we will find more of the true spirit of the actions of the day, and the men engaged in them, in his letters and memoirs, than almost anywhere else. He was one of those statesmen whose fate it is to struggle for great ends, which their masters, the heads of the government, will not back through with the necessary energy. As M. Chéruel says, he had in the interests of France to fight Elizabeth in Scotland, and Philip of Spain in the Netherlands. His memoirs show that he beheld with a grave sorrow, partaking of despondency, the exterminating spirit and bloody deeds of both the parties, the League and the Huguenots, who each struggled in his own country, not merely for existence, but for mastery; and his experience of this rude contest gives an air of practical wisdom and staid sagacity to his remarks on our own quarrels, which, fierce as they were, hold altogether a smaller space in the world's history than the contemporaneous quarrels of the French. Hence he

* Chéruel, p. 111.

narrates some of the most marvellous incidents of Scottish history with a quiet distinctness, which, instead of subduing, rather tends to give power and emphasis to the narrative, when it is felt throughout that it is by an onlooker deeply grounded in a practical knowledge of similar events.

He it was who came to Britain charged by Catherine of Medici with two matrimonial missions—whether they were sincere or sarcastic, let him tell who can. In the one, she proposed to the austere Elizabeth an alliance with Charles IX. of France, then a boy of thirteen. Whether Catherine knew it or not, the virago had that peculiar weakness when anything matrimonial was proposed, that she would play with the suggestion as long as it would keep alive without serious discussion. She remarked cleverly enough to Castelnau, that the King of France was both too great and too little a match for her—too great in his power, too little in his youth. But she did not let the affair drop for some time, writing herself to Catherine, and otherwise bandying it about in a manner sometimes bordering on, but never transgressing, the serious.

His other matrimonial commission was to offer Mary the Duke of Anjou as a husband. It was not very well received, and he observed in the beautiful widow the haughty and restless spirit of her uncle the Cardinal. She was angry, he thought, with the Court of the French Regent, for having come between her and the match with Don Carlos.

While it was in her mind to make an ambitious match, she would have none but a truly great one, and she freely spoke of Don Carlos's younger brother, who was subsequently offered to her, as the selfish fortune-seeking beauties in fashionable novels speak of detrimental second sons. To drop from the heir of the Spanish empire to a prince with neither dominions nor prospects, was not a destiny to which she could reconcile herself.

Yet it was while Mary was dealing in this way with a second offer of the same kind, that the acute diplomatist saw growing in her bosom an attachment for a far more obscure youth, whom his mother the Countess of Lennox had brought up very oddly, having taught him from his youth to dance and play on the lute. The man of the world was puzzled somewhat by this phenomenon, and looked for an explanation of it to a cause deemed in his day, among sensible men, a very practical one—he thought that there was some influence *d'enchantements artificiels* in the passion of Mary for Darnley. Of the sad and tragic events which followed he was a careful observer, and in some respects indeed he was an actor in them, having frequently to attempt the vain task of the peacemaker.

La Mothe Fĕnĕlon, an ancestor of the great bishop, is another French diplomatist whose papers contain interesting vestiges of the history of the period. He it was who was received, after the massacre of St Bartholomew, at the Court of Elizabeth with a solemn and ominous gloom, which had more effect on him than all the virago's furious scoldings. He was a personal friend of Queen Mary, holding a kindly intercourse with her in her captivity. It was from him that she commissioned the costly foreign tissues which she employed in her renowned needlework; and he performed for her many other little services. Some of the letters relating to such matters are a refreshing contrast with the formidable documents among which they are scattered.

Casual mention of Castelnau and Fénélon may be found in our ordinary histories. In these the reader will probably look in vain for anything whatever about Charles de Prunelé, Baron of Esneval and Vidame of Normandy. Yet he was sent to Scotland on a mission so critical, that, as far as externals go, the subsequent fate and history of the British empire might be said to turn on its results. He was sent over to Scotland in the critical year 1585, to make a last effort to continue the ancient alliance of Scotland and France. Were it merely as the parting scene between two old national friends, the last effort to keep up the friendship of France would have its interest. But in reality it was a mission of real practical importance, since it put the question to issue, as lawyers say, which was to fix the destinies of Scotland, and in a great measure those of England. That such a mission should pass unnoticed by historians, and wait for centuries to be spoken of, is one of the illustrations of the truth that the tendency of history is not fully seen by contemporaries; the importance of many events has to be fixed by the posterity which sees the development, and can proportion to each other the relative importance of the several parts.

The instructions to D'Esneval urge on him with reiterated emphasis the support, or rather the restoration, of "l'antienne amytié, alliance et voisinance qui ont toujours esté entre la France et l'Escosse." The tone of the document partakes somewhat of the patronising spirit which had characterised the French treatment of her ally for some half-a-century. The ambassador is not merely accredited to a sovereign prince; he has to do with the people too, as if he were sent from a superior authority entitled to adjust their relations to each other; and he is directed to use his influence to bring the people to obedience, and a proper sense of their duty to their sovereign.

This effort was made at a juncture when the French Government could not afford to quarrel with England, and was in mortal terror of the Guises at home. It came upon King James at that ticklish time when his mother was in imminent danger, and yet when there were strengthening in his favour the chances that, if he behaved well, and committed no piece of folly, he would some day be king of England. In the whole affair, as in all others, he behaved like an exaggeration of a heartless, greedy, grasping schoolboy, snatching at whatever he could get without caring for consequences.

He had half-authorised emissaries at the courts of France and Spain, and at several other places—Romanists who could not obtain actual diplomatic credentials, and whose acts he could disavow if he thought fit; nor was it all to his inconvenience that these zealous men were apt to go far beyond the bounds of his dubious verbal instructions, since that gave him the better excuse for repudiating their proceedings when it was necessary.

Not a year before the mission of D'Esneval, the Lord Seton, the ardent, uncompromising supporter of Mary and Catholicism, appeared at the French Court, commissioned, as he maintained, by the actual ruling power in Scotland, to ask certain aids and concessions from France. He pleaded that the old League should be restored, and that France, like an honest, faithful ally, should rescue the Scottish Queen from her captivity. Among other stipulations were the restoration of the Scottish Guard to the full enjoyment of those privileges in France which they had bought with their blood, the payment by France of a body of Scotsmen serving in Scotland—a very unreasonable-looking proposal—and certain privileges of trading.

These proposals were coldly received; all that Henry III. would give to the juvenile Solomon was a pension of twenty thousand livres, which M. Chéruel, who has seen the brevet granting it, supposes was very ill paid. This embassy, whatever was the authority for it, took place a year before

Esneval's to Scotland. There had been great changes in the mean time, which, if they rendered Mary's condition more dangerous, had increased the chance of her son's succession to the throne of England. The same series of events—the fall of Arran, namely, and the league with England—alarmed the Court of France, by pointing to the total extinction of the French alliance; and it was hence that D'Esneval was sent to offer as much of the rejected Scottish demands as France could afford to give.

It will be of course remarked that, in all these matters, there were longer heads at work than those of the youthful King; but the instincts of his selfish, narrow heart taught him to co-operate in them. He could, if he had thought fit, have broken through all the diplomatic trammels surrounding him, and struck a blow for his mother's life. He had no conscientious principle to restrain him from such an act, though he had a strong dislike for Popery on the ground on which he hated Presbyterianism—because it interfered with the will of kings. His ruling principle was well enough expressed in his remarks to Courcelles—interim ambassador in the absence of D'Esneval—that he liked his mother well enough, but she had threatened, if he did not conform with her religious views, that he should have nothing but the lordship of Darnley like his father—that she must drink the ale she had brewed—that her restless machinations had nearly cost him his crown—and he wished she would meddle with nothing but prayer and serving God. The chief figure in this group of selfishness, meanness, and cruelty, has to be supplied in Queen Elizabeth seizing and committing to the dungeon an unfortunate who had fled to her for protection—grudging her the expense of suitable clothing and food in her captivity—insulting her religion—wanting to get somebody to assassinate her; and at length, when the wished-for death could not be brought about without the forms of law, pretending that she desired it not, and endeavouring to throw on others the blame of the deed.

And yet how wonderfully has all this, which seems so foul and unseemly in romance, tended to one of the most wonderful and blessed of historical developments! Let us suppose King James, under the generous impulse of youthful heroism, drawing the sword in his mother's cause, and France, with chivalrous devotion, sending her armies to avert insult and cruelty from one who had sat as a queen on the throne of St Louis. Let us imagine Queen Elizabeth, endowed with the natural instincts and impulses of her sex, kindly disposed to a persecuted sister, and, in obedience to the impulses of her heart, marrying, and leaving a progeny behind her. Had the dark annals of the age been thus brightened, the glorious history of British power and progress would have remained unwritten—at least in its present shape. With how much longer waiting—through what series of events—the two kingdoms would have fulfilled their natural destiny and come together, are speculations in the world of the unreal which can receive no definite answer. We only know that, however it might have otherwise come to pass, the beneficent conclusion arose out of acts of baseness, selfishness, and cruelty, as a tree grows from decay and putrescence.

It is fortunate, after all, that those who like to see a little of the good that is in the world can pass over that fermentation of the evil passions and selfish propensities, and look back upon the long, stern, honest struggle for independence which was the real operative cause of the desired result. Had it been otherwise, Scotland may read the fate she would have had in Ireland. The Scots repaid the oppressors in the bloody retaliation of the three hundred years' war—the Irish are still taking it out. A sort of general balance of victories and defeats—of injuries and retaliations—put the two enemies in a position for bargaining, which they did with surly suspicion at first, with cordiality when they came better to know each other as friends. Their amity was recorded in a state paper such as no other part of the world can show—a fusion, by mutual consent, between two nations, the one six or eight times as powerful and populous as the other, with no other inequality save the placing of the centre of government in that spot within the larger of the two to which it would naturally have gravitated.

There are some less reasonable ethnological theories afloat in the world, than that we may to some extent attribute to this long struggle the national characteristics which make the Scots appear a dry, hard, stern, unamiable, practical people, with little capacity for cheerful enjoyments or susceptibility to the lighter and more transient excitements. Perhaps the original nature of the people, and the work they had to do, may have reacted on each other, leaving these characteristics deepened and hardened in the end. That the people had a nature susceptible to the deeper enthusiasm, the character of the struggle itself sufficiently tells. And in the tragedies and bereavements that it caused, the devotion it demanded, and the deep love for home and country to which it testified, we may, perhaps, attribute a certain sweetness and plaintive tenderness in the lyrical literature of the country, a vein of gentleness and beauty running through her rugged nature, like the lovely agates which nestle in the hollows of the black trap rocks, or the purple amethysts that sparkle in her granite corries.

So came the kindly old French alliance to its natural conclusion. It was nominally re-established in a friendship between King James and Henry IV., who established a special company of Scots gensdarmes, and afterwards there were some curious dealings between Cardinal Richelieu and the Covenanters; but these were casual affairs having no influence on national destinies. The story of the alliance is now an old one, but it leaves a mellow tinge upon the long annals of medieval brutality and violence. Scotland at last became reconciled to that great relation which, let us suppose, in the usual misunderstanding which creates the quarrels in the romances, had treated her as an alien enemy. But while the reconciliation has been long consolidated, and has proved as natural a national adjustment as the restoration of an exiled child is a natural family adjustment, there is still a pleasing sentiment in recalling the friends found in the wide world when kindred were unkind; and the hospitable doors opened to our wandering countrymen among those who stood at the head of European civilisation in the middle ages, must ever remain a memorable record of the generosity of the patrons, and of the merits of those who so well requited their generosity by faithful and powerful services.*

---

* M. Chéruel (p. 175) puts the sentiment of the conclusion very effectively: "L'Ecosse s'est de plus en plus identifiée avec l'Angleterre, et, il faut bien le reconnaître, toutes deux y ont gagné. L'Ecosse a reçu, en compensation de l'indépendance nationale, une puissante impulsion : industrie, sciences, littérature, philosophie, tout y a prospéré. Une sage regularité, une observation patiente et ingénieuse, une probité proverbiale, ont remplacé la loyauté un peu sauvage, le fanatisme puritain, la fougue indisciplinée des anciens Ecossais. De son côté l'Angleterre a conquis la securité : tranquille dans son île, elle a pu porter au loin son activité guerrière et commerciale. Une alliance de moins

It is a significant token of the enduring interest of this episode in history, that, besides lighter memorials, to many of which I have referred, two eminent French archæologists have bestowed what must have been a large portion of the labour of their days to the production each of a great book after his own kind, bearing on the old relations between France and Scotland.* To the volumes which contain the record of this attachment, something more is due than the mere recognition of their literary merits—they deserve at the hands of our countrymen an affectionate recognition as national memorials. The quantity of curious and interesting matter contained in them, but for the special zeal of the two men who have thus come forward, might have remained still buried under archæo-

---

pour la France, une province de plus pour l'Angleterre, voilà le résultat d'une politique tour à tour faible ou passionnée, fanatique ou indifférente." In strict propriety, the import of these remarks should have suggested the metamorphosis of l'Angleterre into Grande Bretagne before their conclusion; but where there is so much that is honest and generous in sentiment, it would be invidious to criticise the nomenclature too closely.

* 'Relations Politiques de la France et de l'Espagne avec l'Ecosse au xvie Siècle—Papiers d'état, Pièces, et Documents inédits ou peu connus, tirés des Bibliothêques et des Archives de France. Publiés par Alexandre Teulet, Archiviste aux Archives de l'Empire.' Nouvelle edition, 5 vols. Paris: Renouard. Edinburgh: Williams & Norgate.

'Les Ecossais en France—Les Français en Ecosse.' Par Francisque Michel, Correspondant de l'Institut de France, &c. &c. 2 vols. London: Trübner & Co.

logical rubbish—might have remained so for ever, even until oblivion overtook them.

Setting before one on the library table the two volumes of M. Michel, and the five of M. Teulet, is a good deal like receiving one guest in full court costume, prepared to meet distinguished company, while another comes to you in his lounging home vestment of serge, with slippers and smoking-cap, as if he had just stepped across the way from the scene of his laborious researches. There is throughout M. Michel's two brilliant-looking volumes the testimony to an extent of dreary reading and searching which would stimulate compassion, were it not that he who would be the victim, were that the proper feeling in which he should be approached, evidently exults and glories, and is really happy, in the conditions which those who know no better would set down as his hardships. There are some who, when they run the eye over arrêts and other formal documents, over pedigrees, local chronicles telling trifles, title-deeds, and suchlike writings, carry with them a general impression of the political or social lesson taught by them, and discard from recollection all the details from which any such impression has been derived. M. Michel is of another kind; he has that sort of fondness for his work which induces him to show you it in all stages, from the rude block to the finished piece of art, so far as it is finished. You are entered in all the secrets of his workshop—you participate in all his disappointments and difficulties as well as his successes. The research which has had no available result is still reported, in order that you may see how useless it has been. One who has not much sympathy with this kind of literature, would yet not desire to speak profanely of it, since some consider it the only perfect method of writing books on subjects connected with history or archæology. The "citation of authorities," in fact, is deemed, in this department of intellectual labour, something equivalent to records of experiments in natural science, and to demonstrations in geometrical science. Those whose sympathy is with the exhibition rather of results than of the means of reaching them, have not that high respect for footnotes filled with accurate transcripts of book-titles which is due to the high authorities by whom the practice has been long sanctioned. They can afford it, however, the sort of distant unsympathising admiration which people bestow on accomplishments for which they have no turn or sympathy—as for those of the juggler, the acrobat, and the accountant. M. Michel's way of citing the books he refers to, is, indeed, to all appearance, a miracle of perfection in this kind of work. Sometimes he is at the trouble of denoting where the passage stands in more than one, or even in every, edition of the work. He gives chapter or section as well as page and volume. In old books counted not by the page but the leaf, he will tell you which side he desires you to look at, right or left; and where, as is the way in some densely printed old folios, in addition to the arrangement of the pages by numeration, divisions on each page are separated by the letters A B C, he tells you which of these letters stands sentry on the paragraph he refers to. There is, at all events, a very meritorious kind of literary honesty in all this, and however disinclined to follow it, no one has a right to object to it. And, after all, a man who has gone through so much hard forbidding reading as M. Michel has, is surely entitled to let us know something about the dreary wastes and rugged wildernesses through which he has sojourned—all for the purpose of laying before his readers his two gay attractive-looking volumes. Towards his foreign reading, I in the general instance lift the hat of respect, acknowledging, without professing critically to test, its high merits. Upon the diligent manner in which he has, in our own less luxuriant field of inquiry among Scots authorities, turned over every stone to see what is under it, one can speak with more distinct assurance. Take one instance. The young Earl of Haddington, the son of that crafty old statesman called Tam o' the Cowgate, who scraped together a fortune in public office under James VI., was studying in France, when he met and fell in love with the beautiful Mademoiselle de Chatillon, grand-daughter of the Admiral Coligny. When only nineteen years old he went back to France, married her, and brought her home. He died within a year, however; and the Countess, a rich beautiful widow, returned to her friends. She was, of course, beset by admirers, and in reference to these, M. Michel has turned up a curious passage in 'Les Historiettes de Tallemant des Réaux,' which, if true, shows the persevering zeal with which our Queen, Henrietta Maria, seized every opportunity to promote the cause of her religion. The Countess being Huguenot, and of a very Huguenot family, the Queen was eager that she should be married to a Roman Catholic, and selected the son of her friend Lady Arundel. The dominion over her affections was, however, held by "un jeune Ecossois nommé Esbron, neveu du Colonel Esbron." The name is French for the Chevalier Hepburn, one of the most renowned soldiers in the French service in the early part of the seventeenth century. The mamma Chatillon was dead against either connection. She got a fright by hearing that her daughter had been carried off to the Tenêbres, or the services of Easter-week which inaugurate Good-Friday; she consequently gave her a maternal box on the ear, carried her off, and, to keep her out of harm's way, forthwith married her to the Count de la Suze, *tout borgne, tout ivrogne, et tout indetté qu'il étoit.*

M. Michel's purpose is not with this desirable husband, nor with his wife after she ceases to be connected with Scotland, but with the young Hepburn who comes casually across the scene. Following in his track entirely, the next quarter where, after appearing in the 'Historiettes,' he turns up, is Durie's 'Decisions of the Court of Session.' This is by no means one of the books which every well-informed man is presumed to know. So toughly is it stuffed with the technicalities and involutions of old Scots law, and so confused and involved is every sentence of it by the natural haziness of its author, that probably no living English writer would dare to meddle with it. No Scotsman would, unless he be a lawyer—nor, indeed, would any lawyer, unless of a very old school—welcome the appearance of the grim folio. In citing from it the decision of Hepburn *contra* Hepburn, 14th March 1639, even the courageous M. Michel subjoins: "Si j'ai bien compris le texte de cet *arrêt* conçu dans une langue particulière." This peculiar arrêt begins as follows:—"The brethren and sisters of umquhile Collonel Sir John Hepburn having submitted all questions and rights which they might pretend to the goods, gear, and means of the said umquhile Sir John, to the laird Wauchton and some other friends, wherein the submitters were bound and did refer to the said friends to determine what proportion of the said goods should be given to George Hepburn, the son of the eldest brother to the said Sir John, which George was then in France at the time of the making of the said submission and bond, and did not subscribe the same, nor none taking the burden for him; upon the which submission, the said friends had given their decreet arbitral. The living brethren and sisters of the said Sir John being confirmed executors to him, pursue one Beaton, factor in Paris, for payment of 20,000 pounds addebted by him to the said umquhile Sir John, who, suspending upon double poinding," &c.

Perhaps enough has been said to exemplify the dauntless nature of M. Michel's researches. It is impossible to withhold admiration from such achievements, and I know that, in some quarters, they are deemed the highest to which the human intellect can aspire. But I confess that, to my own taste, the results of M. Teulet's labours are more acceptable. True, he does not profess to give the world an original book. He comes forward as the mere transcriber and editor of certain documents. But in the gathering of these documents from different quarters, through all the difficulties of various languages and alphabets, in their arrangement so as to bring out momentous historical truths in their due series, and in the helps he has afforded to those who consult his volumes, he has shown a skill and scholarship which deserve to be ranked with the higher attainments of science. Reference has already been made to his volume on Queen Mary. Among not the least valued of the contents of any good historical library, will be six octavo volumes containing the correspondence of La Mothe Fěnélon, and the other French ambassadors to England and Scotland during the latter years of Queen Elizabeth's reign, for which the world is indebted to M. Teulet's researches. The book at present especially referred to is a reprint, with some additions, of the papers—at least all that are worth having—which were previously an exclusive luxury of the Bannatyne Club, having been printed in three quarto volumes, as a gift to their brethren, by certain liberal members of that Club. These papers go into the special affairs of this country as connected with France and Spain from the beginning of our disputes with our old ally down to the accession of James VI. In the hands of the first historian who has the fortune to make ample use of them, these documents will disperse the secluded and parochial atmosphere that hangs about the history of Scotland, and show how the fate of Europe in general turned upon the pivot of the destinies of our country. It is here that, along with many minor secrets, we have revealed to us that narrow escape made by the cause of Protestantism, when the project on the cards was the union of the widowed Queen Mary to the heir of Spain, and those political combinations already referred to as centering round the interests and the fate of the Queen of Scots, which led to the more signal and renowned escape realised in the defeat of the Armada.

Chapter V.

Relics of the League in Scots Habits and Practices—The Law—The Bonnet Vert and the Dyvour's Habit—The States-General and the Three Estates—The Huguenots and the Covenanters—Religious Architecture—The Chateau and the Castle—The Eguimené and the Hogmanay—The Fêtes des Foux and the Daft Days—French Education and Manners.

THE long and close connection with France could not fail to leave some specialties in the constitution and social condition of Scotland. A glance at these may prove curious, and may also be instructive as showing how far a political alliance with a nation essentially differing in character will go, in changing the fundamental nature of a people.

However much the infusion of Scots blood into her veins may have affected the inner life of France, in externals the great central territory, the inheritor of Roman civilisation, was naturally the teacher—

the rude northern land the pupil. France thus infused into Scotland her own institutions, which, being those of the Roman Empire, as practised throughout the Christian nations of the Continent, made Scotsmen free of those elements of social communion—of that *comitas gentium*—from which England excluded herself in sulky pride. This is visible, or rather audible, at the present day, in the Greek and Latin of the Scotsmen of the old school, who can make themselves understood all over the world; while the English pronunciation, differing from that of the nations which have preserved the chief deposits of the classic languages in their own, must as assuredly differ from the way in which these were originally spoken.

The Englishman disdained the universal Justinian jurisprudence, and would be a law unto himself, which he called, with an affectation of humility, "The Common Law." It is full, no doubt, of patches taken out of the 'Corpus Juris,' but, far from their source being acknowledged, the civilians are never spoken of by the common lawyers but to be railed at and denounced; and when great draughts on the Roman system were found absolutely necessary to keep the machine of justice in motion, these were entirely elbowed out of the way by common law, and had to form themselves into a separate machinery of their own, called Equity.

Scotland, on the other hand, received implicitly from her leader in civilisation the great body of the

civil law, as collected and arranged by the most laborious of all labouring editors, Denis Godefroi. There came over also an exact facsimile of the French system of public prosecution for crime, from the great state officer at the head of the system to the Procureurs du Roi. It is still in full practice, and eminently useful; but it is an arrangement that, to be entirely beneficial, needs to be surrounded by constitutional safeguards; and though there has been much pressure of late to establish it in England, one cannot be surprised that it was looked askance at while the great struggles for fixing the constitution were in progress.

Saying that Scotland took from France the civil law entire, supersedes all particulars as to the similarity of the forms of the administration of justice in the two countries, unless one were writing an extensive work dedicated to the comparative anatomy of the civil law as exemplified in both. In such a pursuit the closest parallel might be found in books without any resemblance whatever in practice. It was long an almost necessary qualification for the bar in Scotland, that one had studied the civil law abroad. There are, perhaps, lawyers old enough to remember when the saying of some Continental civilian of the sixteenth or seventeenth century, Viglius Zuichemus, Rittershusius, Puffendorf, Noodt, Voet, and the like, might be cited just as aptly as a decision a few years old, in some case about a breach of warranty in the insurance of a vessel, or the import of a contract for the sale of goods in a bonded warehouse.

Such things are typical of the sort of law that the French alliance brought to Scotland. It was all words and scholarship—not reality. Of the Code and the Pandects, and of the hundred and fifty thousand volumes calculated to be about the sum total of the commentaries on them, all the intricacies and wanderings were more or less law in Scotland; but, at the same time, with so tremendous a mass of written law, there was very little real and practical law. The Roman law, in fact, from its exceeding symmetry and minute logical organisation, has proved extremely ductile and accommodating. Whether or not it be because it grew in a republic and was perfected in a despotism, it has been practically found that it suits admirably for either. It has just three grades: an emperor over all; the free citizens; and the slaves, who are disposed of as property. In a country like Scotland, where there was neither an absolute emperor nor slavery in the old Roman sense, and where feudal institutions broke in upon the symmetry of the analytical adjustments of the civilians, there was room for a great deal of freedom; and the fact is, that the Scots, being fond of it and unruly, got rather more freedom under the law of the despotic Roman Empire than the English achieved by that laborious structure, their Common Law.

In other respects it is curious to observe with

what nicety, when they were about it, our lawyers would adopt some small specialty of practice from France. Before leaving the department of jurisprudence, let me mention just one little example of this. Long before England had an insolvency statute there existed in Scotland the "cessio," or cession to his creditors of all his worldly means by a prosecuted and persecuted debtor, who in return obtained a protection from further personal pursuit. By an old regulation, put into shape in an Act of Sederunt, or rule of court, in the year 1606, dyvours or debitors, when they obtained this protection, had "to caus mak and buy ane hatt or bonnet of yellow coloure," to be worn "in all tyme thairefter, swa lang as they remane and abide dyvoris; with speciall provision and ordinance, if at ony tyme or place efter the publication of the said dyvoris at the said mercat-croce, ony person or personis declarit dyvoris beis fundin wantand the foresaid hatt or bonnet of yellow colour, *toties* it sall be lawful to the baillies of Edinburgh, or ony of his creditoris, to tak and apprehend the said dyvor," &c. This cap was called the dyvour's habit, and may be traced in use after the middle of last century.

In France there was the "cession"—a pretty exact parallel to the Scots cessio. There, too, a special head-covering was worn by the privileged debtor to distinguish him from those who either were not in debt, or, being so, had no special protection from the inflictions of their creditors. There was, however, a difference, as if to rebut the charge of slavish imitation: in Scotland, as we have seen, it was a yellow cap; in France, whence the example was taken, the cap was green.*

Since the Union, legislation for Scotland has been adapted to the old practice of the English Parliament; anything derived by the old Scots Parliament from French practice cannot, therefore, be spoken of as an existing influence of France, yet this is the place in which a word or two may be most appropriately said about it.

The Parliament of Scotland, when it came to an end at the Union, differed in constitution from that of England, having three estates—the nobles, the county members, and the representatives of the municipal corporations—all sitting together in one house. This came from the old practice of the States-General of France; but so little could the shape

---

* "Le bonnet vert est le marque de ceux qui ont fait cession. L'usage du bonnet vert n'a été introduit en France par aucunes ordonnances, mais par les arrêts des cours supérieures, notamment par celui du parlement du 26 juin 1582 en forme de réglement: cet arrêt ordonne que ceux que seront admis au bénéfice de cession, après avoir justifié la perte de leurs biens sans fraude, seront tenus de porter le *bonnet vert:* et que s'ils sont trouvés ne l'ayant pas, ils seront déboutés du bénéfice de la cession, et permis à leur créanciers de les emprisonner."—Denisart, 'Collection de Décisions Nouvelles:' *voce*, Bonnet vert.

thus given to the institution affect the condition of the community, that had the shape of the English Parliament been substituted for that of the French States-General, the country could not have been freer than it was. In fact, there arose this mighty difference between the French institution and its Scots offspring, that the parent died, while its progeny lived.

The practice of the long-forgotten States-General of France was an object of rather anxious inquiry at the reassembling of that body in 1789, after they had been some four centuries and a half in a state of adjournment or dissolution. The investigations thus occasioned brought out many peculiarities which were in practical observance in Scotland down to the Union. All the world has read of that awful crisis arising out of the question whether the Estates should vote collectively or separately. Had the question remained within the bounds of reason and regulation, instead of being virtually at the issue of the sword, much instructive precedent would have been obtained for its settlement by an examination of the proceedings of that Parliament of Scotland which adjusted the Union—an exciting matter also, yet, to the credit of our country, discussed with perfect order, and obedience to rules of practice which, derived from the custom of the old States-General of France, were rendered pliant and adaptable by such a long series of practical adaptations as the country of their nativity was not permitted to witness.*

There was a very distinct adaptation of another French institution of later origin, when the Court of Session was established in 1533. Before that year, the king's justices administered the law somewhat as in England, but there was an appeal to Parliament; and as that body did its judicial work by committees, these became virtually the supreme courts of the

* "The riding of the Parliament," as it was called—the procession with which a session opened and closed—was a great state ceremony, with many minute and strict traditional details which it behoved Lyon King-at-Arms to be minutely acquainted with. I do not know how far a comparison of these with the formalities of the old French States-General might reward research. The only attempt to represent the ceremonial of the Scots Parliament I have ever met with is in a French book, the beautiful 'Atlas Historique' of Guendeville (II. No. 56); we have here the procession and the sitting, and each figure with robes, insignia, and appropriate gesture separately articulated. There is enough of special costume and other characteristics to let one see that, although not taken from life, the picture was done at the direction of one acquainted with the reality. Though published in the year 1718, eleven years after the Parliament of Scotland had ceased to exist, it must have been made up from materials some forty years earlier, since we have "les archevesques" and "les evesques." The bulk of the procession is made up of "le commissaires des comtez, et de bourgs, et des villes." The national emblems, besides the heraldic lion, are a gigantic thistle surmounted by an armed Pallas, who has quietly deposited on her knee "le chapeau de la liberté"—the same Phrygian nightcap which subsequently had so horrible a renown in France.

realm. Their proceedings, under the title of 'The Acts of the Lords Auditors of Causes and Complaints,' may be purchased from the Government, with the other volumes issued by the Record Commission. The Court of Session, established to supersede this kind of tribunal, was exactly a French parliament—a body exercising appellate judicial functions, along with a few others of a legislative character. These were few in this country, but in France they became sufficiently extensive to render the assembling of the proper Parliament of the land—the States-General—unnecessary for all regal purposes.

Let us turn now to the Universities. It was undoubtedly the influence of France that stamped on those of Scotland the form and character of their Continental parentage, so accurately that to this day they supply the best living specimens from which we may study the structure of the medieval university. The University of King's College in Aberdeen was constructed on the model of that of Paris, the metropolitan of the universities of the world, whose usages were the authority in all questions of form and practice.* There the founder of King's College, Bishop Elphinston, had taught

* In 1634, when Charles I. noted Presbyterian innovations in King's College, and expressed a desire "for re-establishing of this university in her jurisdiction, conservation, and privileges, according to her ancient rights granted thereanent," application was directed to be made to "the

for many years; so had the first principal, Hector Boece, of whom hereafter. The transition from the Paris to the Aberdeen of that day must have been a descent not to be estimated by the present relative condition of the two places; and one cannot be surprised to find Hector saying that he was seduced northwards by gifts and promises. Yet it is probable that we would find fewer actual living remnants of the old institution in Paris itself, than in this northern offspring and its brother universities in Scotland.

In these the forms, the nomenclature, and the usages of the middle ages are still preserved, though some of them have naturally changed their character with the shifting of the times. Each of them has still its chancellor, and sometimes a high state dignitary accepts of the office. It was of old a very significant one, for it was the link which allied the semi-republican institutions of the universities to the hierarchy of St Peter. The bishop was almost invariably the chancellor, unless the university were subordinated to some great monastic institution, the head of which became the chancellor—so in Paris the Prior of St Genevieve held this high office. In the Scottish universities the usual Continental arrange-

---

rector and University of Paris for a just and perfect written double of the rights and privileges of that University of Paris, for the better clearing and setting in good order the rights and privileges belonging to this University of Aberdeen."—'Fasti Aberdonenses,' p. 400.

ment seems to have been adopted prior to the Reformation—as a matter of course, the bishop was the chancellor.

But while the institution was thus connected through a high dignitary with the Romish hierarchy, it possessed, as a great literary community with peculiar privileges, its own great officer electively chosen for the preservation of those privileges. It had its Rector, who, like the chief magistrate of a municipal corporation, but infinitely above him in the more illustrious character of the functions for which his constituents were incorporated, stood forth as the head of his republic, and its protector from the invasions either of the subtle churchmen or the grasping barons. The rector, indeed, was the concentration of that peculiar commonwealth which the constitution of the ancient university prescribed. Sir William Hamilton has shown pretty clearly that, in its original acceptation, the word Universitas was applied, not to the comprehensiveness of the studies, but to that of the local and personal expansion of the institution. The university despised the bounds of provinces, and even nations, and was a place where ardent minds from all parts of the world met to study together, and impart to each other the influence of collective intellect working in combination and competition. The constitution of the Rectorship was calculated to provide for the protection of this universality, for the election was managed by the Procurators or Proctors of the Nations, or geographical clusters into which the students were divided, generally for the purpose of neutralising the naturally superior influence of the home students, and keeping up the cosmopolitan character imparted to the system by its enlightened founders. Hence in Paris the nations were France, Picardy, and England, afterwards changed to Germany, in which Scotland was included. Glasgow is still divided into four nations: the Natio Glottiana, or Clydesdale, taken from the name given to the Clyde by Tacitus. In the Natio Laudoniana were originally included the rest of Scotland, but it was found expedient to place the English and the colonists within it; while Albania, intended to include Britain south of the Forth, has been made rather inaptly the nation of the foreigners. Rothesay, the fourth nation, includes the extreme west of Scotland, and Ireland. In Aberdeen there is a like division into Marenses, or inhabitants of Mar, the central or metropolitan district; Angusiani, or men of Angus, which, however, includes the whole world south of the Grampians; while the northern districts are partitioned into Buchanenses and Moravienses, the people of Buchan and Moray.

The Procurators of the Nations were, in the University of Paris, those high authorities to whom, as far separated from all sublunary influences, King Henry of England proposed, in the twelfth century, to refer his disputes with the Papal power. In England they are represented at the present day by the formidable Proctor, who is a terror to evil-doers without being any praise or protection to them that do well. But it may safely be said that the ingenious youths who in Glasgow and Aberdeen go through the annual ceremony, as *procuratores nationum*, of tendering the votes of the nations in the election of a rector, more legitimately represent those procurators of the thirteenth and fourteenth century, who maintained the rights of their respective nations in the great intellectual republic called a Universitas. The discovery, indeed, of this latent power, long hidden, like some palæozoic fossil, under the pedagogical innovations of modern days—which tended to make the self-governing institution a school ruled by masters — created astonishment in all quarters, even in those who found themselves in possession of the privilege. In Aberdeen especially, when some mischievous antiquary maintained that, by the charter of the younger college, the election of a lord rector lay with the students themselves, the announcement was received with derision by a discerning public, and with a severe frown, as a sort of seditious libel, enticing the youth to rebellion, by the indignant professors. But it turned out to be absolutely true, however astounding it might be to those who are unacquainted with the early history of universities, and think that everything ancient must have been tyrannical and hierarchical. The students made a sort of saturnalia of their fugitive power, while the professors looked on as one may see a solemn mastiff contemplate the gambols of a litter of privileged spaniel pups.

Those who are logically the very worst distributors of patronage or honours sometimes turn out to be the best, because, distrusting their own capacity to judge correctly, they fix their choice so high up in the hierarchy of merit as to be beyond cavil. Hence the catalogue of Lord Rectors soars far above respectability and appropriateness: it is brilliant. From Burke to Bulwer Lytton and Macaulay, they have, with a few exceptions, been men of the first intellectual rank. What is a still more remarkable result than that they should often have been men of genius, there is scarcely an instance of a lord rector having been a clamorous quack or a canting fanatic.

In Edinburgh there was no such relic of the ancient university commonwealth, and the students had instinctively supplied the want by affiliating their voluntary societies, and choosing a distinguished man to be the president of the aggregate group. The constitution of the College of Edinburgh, indeed, was not matured until after the old constitution of the universities had suffered a reaction, and, far from any new ones being constructed on the old model, the earlier universities with difficulty preserved their own constitutions. It is a tribute to the worth of these, that their example has been followed in the late readjustments in Edinburgh.

That principle of internal self-action and independence of the contemporary constituted powers, of which the rectorship and some other relics remain to us at this day, is one of the most remarkable, and in many respects admirable, features in the history of the middle ages. It is involved in mysteries and contradictions which one would be glad to see unravelled by skilful and full inquiry. Adapted to the service of pure knowledge, and investing her with absolute prerogatives, the system was yet one of the creatures of that Romish hierarchy, which at the same time thought by other efforts to circumscribe human inquiry, and make it the servant of her own ambitious efforts.

It may help us in some measure to the solution of the phenomenon to remember that, however dim the light of the Church may have shone, it was yet the representative of the intellectual power, and was in that capacity carrying on a war with brute force. Catholicism was the great rival and controller of the feudal strength and tyranny of the age. As intellect and knowledge were the weapons with which the blind colossus was to be attacked, it was believed that the intellectual arsenals could not be too extensive or complete—that intellect could not be too richly cultivated. Like many combatants, the churchmen perhaps forgot future results in the desire of immediate victory, and were for the moment blind to the effect so nervously apprehended by their successors, that the light thus brought in by them would illuminate the dark corners of their own ecclesiastical system, and lead the way to its fall. Perhaps such hardy intellects as Abelard or Aquinas may have anticipated such a result from the stimulus given by them to intellectual inquiry, and may not have deeply lamented the prospect.

But however it came about—whether in the blindness of all, or the far-sightedness of some—the Church, from the thirteenth to pretty far on in the fifteenth century, encouraged learning with a noble reliance and a zealous energy which it would ill become the present age to despise or forget. And even if it should all have proceeded from a blind confidence that the Church placed on a rock was unassailable, and that mere human wisdom, even trained to the utmost of its powers, was, after all, to be nothing but her handmaiden, let us respect this unconscious simplicity which enabled the educational institutions to be placed in so high and trusted a position.

The Church supplied something then, indeed, which we search after in vain in the present day, and which we shall only achieve by some great strides in academic organisation, capable of supplying from within what was then supplied from without. What was thus supplied was no less than that cosmopolitan nature, which made the university not merely parochial, or merely national, but universal, as its name denoted. The temporal prince might endow the academy with lands and riches, and might confer upon its members honourable and lucrative privileges; but it was to the head of the one indivisible Church that the power belonged of franking it all over Christendom, and establishing throughout the civilised world a freemasonry of intellect, which made all the universities, as it were, one great corporation of the learned men of the world.

It must be admitted that we have here one of those practical difficulties which form the necessary price of the freedom of Protestantism. When a great portion of Europe was no longer attached to Rome, the peculiar centralisation of the educational systems was broken up. The old universities, indeed, retained their ancient privileges in a traditional, if not a practically legal shape, carrying through Lutheranism and Calvinism the characteristics of the abjured Romanism, yet carrying them unscathed, since they were protected from injury and insult by the enlightened object for which they were established and endowed. When, however, in Protestant countries, the old universities became poor, or when a change of condition demanded the foundation of a new university, it was difficult to restore anything so simple and grand as that old community of privileges which made the member of one university a citizen of all others, according to his rank, whether he were laureated in Paris or Bologna, Upsala or St Andrews.

The English universities, by their great wealth and political influence, were able to stand alone, neither giving nor taking. Their Scottish contemporaries, unable to fight a like battle, have had reason to complain of their ungenerous isolation; and as children of the same parentage, and differing only from their southern neighbours in not having so much worldly prosperity, it is natural that they should look back with a sigh, which even orthodox Presbyterianism cannot suppress, to the time when the universal mental sway of Rome, however offensive it might be in its own insolent supremacy, yet exercised that high privilege of supereminent greatness to level secondary inequalities, and place those whom it favoured beyond the reach of conventional humiliations.

Besides that great officer the rector, we have in Scotland a Censor too; but for all the grandeur of his etymological ancestry in Roman history, he is but a small officer—in stature sometimes, as well as dignity. He calls over the catalogue or roll of names, marking those absent—a duty quite in keeping with that enumerating function of the Roman officer, which has left to us the word census as a numbering of the people.

So lately as the eighteenth century, when the monastic or collegiate system which has now so totally disappeared from the Scottish universities yet lingered about them, the censor was a more important, or at least more laborious officer, and, oddly enough, he corresponded in some measure with the character into which, in England, the proctor had so strangely deviated. In a regulation adopted in

Glasgow in 1725, it is provided "that all students be obliged, after the bells ring, immediately to repair to their classes, and to keep within them, and a censor be appointed to every class, to attend from the ringing of the bells till the several masters come to their classes, and observe any, either of his own class or of any other, who shall be found walking in the courts during the above time, or standing on the stairs, or looking out at the windows, or making noise." * This has something of the mere schoolroom characteristic of our modern university discipline ; but this other paragraph, from the same set of regulations, is indicative both of more mature vices among the precocious youth of Glasgow, and a more inquisitorial corrective organisation :—

"That for keeping order without the College, a censor be appointed to observe any who shall be in the streets before the bells ring, and to go now and then to the billiard-tables, and to the other gaming-places, to observe if any be playing at the times when they ought to be in their chambers ; and that this censor be taken from the poor scholars of the several classes alternately, as they shall be thought most fit for that office, and that some reward be thought of for their pains." † In the fierce street-conflicts to which we may have occasion to refer, the poor censors had a more perilous service.

---

* 'Munimenta Univ. Glasguensis,' ii. 429.
† Ibid., 425.

In the universities of central Europe, and that of Paris, their parent, the censor was a very important person; yet he was the subordinate of one far greater in power and influence, the Regent or monarch of a department.* The regents still exist in more than their original potency; for they are that essential invigorating element of the university of the present day, without which it would not exist. Of old, when every magister was entitled to teach in the university, the regents were persons selected from among them, with the powers of government as separate from the capacity and function of instructing; at present, in so far as the university is a school, the regent is a schoolmaster—and therefore an essential element of the establishment. The term Regent, like most of the other university distinctions, was originally of Parisian nomenclature, and there might be brought up a good deal of learning bearing on its signification as distinct from that of the word Professor—now so desecrated in its use that we are most familiar with it in connection with dancing-schools, jugglers' booths, and veterinary surgeries. The regency, as a university distinction conferred as a reward of capacities shown within the arena of the university, and judged of according to its republican

---

* In the words of the writers of the 'Trevoux,' so full of knowledge about such matters, "Un régent est dans sa classe comme un souverain; il crée des charges de *censeurs* comme il lui plait, il les donne à qui il veut, et il les abolit quand il le juge à propos."

principles, seems to have lingered in a rather confused shape in our Scottish universities, and to have gradually ingrafted itself on the patronage of the professorships. So in reference to Glasgow, immediately after the Revolution, when there was a vacancy or two from Episcopalians declining to take the obligation to acknowledge the new Church Establishment, there appears the following notice:—

"*January* 2, 1691.—There had never been so solemn and numerous an appearance of disputants for a regent's place as was for fourteen days before this, nine candidates disputing; and in all their disputes and other exercises they all behaved themselves so well, as that the Faculty judged there was not one of them but gave such specimens of their learning as might deserve the place, which occasioned so great difficulty in the choice that the Faculty, choosing a leet of some of them who seemed most to excel and be fittest, did determine the same by lot, which the Faculty did solemnly go about, and the lot fell upon Mr John Law, who thereupon was this day established regent." *

---

* 'Munimenta,' iii. 596. Sir William Hamilton explains the position of the regents with a lucid precision which makes his statement correspond precisely with the documentary stores here referred to. "In the original constitution of Oxford," he says, "as in that of all the older universities of the Parisian model, the business of instruction was not confided to a special body of privileged professors. The university was governed, the university was taught, by the graduates at large. Professor, master, doctor, were

The term Regent became obsolete in other universities, while it continued by usage to be applied to a certain class of professors in those of Scotland. Along with other purely academic titles and func-

---

originally synonymous. Every graduate had an equal right of teaching publicly in the university the subjects competent to his faculty and to the rank of his degree; nay, every graduate incurred the obligation of teaching publicly, for a certain period, the subjects of his faculty—for such was the condition involved in the grant of the degree itself. The bachelor or imperfect graduate, partly as an exercise towards the higher honour, and useful to himself, partly as a performance due for the degree obtained, and of advantage to others, was bound to read under a master or doctor in his faculty a course of lectures; and the master, doctor, or perfect graduate was in like manner, after his promotion, obliged immediately to commence (*incipere*), and to continue for a certain period publicly to teach (*regere*) some at least of the subjects appertaining to his faculty. As, however, it was only necessary for the university to enforce this obligation of public teaching, compulsory on all graduates during the term of their *necessary regency*, if there did not come forward a competent number of *voluntary regents* to execute this function; and as the schools belonging to the several faculties, and in which alone all public or ordinary instruction could be delivered, were frequently inadequate to accommodate the multitude of the incepters, it came to pass that in these universities the original period of necessary regency was once and again abbreviated, and even a dispensation from actual teaching during its continuance commonly allowed. At the same time, as the university only accomplished the end of its existence through its regents, they alone were allowed to enjoy full privileges in its legislature and government; they alone partook of its *beneficia* and *sportulæ*. In Paris the non-regent graduates were only assembled on rare and extraordinary occasions:

tions, it fell in England before the rising ascendency of the heads and other officers of the collegiate institutions—colleges, halls, inns, and entries. So, in the same way, evaporated the Faculties and their Deans, still conspicuous in Scottish academic nomenclature. In both quarters they were derived from the all-fruitful nursery of the Parisian university. But Scotland kept and cherished what she obtained from a friend and ally; England despised and forgot the example of an alien and hostile people. The Decanus seems to have been a captain or leader of ten—a sort of tything-man; and Ducange speaks of him as a superintendent of ten monks. He afterwards came into general employment as a sort of chairman and leader.

The *Doyens* of all sorts, lay and ecclesiastical, were a marked feature of ancient France, as they still are of Scotland, where there is a large body of lay deans, from the lawyer, selected for his eminence at the bar, who presides over the Faculty of Advocates, down to "my feyther the deacon," who has gathered behind a "half-door" the gear that is to make his son a capitalist and a magistrate. Among

---

in Oxford the regents constituted the house of congregation, which, among other exclusive prerogatives, was anciently the initiatory assembly through which it behoved that every measure should pass before it could be admitted to the house of convocation, composed indifferently of all regents and non-regents resident in the university."—'Dissertations,' pp. 391, 392.

the Scottish universities the deans of faculty are still nearly as familiar a title as they were at Paris or Bologna.

Their exemption from the authority of the ordinary legal or correctional tribunals was one of the remarkable features of the ancient universities, and the relics of it which have come down almost to the present day in Scotland are very curious. The University was a state in itself, where the administrators of the ordinary authority of the realm had no more power than in a neighbouring independent republic. So jealously was this authority watched and fenced, that usually when the dispute lay between the liegemen of the university and those of the state—between gown and town—the university haughtily arrogated the authority over both. To be sure, it was very much the practice of the age to adjust rights and privileges by balancing one against another—by letting them fight out, as it were, every question in a general contest, and produce a sort of rude justice by the antagonism and balance of forces, just as in some Oriental states at this day the strangers of each nation have the privilege of living under their native laws; a method which, by pitting privilege against privilege, and letting the stronger bear down the weaker, saves the central government much disagreeable and difficult work in the adjustment of rights and duties.

So, in the middle ages, we had the ecclesiastical competing with the baronial interests, and the burghal or corporate with both. Nay, in these last there was a subdivision of interests, various corporations of craftsmen being subject to the authority of their own syndics, deans, or mayors, and entitled to free themselves from any interference in many of their affairs by the burghal or even the royal courts. Ecclesiastical law fought with civil law, and chancery carried on a ceaseless undermining contest with common law; while over Europe there were inexhaustible varieties of palatinates, margravates, regalities, and the like, enjoying their own separate privileges and systems of jurisprudence. But over this Babel of authorities, so complexly established in France that Voltaire likened it to a traveller changing laws as often as he changed horses, what is conspicuous is the homage paid by all the other exclusive privileges to those of the universities, and the separation of these grand institutions by an impassable line of venerated privileges from the rest of the vulgar world. Thus, the State conceded freely to literature those high privileges for which the Church in vain contended, from the slaughter of Becket to the fall of Wolsey. In a very few only of the states nearest to the centre of spiritual dominion could an exclusive ecclesiastical jurisdiction extending to matters both spiritual and temporal be asserted; and France, which acknowledged the isolated authority of the universities, bade a stern defiance to the claims of the Popedom.

It can hardly be said that, invested with these high

powers, the universities bore their honours meekly. Respected as they were, they were felt to be invariably a serious element of turbulence, and a source of instability to the government of the cities in which they were. In the affairs of the League, the Fronde, and in the various other contests which, in former days, as in the present, have kept up a perpetual succession of conflicts in turbulent Paris, the position to be taken by the students was extremely momentous, but was not easily to be calculated upon; for these gentry imbibed a great amount both of restlessness and capriciousness along with their cherished prerogatives. During the centuries in which a common spirit pervaded the whole academic body, the fame of a particular university, or of some celebrated teacher in it, had a concentrating action over the whole civilised world, which drew a certain proportion of the youth of all Europe towards the common vortex. Hence, when we know that there were frequently assembled from one to ten thousand young men, adventurous and high-spirited, contemptuous of the condition of the ordinary citizen, and bound together by common objects and high exclusive privileges—well armed, and in possession of edifices fortified according to the method of the day—we hardly require to read history to believe how formidable such bodies must have proved.

Although the Scottish universities never boasted of the vast concourse of young men of all peoples, nations, and languages, which sometimes flocked to the Continental schools, and thus with their great privileges created a formidable *imperium in imperio* —yet naturally there has existed more or less of a standing feud between the citizen class and the student class. Their records show repeated contests by the authorities of universities, against an inveterate propensity in the students to wear arms, and to use them. The weapons prohibited by the laws of King's College, Aberdeen, are so varied and peculiar that one need not attempt to convert them into modern nomenclature, but must be content to derive, from the terms in which they are denounced, a general notion how formidable a person a student putting the law at defiance must have been. The list reminds one of Strada's celebrated account of the armature of the Spanish Armada.*

As to the rights of exclusive university jurisdiction which made the turbulent students of old so formidable, the universities of Scotland were not strong enough to retain so much of them as their English neighbours have preserved. There are curious notices, however, here and there, of efforts to

* "Gladios pugiones sicas machæras rhomphæas acinaces fustes, præsertim si præferrati vel plumbati sint, veruta missilia tela sclopos tormenta bombardas balistas, ac arma ulla bellica nemo discipulus gestato."—'Fasti Aberdonienses,' 242. The Glasgow list is less formidable: "Nemo gladium pugionem tormenta bellica aut aliud quodvis armorum et telorum genus gestet; sed apud præfectum omnia deponat."—'Instituta,' 49.

maintain them. In Glasgow, in the year 1670, a sudden and singularly bold attempt appears to have been made for their revival, a court of justiciary being held by the university, and a student put on trial on a charge of murder. The weighty matter is thus introduced :—" Anent the indytment given in by John Cumming, wryter in Glasgow, elected to be Procurator-Fiscal of the said university; and Andrew Wright, cordoner in Glasgow, neirest of kin to umquhile Janet Wright, servetrix to Patrick Wilson, younger, gairdner there, killed by the shot of ane gun, or murdered within the said Patrick his dwelling-house, upon the first day of August instant, against Robert Bartoun, son lawful of John Bartoun, gairdner in the said burgh, and student in the said university, for being guilty of the said horrible crime upon the said umquhile Janet." *

A jury was impannelled to try the question. The whole affair bears a suspicious aspect of being preconcerted to enable the accused to plead the benefit of acquittal; for no objection is taken on his part to the competency of the singular tribunal before which he is to be tried for his life; on the contrary, he highly approves of them as his judges, and in the end is pronounced not guilty.

Half a century later, in the year 1721, the 'Glasgow Records' bear that—" The faculty, being informed that some of the magistrates of Glasgow,

* 'Glasgow Records,' ii. 341.

and particularly Bailie Robert Alexander, has examined two of the members of the university—viz., William Clark and James Macaulay, students in the Greek class—for certain crimes laid to their charge some time upon the month of February last, and proceeded to sentence against these students, contrary to and in prejudice of the university and haill members, do therefore appoint Mr Gershom Carmichael, &c., to repair to the said magistrates of Glasgow, and particularly Bailie Alexander, and demand the cancelling of the said sentence, and protest against the said practice of the said bailie, or any of the magistrates for their said practice, and for remeid of law as accords." *

It was the principle, not the persons—the protection of their privileges, not the impunity of their students—that instigated the faculty on this occasion, since in their next minute they are found visiting William Clark and James Macaulay with punishment for heavy youthful offences.

César Egasse du Boulay, commonly called Bulæus, in the vast labyrinth of documents running through six folios which he was pleased to call a History of the University of Paris, has much to say here and there about the Bursus and the Bursarius—the bursary and its holder. The word comes from the same origin, indicative of connection with money, as the French "bourse" and our own "purse." The term

* 'Glasgow Records,' p. 422.

has various meanings in ecclesiastical history, but in the universities it referred to endowments or scholarships. In nothing, perhaps, is the old spirit of the university—the spirit of opening the fountain of knowledge to all who are worthy of it and desire it —more conspicuous than in the bursary system which has existed in Scotland, and especially in that northern institution formed on the Parisian model, and its neighbour. These foundations, some of them of ancient date—unless some recent change has crossed them—are open to general competition, and those who gain them obtain what carries them through the curriculum of the university, and supplies them during the course with an annual surplus, less or more. When I remember the competition for bursaries, the door was open to all comers. It was curious to see at the long tables the variety in the tone and character of the intellectual gladiators, each trying his strength against the rest—long, red-haired Highlanders, who felt trousers and shoes an infringement on the liberty of the subject—square-built Lowland farmers—flaxen-haired Orcadians—and pale citizens' sons, vibrating between scholarship and the tailor's board or the shoemaker's last. There was nothing to prevent a Bosjesman, a Hottentot, or a Sioux Indian from trying his fortune in that true republic of letters. Grim and silent they sat for many an hour of the day, rendering into Latin an English essay, and dropped away one by one, depositing the evidence of success or failure as the case might be.

There was an instruction that each should write his name on his thesis, but write nothing behind the name, so that it might be cut off and numbered to tally with the thesis—a precaution to make sure that the judges who decided on the merits of each performance should be ignorant of its author's name.*

The employment in the universities of a dead language as the means of communication was not only a natural arrangement for teaching the familiar use of that language, but it was also evidently courted as a token of isolation from the illiterate, and a means of free communication throughout the

* There are, besides these competitive bursaries, others endowed for students of specific names or qualities. Some Highland endowments of this kind are curious. Thus, the Laird of Macintosh, who begins in the true regal style, "We, Lachlan Macintosh of that Ilk," and who calls himself the Chief and *Principall* of the Clan Chattan—probably using the term which he thought would be the most likely to make his supremacy intelligible to university dignitaries—dispenses to the King's College two thousand merks, "for maintaining hopeful students thereat." He reserves, however, a dynastic control over the endowment, making it conducive to the clan discipline and the support of the hierarchy surrounding the chief. It was a condition that the beneficiary should be presented "by the lairds of Macintosh successively in all time coming; that a youth of the name of Macintosh or of Clan Chattan shall be preferred to those of any other name," &c.—'Fasti,' 206. This document is titled in the records, "Macintosh's Mortification," according to a peculiar technical application of that expression in Scotland, to the perpetuity of possession which in England is termed mortmain.

learned, world. In Scotland, as perhaps in some other small countries, such as Holland, the Latin remained as the language of literature after the great nations England, France, Germany, Italy, and Spain, were making a vernacular literature for themselves. In the seventeenth century the Scot had not been reconciled to the acceptance of the English tongue as his own; nor, indeed, could he employ it either gracefully or accurately. On the other hand, he felt the provincialism of the Lowland Scottish tongue, the ridicule attached to its use in books which happened to cross the Border, and the narrowness of the field it afforded to literary ambition.

The records just cited afford some amusing instances of the anxious zeal with which any lapse into the vernacular tongue was prevented, and conversation among the students was rendered as uneasy and unpleasant as possible. In the visitorial regulations of King's College, Aberdeen, in 1546, it is provided that the attendant boys—the gyps, if we may so call them—shall be expert in the use of Latin, lest they should give occasion to the masters or students to have recourse to the vernacular tongue.* If Aberdeen supplied a considerable number of waiting-boys thus accomplished, the stranger wandering to that far northern region, in the seventeenth century, might have been as

---

* "Ne dent occasionem magistris et studentibus lingua vernacula uti."

much astonished as the man in 'Ignoramus,' who tested the state of education in Paris by finding that even the dirty boys in the streets were taught French. It would, after all, have perhaps been more difficult to find waiting-boys who could speak English. The term by which they are described is a curious indication of the French habits and traditions of the northern universities: they are spoken of as *garciones*—a word of obvious origin to any one who has been in a French hotel.

The object of these regulations seems to have been not so much to teach the Latin as to discountenance the vernacular language of the country. In some instances the language of France is admitted; and here the parallel with the parent University of Paris is lost, by the necessity that the language could not there have the privilege of a foreign tongue. The reason for the exception in favour of this modern language was the ancient French League.*

It would be easy to note several other relics of French university phraseology which still cling round the usages of our humble institutions in Scotland. The Lauration is still preserved as the apt and classical term for the ceremony of admission to a de-

---

* "Sermo omnium et singulorum ubique Latinus, Græcus, aut Hebræus esto: propter antiquum inter Scotos et Gallos fœdus Gallicum nostra addit fundatio."—'Fasti Aberd.,' 241.

gree; and even Dr Johnson, little as he respected any Scottish form, especially when it competed with the legitimate institutions of England, has given in his dictionary the word Laureation, with this interpretation attached thereto: "It denotes in the Scottish universities the act or state of having degrees conferred, as they have in some of them a flowery crown, in imitation of laurel among the ancients."

Elsewhere we are honoured in the same work with a more brief but still a distinctive notice. Among the definitions of "Humanity," after "the nature of man," "humankind," and "benevolence," we have "Philology—grammatical studies; in Scotland, *humaniores literæ.*" The term is still as fresh at Aberdeen as when Maimbourg spoke of Calvin making his humanities at the College of La Mark. The "Professor of Humanity" has his place in the almanacs and other official lists as if there were nothing antiquated or peculiar in the term, though jocular people have been known to state to unsophisticated Cockneys and other simple persons, that the object of the chair is to inculcate on the young mind the virtue of exercising humanity towards the lower animals; and it is believed that more than one stranger has conveyed away, in the title of this professorship, a standing illustration of the elaborate kindness exercised towards the lower animals in the United Kingdom, and in Scotland especially.

Accuracy is tested by the smallest particulars. To find if it is in a gazetteer you look up your own parish—in a book of genealogy you search for your own respectable relations. Having noticed a parallel with Parisian practice in the higher dignitaries of the northern universities, I propose to go to the humblest grade—the fresh new-comer—and find it as distinct there as anywhere. During the first year of attendance, the student in Aberdeen is called a Bejeant; three hundred years ago he was called in Paris a Bejaune. He frequently comes up in the pages of Bulæus. Thus, in the year 1314, a statute of the university is passed on the supplication of a number of the inexperienced youths *qui vulgo Bejauni appellebantur*. Their complaint is an old and oft-repeated tale, common to freshmen, greenhorns, griffins, or by whatever name the inexperienced, when alighting among old stagers, are recognised. The statute of the Universitas states that a variety of predatory personages fall on the newly-arrived bejaune, demanding a *bejaunica*, or gratuity, to celebrate a *jocundus adventus;* that when it is refused, they have recourse to insults and blows; that there is brawling and bloodshed in the matter, and thus the discipline and studies of the university are disturbed by the pestiferous disease. It is thence prohibited to give any *bejaunica*, except to the bejaun's companions living in the house with him, whom he may entertain if he pleases; and if any efforts are made by others to impose on him, he is solemnly enjoined to give secret information to the procurators and the deans of the faculties.*

We have elsewhere come across a few specialties about the connection of the old Church with France.

---

* 'Hist. Univ. Paris,' iv. 266. The etymology attributed to the word bejaune is rather curious. It is said to mean yellow neb—*béc jaune*—in allusion to the physical peculiarity of unfledged and inexperienced birds, to whose condition those who have just passed from the function of robbing their nests to the discipline of a university are supposed to have an obvious resemblance. "Ce mot," says the 'Trevoux,' "a été dit par corruption de béc jaune, par métaphore de oisons et autres oiseaux niais qui ont le béc jaune—ce qu'on a appliqué aux apprentis en tous les arts et sciences—*rudis tiro imperitus*." Yet in the same dictionary there are such explanations about the use of the words *begayer*, to stutter, and *begayement*, stuttering, as might have furnished another origin. "Les enfans," we are told, "begayent en apprenant à parler. Ceux qui ont la langue grasse begayent toute leur vie. Quand un homme a bû beaucoup il commence a *begayer*." But it is used also figuratively: "Des choses qu'on a peine d'expliquer, ou de faire entendre—Ce commentateur n'a fait que begayer en voulant expliquer l'Apocalypse." The genealogy of the word is, unfortunately, rather perplexed than cleared up by Ducange carrying it into Germany. He tells us that *Beanus* means a new student who has just come to the academy, and cites the statutes of the University of Vienna, like that of Paris prohibiting all persons from cheating or overcharging the new-comers, who are called Beani, or assailing them with other injuries or contumelies. Lambecius, in the 'Epistolæ Obscurorum,' finds Beanus in an acrostic—"Beanus Est Animal Nesciens Uitam Studiosorum."

Many changes, known to every one, intercepted the descent to modern times of any peculiarities that can through this channel be traced to France. I do not think, however, that sufficient emphasis has hitherto been given to the influence which the French Huguenots had on Presbyterianism in Scotland. The system, both in its doctrines and its forms, was brought over ready-made, and the root of it is still to be found in the Synodicon, or 'The Acts, Decisions, Decrees, and Canons of those famous National Councils of the Reformed Churches in France,' gathered together through the diligent zeal of the English Nonconformist John Quick. Passing over, as unsuitable for discussion here, the larger matters of coincidence or of special difference, advisedly adopted by those who adjusted the Continental model for use in Scotland, some of the trifling details may be aptly referred to as evidence of accuracy in the adaptation. "The Moderator" is to this day the head of every Presbyterian ecclesiastical body in Scotland. There is the Moderator of the presbytery, the Moderator of the synod, and the great temporal head of the Church for the time being, "the Very Reverend the Moderator of the General Assembly." The term has scarcely a native tone. It was of old use in specialties in the Gallican Church. There was, for instance, a Moderateur of the celebrated Oratory in Paris; but after the Reformation the name came to be almost exclusively applied to the presidents of the Huguenots' ecclesiastical courts or assemblages.* So, too, the form in which any legislative measure is initiated in the General Assembly is "an overture"—a term still more expressive of foreign origin. It is used as foreign terms are in our tongue, and made a verb of, without consideration for its native structure; and so a motion is made in a presbytery "to overture" the General Assembly. This is the direct descendant of the solemn "œuverture" by which important pieces of business were opened in the Parliament of Paris and other august bodies.† The term has had an odd history, having split, and divided in two opposite directions—the one attaching itself to ecclesiastical business entirely, the other to the initial steps of certain theatrical performances.

I think it is to its source among these Huguenots, chiefly the children of the fiery south of France, that we must attribute some puzzling inconsistencies in the religious history of Scotland, and among them an intolerance and ferocity in profession and language which were not carried into practice, because they were inconsistent with the nature of the

* "Ce mot est plus Latin que François, pour signifier le président d'un assemblée. Il étoit surtout en usage par les Réformez de France, pour signifier le président de leurs synodes. Ils élisoient le *moderateur* à la pluralité des voix."—'Dict. de Trevoux.'

† Whoever wants to know all about it may read a thick quarto, called 'Les Ovvertvres des Parlements faictes par les Roys de France tenant pour Lict de Justice, &c.,' par Lovys d'Orleans, 1612.

people. Scarcely any religious body has lifted up more intolerant testimonies than the Covenanters, yet it would be difficult to point to any other large communion—save the Church of England—with fewer stains of blood upon it than Presbyterianism in Scotland. Had the Huguenots ever possessed the opportunity for vengeance enjoyed by "the wild Whigs of the West" at the Revolution, they would have made an anti-Bartholomew of it. There is an old homely metaphor applied to men with sharp tongues or pens but soft hearts, that with them "the bark is worse than the bite." It has been much so with Presbyterianism in Scotland.* There is hardly a more liberal ecclesiastical body to be found anywhere than the United Presbyterian Church. Yet on coming forth it lifted its testimony against what it called "the almost boundless toleration" which was vexing its righteous heart, and rendering the Established Church a hissing and a reproach.

It is conspicuous among strange historical con-

---

* Witness the doctrine thus announced in the 'Cloud of Witnesses' as something so palpably evident that even a reasonable opponent cannot reject it as a basis of discussion: "It is acknowledged by all rational royalists that it is lawful for any private person to kill an usurper or a tyrant *sine titulo*, and to kill Irish rebels and Tories, or the like, and to kill bears and wolves, and catch devouring beasts, because the good of his action doth not only redound to the person himself, but to the whole common-wealth, and the person acting incurs the danger himself alone."

tradictions, that in the country supposed to be the least earnest and the most apt to take all things with an easy, light epicureanism, intolerance should have broken forth in so many and so powerful shapes as to seem a nature of the people. At one period aristocracy and government are intolerant of the poor and of liberty—at another, the populace are intolerant of rank and order. At one period the Church is domineering and persecuting — at another, it is trodden under bloody feet, and religion with it. The philosophers of the Encyclopedia themselves were intolerant of seriousness and religion, and any one admitted within their circle who happened to retain a turn for devotion had to slink secretly to his place of worship like a dram-drinker to his tavern.

It is the intolerance on both sides that communicates so much of the horrible to the French wars of religion. The Huguenots were not less bloody and ferocious than their opponents. Of liberty of conscience they had not the faintest notion. Of internal intolerance—"discipline," as it was termed —or compulsory conformity with their own special sectarian rules, they had a far larger share than the Church of Rome. They held the internal rule all the more severely the more they were persecuted, for it is incident to persecuted bodies to be more relentless among each other than the prosperous. A persecuted Church is like an army passing through an enemy's country, in which difference from the opinion of the leaders is mutiny and desertion. The Edict of Nantes was not an act of toleration—it was a compulsory pacification between two hostile forces, each ready when the opportunity came to fly at the other's throat. To keep them from doing so, each was assigned its own place, with barriers between them. The Huguenots had their own fortified towns, their own municipalities, their own universities; and, what is so difficult to comprehend as a working machinery, their own courts of justice. The "Revocation" was, no doubt, a crime and a folly, but it was an act which the sufferers in it would have done had they got an opportunity.

There was something, indeed, in the profession of the new Church more tyrannical than that of the old. The Papal hierarchy drew a line between its own function, which was spiritual, and that of the State, which was temporal—a line, doubtless, not always observed. The Church of Calvin, however, as enacted for a short time on its small stage of Geneva, professed to rule everything. It was a theocracy dictating to all men the rule of the Deity as to their daily life and conversation through His ministers. Hence the domineering propensities of the church-courts of Scotland, which have made so many people angry, are but a poor and ineffectual mimicry of the iron rule of Calvin and Farel. Knox, the fiercest and hottest of their Scots followers, though in the spirit of party he vindicated many a rough act, was not a man of blood. It was not in his nature to have tracked like a detective a controversial opponent through obscure acrimonious criticisms hidden in corners, to have lured their writer within his reach, and then to have put him to death. Thus were there many things done which the Scots followers of the school, though themselves incapable of committing, had yet, with a sort of heroic devotion to their party, to vindicate in others—a practice which has brought on them much undeserved odium.*

Knox brought over with him the words, perhaps in some measure the thoughts, of his cruel teachers, but not their natures. His cry was, that "the idolatrous priest shall be slain at the altar," but he did not bring the threat to the test of practice. It is one of the most curious instances of human frailty and inconsistency, that he afterwards professed bitterly to repent of his moderation, mentioning, as an aggravation of his offence, that he had

---

* It is difficult to estimate the extent of heroic generosity which must have actuated an amiable and accomplished divine of the present day in prevailing on himself to say of the burning of Servetus: "According to modern opinions, such a sentence was too severe; but when it is remembered that only a few years have passed since, in the most enlightened countries in Christendom, it was deemed proper to inflict capital punishment for such offences as forgery and robbery to a small amount, it will not, perhaps, appear so surprising that pious and earnest men three centuries ago should have thought it right to deal in the same way with an offence greatly more wicked in itself and more injurious to society than any act of dishonesty however great."—'Enc. Brit.', article Calvin.

credit with many who would have enforced God's judgments had he urged them to the task, but he held back, and so had from the bottom of his heart to ask God's pardon that he did not do what in him lay to suppress the idol from the beginning. He would have found the sort of work he referred to, however, more difficult to accomplish than he supposed. The elements he had to deal with were far more worldly and selfish than the fiery zeal he had witnessed in the south. Away from that furnace into which he had gone hardened by persecution, he chafed furiously against the Laodicean latitudinarianism of his lay followers, who flung his 'Book of Discipline' back with contempt, and poured out the vials of his wrath copiously on those rags of Popish mummeries which Elizabeth permitted to hang round the Reformation in England.

It is pretty clear that he and others of the fiery spirits of the age liked France, where they found themselves among hearts full of the zeal that was lacking at home. It was somewhat the same on the other side; so, as the valorous supporters of either cause found fields of battle in the French wars, the hot controversialists found there also a congenial arena of strife. Some of the Popish refugees let fly from the safe distance of French soil a few pungent arrows, which they dared not have shot nearer home, and they did not hesitate to make the powerful John Knox their peculiar aim. Among these John Hamilton, a restless and versatile priest—not to be confounded with his namesake the Archbishop—in a general volley against the reformers at large, states with much succinctness, and less than the usual indecorum, a favourite charge of that day against Knox.*

---

* "A facile traictaise, contenand first ane infallible reul to discerne trevv from fals religion; nixt a declaration of the nature, numbre, vertew, and effects of the sacraments, togiddir with certain prayers of devotion, be Maister Jhone Hamilton, Doctor in Theologie at Lovan. Imprinted be Laurence Kellam.

"The first autheurs of thir neu sectes vvar of this qualitie, to vvit, Martin Luther, a privat monk in Germanie: Zuinglius, a particular preist in Sweisseland: Caluin, a privat chanoine of Noyon in France: Beze, a prieur of Longemean, besyde Paris, vvha sauld his priorie tuyse and tuike Candida a mans vvyf vvith him to Geneue. Knox, a renegat prest of Haddintoun, in Scotland, vvha vvas excomunicat for having ado vvith the mother and the daughter in ane killoggy, and theireftir vvas banisit for the assisting to the murthere of the Cardinal Beton in the castel of Saint Andres; and his predecessor, Paul Methuen, a privat baxter in Dundie: and VVillie Harlay, a tailzour in Edinbourg: sik lyk the first autheurs of al vther particular sectes erectit within thir three or four scoir zearis, vvar priuat men, vvha maed apostacie frem the Catholik, Apostolik, and Romane Kirk, and forgit nevv opinions in religion."

Had Hamilton waited a little, he would have had a far stronger case against Paul Methven than his humble origin. He became a sadly fallen star, and the story of his lapse, which blazes in Knox's history and the Protestant works of the day, is significant in a way different from the usual influence of scandals, in making the impartial reader feel that, where so tremendous a fuss was made about the sin of one man, there must have been a remarkable amount of moral purity, unless in the supposition of a hypocrisy too great for belief.

In literature as well as religion Hamilton affected the part of the conservative, who stood on old assured standards. But like many others assuming that character, he made his protest against the movement onwards more emphatic by going backwards. In his controversial tracts, such as his 'Catalogue of ane hundret and sixty-seven heresies, lies, and calumnies, teachet and practicit by the ministers of Calvin's sect,' after exhausting his polemical rage, he girds himself anew for frantic attacks on the innovations brought by Knox and others from the English idiom of the day, and in scolding them for "knapping saddrone," as he chose to call their use of a southern idiom, he used a form of expression which seems to have become obsolete in his own country. A gentler opponent of Knox, Nynian Winzet, twits him with the southern affectation of his style, calling it "quaint inglis." The whirlwind of the Reformation seems to have stirred the vernacular languages of the day. Luther's Bible makes an epoch in the formation of the German language, and Pasquier, no partisan of Calvin, admits the great debt to him of the French language.*

Hamilton, by the way, was a man violent in his actions as well as his words, and had his right place in the midst of the contests of the League. The student of history is probably acquainted with an

---

* "Auquel nostre langue Françoise est grandement redevable pour l'avoir enrichée d'une infinité de beaux traicts."—'Recherches de la France,' 769.

erudite work on the monarchy of ancient Persia, by a certain Barnabas Brissonius. The student of jurisprudence, digging to the roots of the civil law, as practised throughout Europe, is likely to be still more familiar with the great folio dictionary of law terms — a work of overpowering erudition, which bears the same name on its ample title-page. To few who turn the teeming pages of the laborious student, does it occur that he is the same President Brisson whose stirring life and terrible death are conspicuous even in the bloody annals of the League! When they had chased Henry IV. and his court from Paris in 1591, they made Brisson first president of their Parliament. No one knows exactly how it came to pass, whether he really attempted to sell the cause of the League, or was unjustly suspected, but he came under the denunciation of the Council of Ten—a committee of public safety which might have made the model for that other which worked two hundred years later. He got the popular nickname of Barabbas, and became a doomed man. When the Burger Guard were called out to line the streets for the capture of several traitors to the cause, Brisson, who was one of them, had to be dragged from a sick-bed. Conspicuous among the clerical orators of the League who lashed the fanatic mob to fury by street orations against the heretics, was John Hamilton, the curate of Saint Côme. He was equally conspicuous, armed from head to heel, in the processions of the leaguers; and in this form it was that he dragged Brisson from his bed. The poor scholar put in a touching plea for life, which he might as well have told to the elements—he was just finishing a new book—might he not be allowed to complete it? No. They hanged him from a beam in the council chamber.

Even in those wild days, when it must have been hard for any man to get ahead of his neighbours, Hamilton became a character. In his humble sphere of a parish priest he made himself conspicuous in French history by the noisy ferocity of his zeal for the old religion and the audacity of his acts. He managed to escape when the Duke of Mayenne hanged the others concerned in the death of Brisson, but he turned up when Henry IV. abjured the Reformation. An act so likely to lead to peaceable results was not to Hamilton's taste, and he put himself at the head of a party of desperadoes, who were to attack the grand procession, in which the monarch was to reconcile himself to the Church, and take peaceful possession of the hearts of the Parisian mob. Hamilton was unable, however, to get a sufficient force even to disturb the general peace and joy of the occasion. Whether or not his doings on that occasion reminded people of his precedents, sentence was afterwards passed on him to be broken on the wheel for the affair of Brisson. He wisely permitted the sentence to be executed on his effigy, and sought refuge under the genial shadow of Philip II. in his Flemish dominions. He afterwards visited his native country, where the powerful influence of his relations of the Haddington family seems both to have protected him and kept him quiet.

David Chambers, in his book upon the departed glory of his country, repeats Hamilton's scandal against Knox, couched in Latin—a form which would only give it more publicity in those days.* There is a little volume called 'Mr Nicol Burne's Disputation,' which, although a rarity hunted after by collectors, and therefore in common estimation worthless for literary purposes, will be found by any adventurous reader to contain some rather curious matter, and among them certain particulars regarding John Knox not to be found in the biographical dictionaries.† The book is a Parisian publication,

---

* "Clam a monasterio profugit, et ad domum paternam regressus, cum noverca, vivo adhuc patre rem habuit Camerarii de Scotorum fortitudine," p. 276. See also Reynolds's 'Calvino-turcismus,' p. 260, and the quotations from Laing and others in Appendix GGG to M'Crie's 'Life of Knox.'

† Passing over a preliminary passage rather more indecorous, I offer with some hesitation the following specimen:—

"Heauing laid asyd al feir of the panis of hel, and regarding na thing the honestie of the varld, as ane bund sklaue of the Deuil, being kendillit vith ane inquenshibil lust and ambition, He durst be sua bauld to interpryse the sute of Mariage vith the maist honorabil ladie my ladie Fleming, my lord Dukes eldest dochter, to the end that his seid being of the blude Royal, and gydit be thair fatheris spirit, micht haue aspyrit to the croun. And becaus he receauit ane refusal, it is notoriouslie knauin hou deadlie he haited the hail hous of the Hamiltonis, albeit being deceauit be him trait-

and will be seen, like Hamilton's, to have had a struggle with the difficulties of the foreign press.

It is possible that some respectable Protestants may be so little acquainted with the fashion of polemical controversy in the sixteenth century, as to be shocked by the passages concerning Knox to which I have referred. But there is no occasion for their losing a particle of their faith in their particular saint. These things were matters of routine; controversy was not complete without them. It was as necessary to accuse the adversary of some monstrous crime, as in later times it was to charge him with stupidity, dishonesty, and imbecile male-

---

torouslie it vas the cheif vpsettar and protector of his hæresie: And this maist honest refusal could nather stench his lust nor ambition, bot a lytil eftir he did perseu to haue allyance vith the honorabil hous of Ochiltrie of the kingis M. auin blude, Rydand thair vith ane gręt court on ane trim gelding, nocht lyk ane prophet or ane auld decrepit preist as he vas, bot lyk as he had bene ane of the blude Royal, vith his bendis of taffetie feschnit vith Goldin ringis and precious stanes: And as is planelie reportit in the cuntrey, be sorcerie and vitchcraft did sua allure that puir gentil voman, that sho could not leue vithout him: quhilk appeiris to be of gret probabilitie, sho being ane Damosel of Nobil blud, And he ane auld decrepit creatur of maist bais degrie of onie that could be found in the cuntrey: Sua that sik ane nobil hous could not haue degenerat sua far, except Iohann kmnox had interposed the pouar of his Maister the Deuil, quha as he transfiguris him self sumtymes in ane Angel of licht: sua he causit Iohann kmnox appeir ane of the maist nobil and lustie men that could be found in the varld: Bot not to offend zour earis langar vith the filthie

volence. Moreover, they have the comfort of knowing that the malignant papists by no means had it all their own way. Among the champions on the other side, we cannot call up a more appropriate one than Knox's own son-in-law, famous Mr John Welch. He lived much in France, and was thoroughly at home among the fierce Huguenots, for whom, indeed, he held a pike in the defence of St Jean d'Angely. There is a story, believed by his followers, and strangely enough also by M. Michel, to the effect that Louis XIII. was mightily charmed by the earnest boldness wherewith he preached the truth. He was not content with ministering to his

---

abhominationis of Schir Iohann kmnox, and to returne to tha thingis quhilk ar common to the sect of the Protestaons, lyk as S. Iohne descryuis the Antichrist to haue ane blasphemous mouth aganis god, his sanctis, and halie tabernacle quhilk is his kirk Catholik, Euin sua the blasphemeis ar maist horribil quhilk thir grishopperis and maist noysum serpentis the sonis of Martin Lauter speuis out of thair venemous mouthis, maist impudentlie defending the sam, as gif thay var headdis and articlis of healthsum doctrine."—'The Dispvtation concerning the Controversit Headdis of Religion, haldin in the Realme of Scotland, the zeir of God ane thousand, fyue hundreth fourscoir zeiris. Betuix. The prætendit Ministeris of the deformed Kirk in Scotland. And, Nicol Burne Professor of philosophie in S. Leonardis college, in the Citie of Sanctandrois, brocht vp from his tender eage in the peruerfit sect of the Caluinistis, and nou be ane special grace of God, ane membre of the halie and Catholik kirk. Dedicat to his Souerane the kingis M. of Scotland, King Iames the Saxt. Imprented at Parise the first day of October 1581.'—Pp. 143, 144.

own people, but made aggressive attempts on the great enemy Popery, with results so little to his satisfaction, that he concluded the devil to have entered into the hearts of the people and hardened them against the truth, notwithstanding its plentiful outpouring. A Protestant even can imagine this outpouring to have been unsavoury to those on whom it fell, without any intervention of the devil, by a peep into his 'Popery Anatomised.' If there are some passages from the other side that one might hesitate to publish, there are many here that one dare not publish—the compositors would not set them up. Hence the two sides are pitted against each other unfairly, the one having, as it were, a hand tied. It is one of those provoking books in which, if some one in a mixed company begins to read a grotesque and pithy passage, he finds himself brought to a sudden stop, probably with a red face, and then takes a leap onward, but with no better success—for instance, in the little biographical notices by which he makes out the Pope to be Antichrist.

"Steven VI.—He caused to take out of the grave the carcass of Formosus, who had mansworn himself, and spoils it of the pontifical habit, and commands it be buried again to the burial of the laicks, cuts off two of his fingers and casts them into the Tyber, and abrogates his decreets, and decreed that the ordnance of Formosus should be void, whilk is a point of Donatism, as Sigebert, a monk, noteth. But Romanus I. and Theodosius II., Popes, his successors, they allow Formosus, and abrogate the acts of Stephanus; and so did John X. by a council of seventy-four bishops, restored the acts of Formosus to the full, and abrogated the acts of Stephanus and condemned them. Yet, for all this, Sergius III. having casten down Christopher I. out of his papal seat, afterwards did cast him in prison, where he died, and so obtained the Satanical seat by the help of Marosia his harlot; he causes to take out the body of Formosus, which had lyen eighteen years in the grave, degrades it from the pontifical honour, cuts off the three fingers which Stephanus VI. had left, and with them casts the carcass in the river Tyber, and abrogates his acts, and ordained anew them that was ordained by Formosus (?), whilk is a point of Donatism. And this most filthy——"

Here come a set of naughty words which cause a sudden stop. Try again.

"Sextus IV., that vile and beastly monster.—Wesselus Groningensis, in his 'Treatise of the Pope's Pardons,' writes of him that he permitted the whole family of Cardinal Lucia——"

Stop again.

"Benedictus IX.—He was so skilled in devilish arts of magic, that before he was made Pope, in the woods he called upon these evil spirits, and by his devilry [here the reader, being on his guard, may get on by slipping over a word or two], obtains the Popedom, and makes his former companions magicians, and his most familiar councillors. But he fearing himself, sold the Popedom unto his fellow-magician, called Joannes Gratianus, who was afterwards called Gregory VI., for £1500. Platin saith, that by the judgement of God he is damned for the selling of his Popedom. So after he is deposed, he is suffocate by the devil in the woods, and so he perisheth. Of whom it is reported, that after his death he was seen monstrously to appear to a certain hermit, in his body like a bear, in his head and tail like an ass," &c.

One cannot help admiring the sagacity of the hermit who recognised the deceased pontiff in this sort of masquerade. It is possible to read in peace a full page about the great Hildebrand, how he poisoned his six predecessors, "that he was a notable magician, that when it pleased him he would shake his sleeves and sparks of fire would come out, whereby he deceived the minds of the simple. Of whom Cardinal Benno reports, that coming to Rome at a time he left his book of magical and devilish arts behind him, through forgetfulness, and, remembering himself, he sends two of his most faithful servants about it, charging them straitly, that they opened not the book. But they, the more they were forbidden, were the more curious, and so opening the book and reading it, behold the angels of Satan appeared to them in such a multitude, that scarcely could the two young men remain in their wits."

Proceed we now to "John, whom some call the

thirteenth of that name. He is such a monster, that I know not if ever the earth did bear a greater, who had sold himself to all sorts of licentiousness" (skip a word or two). "Luitprandus, in lib. 6, declares that, of his cardinals, of some he cuts out their tongues; of some he cuts off their hands; of some their noses; of some——"

Pulled up again; and so the book is stowed away in a corner of the library, carefully selected as out of reach of the children.*

Among the preachers whom we sent to France, there were many who not only did battle with the common enemy, but fought among themselves. This feature seems to have surprised the French

---

* The author of these flowers of rhetoric was something closer to a canonised saint than appears quite consistent with sound Protestantism. A brother rummager has given me the following extract from the Wodrow MSS. in the University of Glasgow:—"One night Mr Welch was watching and praying in his own garden, at Air, very late. Some freinds wer waiting upon him in his house, and they beginning to weary upon his long stay, one of them chanced to open a window towards the place wher he walked, and saw clearly a strange light surround him, and heard him speak strange words about his spirituall joy. And tho' these appearances of light may seem strange, and to many may savour of enthusiasme and delusion, yet ther are not a feu creditable instances of them with extraordinary persons, and extraordinary cases."—Wodrow's 'Life of Mr John Welch,' written in 1724. This would give an eikonographer a very good hint for a *nimbus*. To many this will be a far sounder certificate of sanctification than the Acts of the Holy College, or the Records of the Bollandists.

Huguenots, who gave implicit submission to their clerical masters. These Scots clergy, in fact, carried with them that disputatious pragmatic spirit of their native land, a climax of which is furnished by the Secession Church, while yet a small obscure body. The question of administering a burgher's oath after the Porteous Mob split it in two, and then it got a transverse split through both halves, insomuch that there were the Old-Light Burghers and the New-Light Burghers, the Old-Light Antiburghers, and the New-Light Antiburghers. Each protested in a general way against Popery and Prelacy, but was very vehement against the three-quarters of what had once been itself, reserving its special anathemas for that from which it had just separated.*

A deal of curious matter about the disputes

* The Scots are called a priest-ridden people, yet their most esteemed jests are against the clergy, and the vehemence of the native sectarianism. Perhaps this is one of the benefits of competition. When I name the late Alexander Stewart Logan, the Sheriff of Forfar, I will recall a sad remembrance of many a hearty laugh. He was a man of strange grotesque genius, and held a large social place; yet he has left no mark behind him, save in the genial pages of Dr John Brown. Logan had good opportunities of picking up such stories, as he was the son of a Relief minister. One of them I remember, a very curious example of how far down sectarianism can go. Some boys were rioting in a Burgher church—whether Old or New Light not known. The person in charge of the building having seized one of them, a shrill youthful cry comes from a corner—"Hit him hard—hit him hard; his father's an *Anti*-burgher!"

among the Scots Protestants in France will be found in M. Michel's second volume. It was in reference to their contentiousness that Andrew Rivet, a native of Poitou, himself a pretty eager controversialist, used an expression which has come into household use in the shape of the *præfervidum ingenium Scotorum*, a slight variation of the original.*

I propose now to leave the religious bodies themselves, and glance at a topic which will bring up the nature of the places in which they worshipped. Architecture, especially if it be of stone, is the most enduring memorial of the social conditions of any country. The buildings scattered over the surface of Scotland attest to this day with extraordinary precision the long severance from England and attachment to France. We have seen that when the Normans came to Scotland, they left their mark there, as they did everywhere, in feudal castles, bearing special types of the architecture of the period at which they penetrated so far northwards.

---

* After alluding to the acridness of the Scots controversies, Rivetus says, "Id præterea observandum est, si quæ durissimis persecutionum temporibus a Scotis et Anglis nonnullis temerè scripta fuerunt, ea posse imputari non tam religioni quam nationum illarum, Scoticanæ præsertim fervido ingenio et ad audendum prompto; quod tantum valde mitigatum fuisse accensa veritatis evangelicæ luce, ex eo constat quod ex centum quinque regibus suis, usque ad Mariam, tres exautorarant, quinque expulerunt, et triginta duos necarunt."—'Riveti Jesuita Vapulans,' ch. xiii. § 14.

These are just like the English castles of the same period. The churches, too, built before and during the war of independence, are the brethren of the English-Norman, and first pointed. The existing remains, as well as the local histories, show that the war and the poverty it caused throughout the land brought castle and church building to a stop for many a year, and when it was resumed, it diverged towards the example of France. For instance, among those remains of church architecture in Scotland which have not been adulterated by bad restorations, there are no instances of the Tudor, third pointed, or perpendicular style, so prevalent everywhere in England. This style came into use in England in the beginning of the sixteenth century, and continued until it was gradually absorbed by the revival of the classical forms. It has been called occasionally the Tudor or the Elizabethan style; but these names were applied to it rather in its application to civil than to ecclesiastical buildings. Mr Rickman gave it the name of perpendicular, from the propensity of all the lines, whether those of pillars or of mullions, to go straight up and meet some arch or transom, instead of spreading themselves in the easy floral forms of the preceding age. It has also been called the third pointed, because the two epochs which preceded had got the name of the first and second pointed; and it is sometimes called depressed, because the favourite form of arch adapted to it has the ogee shape, as if it were the old pointed arch pressed down at the apex. Lastly, it is called the degenerate Gothic; but people sometimes object to the applicability of the term, when they remember that Henry VII.'s Chapel, the hall of Christ Church, and many of the ornaments both of Oxford and Cambridge, have been built after this style. It will make the exclusion of this style from Scotland more distinct, to mention the one building that most nearly approaches to it, the church of Melrose Abbey. But even here the dominant feature of the style—the depressed arch, as it is called by archæologists, the four-centred arch, as it is termed in architects' offices—is not to be found. At the time when it came into use in England, we here evidently adopted the contemporary style of France, called the flamboyant, from the flame-like shape and character of its details, especially conspicuous in the compartments of the windows when a bright evening sunshine passes through them.

In the baronial or military branch of architecture, the influence of the alliance was still more emphatic. The poverty of their employers compelled Scots masons to go back to the beginning, and produce the mere square block, such as the Normans had raised two centuries earlier. Hence strangers have found puzzling anachronisms in Scots architecture; and in such instances as Borthwick, Elphinston, Niddrie, and Broughty, have only been convinced that they were not looking on ancient Norman work, when, on close examination, they have seen none of the round pillars, ribbed arches, and cheveron or dog-tooth decorations which mark the transition between the classic and the Gothic.

The natural development of castle-building is into flanking works. The owner or other person responsible for the defence wants something beyond the mere wall-plate, with the enemy outside and himself inside. He desires outworks, that he may protract the enemy's approach, and assail him, when he has come up, upon both sides as well as in front. When he has built his first flanking works, he wants to protect these works in the same way—and so the affair has gone on, from those noble round towers which the architects of the Edwards clustered round the square tower of earlier days, to the long ranges of bastions and redans which covered miles of land under the constructive genius of Vauban and Coehorn.

The Scots laird was too poor to build the flanking round towers of his English neighbours, but he found a cheap substitute for them, which does credit to his ingenuity. He perched projecting crenelations or bastions on the top corners of his tower. If he could afford one at each of the four corners, it was well; if not, he put up two at opposite angles of the square, so that each could rake two sides of it.

Meanwhile in France the practice was adopted of topping the flanking round towers with conical roofs, giving their form an approach to that of the steeple;

any bastions or other petty flanking structures that were wanted were topped in the same manner. This has given a peculiar airy richness to French chateau architecture which every traveller notices, both in France and the countries where French taste or influence has predominated. The Scots laird, when he grew rich, enlarged his bastion, and topped it after the French manner. As he grew still richer, he built flanking towers of the same character. So at last his castle, from the original grim square block, sprouted up into a fanciful coronet of lofty crow-stepped gables, high chimneys, and turret-tops, such as we see in Glammis, Pinkie, Fyvie, Midmar, and a hundred other specimens. Indeed two, and perhaps the two finest of those I have named—Fyvie and Pinkie—were built by Seton, Earl of Dunfermline, who came to Scotland, after a foreign education, full of French law and French tastes.*

* The family historian, who says "he was well versed in mathematics, and had great skill in architecture," describes his solemn inauguration to his profession in the *bonnet quarré* of the French bar:—"Shortly after that he came to Scotland, he made his public lesson of the law before King James the VI., the Senators of the College of Justice, and advocates present in the Chapel Royal of Holyroodhouse, in his lawer goun and four-nooked cap, as lawers use to pass their tryalls in the universities abroad, to the great applause of the King and all present." Also, "He acquired the lands of Pinkie, where he built ane noble house, brave stone dykes about the garden and orchard, with other commendable policies about it."—Kingston's Continuation of 'Maitland's House of Seyton.'

Heriot's Hospital, in Edinburgh, is a daring and beautiful attempt to bring the architecture which had thus irregularly grown, into system and symmetry. There has been much random discussion about its architect, who certainly deserves not to be forgotten. It is generally said to have been designed by Inigo Jones, because it is so like the Castle of Friedriksborg, which he undoubtedly designed; and again, it is said that Friedriksborg was certainly the work of Jones, because it is so like Heriot's Hospital. When we get out of this circle, we find that the architect was William Aytoun of Inchdairnie, a namesake and ancestor of our own lyrical poet, so justly loved and lauded.

It is a social specialty of Scotland, that castles after the French fashion were built there long after private dwellings had ceased to be fortresses in England. The wide stretch of area, the broad hospitable doorways, and the cheerful oriel windows of the Tudor architecture prevalent in England, spoke of a country where the law was strong enough to put down private warfare. Though richly decorated externally, however, every passage into the Scots mansions by door or window was dark and intricate. A Tudor oriel or bow window would have been as absurd a thing there as in the embrasure of a fortress—the inmates would have been in constant risk of being fired at through it by their neighbours and hereditary enemies. Down nearly to the Union the Scotsman's house was his castle, not metaphorically or by fiction of law, but by strength of building. It was almost the same in street architecture, where the houses were lofty, inaccessible, and easily fortified. And to this day, in the larger towns of Scotland, house is piled above house in a manner which makes Edinburgh as anomalous to the Englishman as Paris; where the Scot, on the other hand, is surprised to find a close parallel to one of the special practices of his own country.

I now propose to bestow a few pages on the examination of a less solemn, but, in its own way, curious and emphatic relic of the French connection. In Scotland, as in France, the day of chief mark in the winter festivals is the first day of the year, while in England it is Christmas. Scotland too, following the example of France, adopted the 1st of January as the beginning of the year early in the seventeenth century; while in England the 25th of March was the beginning of the year down to the year 1753. Neither of these, however, is the point to which I wish to draw special attention.

The eve that ushers in the new year is called in Scotland Hogmanay Night. The young folks then go about soliciting gifts, with a rhyme in their mouths, of which the most accepted form is—

> "Hogmanay,
> Trollollay,
> Give us of your white bread, and none of your grey."

An amount of austere learning, which it is painful

to contemplate, has been exhausted in a vain search after the parentage of these words. Attempts have naturally been made to trace the first to the Greek word which characterises the virtues of the saints; but no further help could be found in that quarter, for the most daring etymologists could find nothing in it to serve as pedigree for the second word. All the fertile resources of Celtic etymology were next let in by the coincidence between the first word and the name which Lucian says the Celts gave to their Hercules—namely, Ogmios—and this gives the etymologist the rare privilege of getting into that magnificent Irish literary system, the Ogham alphabet and the Ogham inscriptions, of which it is the delightful peculiarity that you can read in them anything you please. Without considerable perversion, however, the Celts could make nothing of the second word, which was readily seized on by the northern antiquaries as having something to do with those beings, of no good repute, known as Trolls. But, indeed, all that has been discovered savouring of the reality in this direction is a memorandum of Torfæus regarding the old heathen festival of midwinter called Jol—merged by the Christians into Christmas: it is, by the way, in Scotland now called Yule. The day which divides the winter, he tells us, is by one old chronicler called Haukunott, and by another called Hekunott. With a candour, however, which affords alike a good example and a striking contrast to our own archæologists, he says he is totally ignorant both of the etymology and the reason of the term.*

Not having courage enough for etymological warfare, I feel much satisfaction in shifting the responsibility, as official people say, and landing it in France, whence we seem to have imported the term, and the curious customs that cluster round it. In two numbers of the French paper 'L'Illustration,' I happen to have seen a representation of children going about on New Year's eve, demanding their eguimené, as it is in some districts, while in others it is eguinené, or eguilané. The word had a sort of rattling accompaniment not unlike our own—thus, "Eguimené, rollet follet, Tiri liri;' and as an equivalent to some petitory lines, which with us generally terminate with, "Oh, give us our hogmanay!" there were verses, of which the following is a specimen :—

> "Le fils du roi s'en va chasser,
> Le fils du roi s'en va chasser,
> Dans la forêt d'Hongrie ;
> Ah donnez-nous la guillanée,
> Monseignieur, je vous prie."†

---

* "Cujus ut etymon ita et rationem ignoro, neque enim alibi legisse memini."—'Historia Rerum Norvagicorum,' ii. 215.

† The date of these numbers of 'L'Illustration' is, as far as I remember, 1850. I regret that I cannot now lay hands on them. The passage was, however, quoted by me in an article in the 'North British Review' for February 1856, in which I took occasion to notice the coincidence of the terms. What follows about the French festival has turned up in the course of subsequent miscellaneous reading.

There is in the writings of Frenchmen of learning, in the sixteenth and seventeenth centuries, a free-and-easy dealing with contemporary matters of common life, rarely to be found among the Scots authors of the period, scarcely to be found at all among the English. It would seem as if our insulars were afraid of their scholarship being questioned if they descended to common things. It gives a charm to the books of even the driest old French writers, that they speak with freedom of national and provincial customs, and thus keep up their history. While there are abundant notices of the corresponding festival in France, as I shall presently show, the only notice behind the present century, which I can find, of the Hogmanay, is in that collection of ribaldry called 'Scotch Presbyterian Eloquence Displayed,' which will not carry us further back than the middle of the seventeenth century. In this passage the etymology is very summarily disposed of in two different ways:—

"It is ordinary among some plebeians in the south of Scotland to go about from door to door, on New Year's eve, crying 'Hogmana!' a corrupted word from the Greek *hagia mene*, which signifies the holy month. John Dickson, holding forth against this custom once in a sermon at Kelso, says, 'Sirs, do you know what Hogmana signifies? It's the devil be in the house—that's the meaning of its Hebrew original.'" Of the French equivalent I shall have presently to say how far it is traced back in practice.

Its oldest use in literature, so far as I am aware, is in Rabelais. While the original might be a little hard on the gentle reader, it is always audacious and generally useless to attempt to explain in one's own terms what Rabelais means, and one is best sheltered by taking the ordinary translation. The eleventh chapter of the second book opens thus :—

" Then began Kissbreech in manner as followeth: 'My lord, it is true that a good woman of my house carried eggs to the market to sell.' 'Be covered, Kissbreech,' said Pantagruel. 'Thanks to you, my lord,' said the Lord Kissbreech; 'but to the purpose. There passed betwixt the two tropics the sum of three pence towards the zenith, and a halfpenny, forasmuch as the Riphœan Mountains had been that year oppressed with a great sterility of counterfeit gudgeons, and shows without substance, by means of the babbling tattle and fond fibs, seditiously raised between the gibble-gabblers and Accursian gibberish-mongers, for the rebellion of the Switzers, who had assembled themselves to the full number of the bumbees, and myrmidons, to go a-handsel-getting at the first day of the New Year, at that very time when they give brewis to the oxen, and deliver the key of the coles to the country girls, for serving in of the oats to the dogs.' "*

---

* In the original, " Au nombre de bombies pour aller à l'aguillan-neuf le premier tru de l'an." There is here a subsidiary etymological difficulty in the " bombies." I take

The words here translated to go a-handsel-getting are *aller à l'ayuillan-neuf.* Here the translator, Sir Thomas Urquhart, has not actually hit the point, though he has come close to it. The aguillan-neuf belonged to the old year, just as the new was coming; the handsel-day belongs to the New Year itself. It is still in full practice in Scotland as a day of largess. Though there is a natural vigilance on the part of the beneficiaries, which saves institutions of this kind from falling to decay, yet the handsel, which was an old custom in England, has fallen into disuse, having been superseded by that great institution the Box-day. In Scotland, both of the old taxative terms are observed; but as the tax-payer will only give once, it has been necessary to make a division, so that youth takes the one and maturity the other. We shall see that the term is of ancient use in the ecclesiastical records of France, and its etymology and import were critically discussed by French

---

it one may search French dictionaries in vain for the meaning of this word. The translator of Rabelais, Sir Thomas Urquhart, having the privilege of being an Aberdeen-awa man, was familiar with the bum-bee as the equivalent of the English humble-bee. He may even have "herreit a bum-bee's byke." But before admitting that his translation is true, one would require some information from France, since Rabelais did not go to Aberdeenshire for a term, just that it might suit a north-country laird. There is a confusion here, reminding one of a juvenile class in natural history, where to the question, "Where do bees get their wax?" the answer comes, "From their ears."

authors as far back as the seventeenth century. It will be seen that in these discussions, and in the older extracts from ecclesiastical records, the Scots word hogmanay is approached from all points, although there is in no instance a parallel to it letter by letter.

The most significant French comment I have found my way to, is that of Menage in his great etymological dictionary. All the world knows him to have been a master of learned gossip, and the very man to pour curious light on such a topic. Under the word Haguignétes he quotes information furnished by M. de Grandemesnil, who says he remembers in his youth that, in Rouen, the word was pronounced hoguignétes, and gives his own theory of the reason for the variation; and he gives a specimen of the way in which he remembers the boys in his own quarter singing it as they solicited their New Year's eve gifts:—

> "Si vous veniez à la dépense,
> A la depénse de chez nous,
> Vous mangeriez de bons choux,
> On vous serviroit du rost—
> Hoquinano."

Menage is further informed by his correspondent that, in Bayeux and Les Vez, the pronunciation is Hoguignames, and then gives a specimen of the way in which he had himself heard it sung in the streets, when practising as an advocate before the Parliament of Rouen. He had very little practice, by the way, being apt, as in the present instance, to occupy himself with matters not relevant to the case before him. The specimen he gives is—

> "Donnez-moi mes Haguignêtes,
> Dans un panier que voici
> Je l'achetai samedi
> D'un bon homme de dehors,
> Mais il est encore à payer—
> Haguinelo."

Menage records his correspondent's theory of the origin of the word, without either impugning or adopting it. The root is *hoc in anno*—in this year—as inferring a hint that it is still time before the year expires to do a small act of generosity to the suppliant, so that the giver may pass into the new year with the benefit of his gratitude.*

---

* "A Rouen ils disoient en ma jounesse non pas Haguignêtes, mais Hoguignêtes; et peut-être a-l-on dit Haguignétes, pour éviter l'equivoque de la signification obscène que les Picards donnent au mot de Hoguigner. Ce mot de Hoguignêtes venoit de *hoc in anno:* car c'est un présent que l'on demande au dernier jour de l'année, Donnez-moi quelque chose *hoc in anno:* encore une fois cette année."

A traditional rumour appears to have existed that the ceremony came from France, and those who desired to find etymology for that view derived the lines from

> "L'homme est nè
> Trois Rois là."

The writer of an oppressively learned paper in the second volume of the 'Transactions of the Antiquaries' Society of Scotland,' "On the Cry of the Maskers at Christmas or Yule"—which, by the way, is not the correct time—gets deep into Norse lore; and in reference to the rumour of a French origin, says, "Had it been in such general use as has

Court de Gebelin, in his 'Monde Primitif,' quotes a portion of Menage's information, and gives as his own derivation *a gui l'an neuf.* This brings us to the border of a vast theory which Cotgrave, in that dictionary so useful to all readers of old French books, thus distinctly announces :—

"Au guy-l'an-neuf.—The voice of country people begging small presents or New Year's gifts on Christmas. An ancient tearm of rejoicing derived from the Druides, who were wont the first of January to goe unto the woods, where, having sacrificed and banqueted together, they gathered mistletow, esteeming it excellent to make beasts fruitful, and most soveraigne against all poyson."

---

been pretended, some vestige of it would have been preserved to the present age ; or at least it would have been mentioned by some of the French historians or antiquaries, as Mezerai, Menage, or Pasquier. But these writers, as well as every other whom I have had occasion to consult, are totally silent as to this usage." It is rash in any one positively to pronounce on what may *not* be found in a book, lest some other searcher may be more fortunate ; but a writer is surely specially unlucky who singles out, as in naming Menage, the very author who gives us a quantity of curious information on a topic, for the purpose of telling that he is "totally silent on it." In Mezerai one would not expect to find anything about it ; yet, as if to confound this learned author, Mezerai does go out of his way to speak of the grotesque ceremonies accompanying the Eguimené, to be presently noticed. I am inclined to concur in Pasquier's silence, having rummaged his 'Recherches de la France'—the book of all others from which I expected most—without finding anything on this topic.

The earliest assertions I happen to have noticed of this theory belong to the middle of the seventeenth century.* We have now got back among the Druids, and therefore at an end both of common sense and common honesty, for it is the fatal effect of any literary dealing with this mysterious fraternity to render some men reckless and mendacious who otherwise are found to be cautious and truthful. This phenomenon might be worthy the investigation of psychologists; in the mean time, I am content to attribute it to that awe and reverence accorded by general consent to a set of people of whom so little is known, if they be not almost altogether creatures of imagination. The investigator who lands his difficulties among them is at once relieved by a sort of supernatural influence, which enables him at once to subdue all the impediments which he would in vain have offered battle to by honest investigation and fair induction. So corruptive is this influence that the compilers of the Trevoux Dictionary, in

* Du Chesne, 'Antiquitez' (164), under the description of Dreux, supposed to have been the Rome or metropolis of the Druids. It is more fully developed a few years afterwards by Borel. "Aguilanleu *au guy l'an neuf*, cri retenu en certaines villes de France, depuis les Druides, qui alloyent couper le guy de chesne avec une serpe d'or en faisant un divinité. Les enfans crient Aguilanneu à Dreux et autres lieux, au premier jour de l'an pour demander les estrennes, selon Du Chesne en ses Antiq. de France. Et Ovide confirme l'antiquité de cette coustoume, lors qu'il dit, 'Ad viscum Druydæ, Druydæ clamare solebant.'"—'Tresor de Recherches et Antiquitez Gauloises est Françoises, 1655.'

general so cool and sagacious, have at once abandoned themselves to it on coming alphabetically to the heading Aguillanneuf, and have, with a minute precision worthy of a Court newsman, given an account of Druidical processions and other ceremonies, for which there is no more authority in any authentic shape than there is for the occurrences narrated in the tales of the Thousand and One Nights.*

---

* "AGUILLANNEUF, s. m.—Vieux mot qu'on crioit autrefois le premier jour de Janvier, en signe de réjouissance. Ce mot vient d'une ancienne superstition des Druides. Les Prêtres alloient, au mois de Décembre, qu'on appeloit sacré, cueillir le gui dû chêne en grande cérémonie. Cela se faisoit avec beaucoup de solennité. Les devins marchoient les premiers, chantant des hymnes, en l'honneur de leurs divinités. Ensuite venoit un héraut, le caducée en main; après lui suivoient trois Druides de front, portant les choses nécessaires pour le sacrifice. Enfin, paroissoit le chef, ou le Prince des Druides, accompagné de tout le peuple. Le chef des Druides montoit sur le chêne, & coupoit le gui avec une faucille d'or. Les autres Druides le recevoient, & au premier jour de l'an on le distribuoit au peuple, comme une chose sainte, après l'avoir beni, & consacré, en criant, *Au gui, l'an neuf*, pour annoncer une année nouvelle. On fait encore ce cri en Picardie, où on ajoute, *Plantez, plantez*, pour souhaiter une année abondante & fertile. De-là est venu le nom d'un fauxbourg de Lyon, qu'on nomme encore à présent *la Guillotière*. En Bourgogne, à Dreux, & autres lieux, les enfans crient, *Aguilanneuf*, pour demander leurs étrennes.

"On donna depuis le nom de *Aguilanneuf* à une quête qui se faisoit le premier jour de l'an, dans quelques diocèses pour les cierges de l'église. Elle se faisoit par des jeunes gens de l'un & de l'autre sexe. Les Synodes ont aboli cette quête, à cause de la licence & du scandale dont elle étoit accompagnée."

To this place of refuge in the sacred groves of the Druids the French archæologists have found their way through a narrow enough path. It is all along of "guy" or "gui," meaning mistletoe; which we are told by one of the most credulous of authors, Pliny junior, that the Druids cut with a golden sickle. With the French writers who believe in the Druidical connection, it is unfortunately necessary to be sceptical about everything, and especially about their spelling of the New Year's Day festival itself.

It is refreshing to pass from such company into that of the accurate Charpentier, who, in his supplement to Du Cange, with something like a gentle sneer, refers to the authorities just cited for an account of the Druidical antiquity of the ceremony, and contents himself with quoting the earliest authentic records in which it is mentioned. Thus, he finds that in Boissière, in Poitou, a vigil was held with lamps and lanterns in the year 1480, and the bachelors of the parish collected an aguillanneuf to defray the cost of the affair. He mentions some instances still earlier, and gives the various readings of Aguilloneu, Aguillenneu, Guillenlieu, Haguirenleux, and Haguimenlo.

A word now about some other practices about the New Year, which I cannot help believing to be faded relics of the French connection. On Hogmanay Night it is customary for the young folks to wear masks and offer petty dramatic surprises.

The height of this sort of effort is to get into a friend's house, without recognition, in personation of some very astounding character far away from the position of the youth who assumes it; but this is a feat rarely accomplished.* Those who thus go a-masking on New Year's eve, or Hogmanay night, are called guisards or guizers. There is very little on record about their mummeries, but we shall presently see that those of their French teachers were an important and formidable affair. †

While the children thus went a-mumming, it be-

---

* For the fullest account of these saturnalia, reference may be made to the conclusion of Chambers's 'Book of Days.'

† Of anything I have heard of the theatrical literature of our Scotch guisards, there is little but sheer common city vulgarity, and little worth noting even for its grotesqueness. An ingenious friend remembers in his youth the beginning of a sort of Hogmanay drama, in which there enter three boys, as appropriately armed and costumed as a village can afford, and commence a trialogue, thus:—

1. "I am Bol Bendo—who are you?"
2. "I am here, the King of France,
Come for a battle to advance."
3. "I am here, the King of Spain,
Come for a battle to maintain."

In any country with less schooling and history-reading than Scotland, there might be something significant in the place where this mummery was noted being in the same parish with "Little France," so called from a tradition that Queen Mary's French attendants lived there in a small colony, at a time when the great contest between France and Spain was the latest important chapter in history.

came the practice of their fathers and other male seniors to take to drinking at the close of the year with a zeal and devotedness reminding one of those ancient rites dedicated to Saturn, from which the practice is said to have arisen. When any man belonging to what are called "the working classes" has a slight touch of dissipation in his temperament, the passing of the New Year is always a serious ordeal. It may chance to send him off into the whirl of eternal dram-drinking, and it seldom fails to start him on a career from which he is not easily recovered. It is usual to call this time of peril "the daft days."*

Our old allies, if they had not so much steady

---

* The temptations of the season, and their influence, are capitally recorded in the following lyric of the late Robert Gilfillan of Leith :—

"I've aye been fou sin' the year cam' in,
I've aye been fou sin' the year cam' in;
It's what wi' the brandy, an' what wi' the gin,
I've aye been fou sin' the year cam' in!

Our Yule friends they met, and a gay stoup we drank;
The bicker gaed round, and the pint-stoup did clank;
But that was a' naething, as shortly ye'll fin'—
I've aye been fou sin' the year cam' in!

Our auld timmer clock, wi' thorl an' string,
Had scarce shawn the hour whilk the new year did bring,
Whan friends an' acquantance cam' tirl at the pin—
An' I've aye been fou sin' the year cam' in!

My auld aunty Tibbie cam' ben for her cap,
Wi' scone in her hand, an' cheese in her lap,
An' drank 'A gude New Year to kith an' to kin'—
Sae I've aye been fou sin' the year cam' in!

businesslike drinking, were, however, in some other respects, still dafter in their Fêtes des Foux.

Of these strange affairs it is difficult to give anything like a distinct conception. We cannot easily, in the Britain of the present day, enter into the solemn earnestness with which the wildest ribaldry and buffoonery were systematised as a direct burlesque not only of the highest solemnities of the old

---

My strong brither Sandy cam' in frae the south—
There's some ken his mettle, but nane ken his drouth!—
I brought out the bottle—losh! how he did grin!—
I've aye been fou sin' the year cam' in!

Wi' feasting at night, and wi' drinking at morn,
Wi' here 'Tak' a kaulker,' an' there 'Tak' a horn,'
I've gatten baith doited, an' donnert, an' blin'—
For I've aye been fou sin' the year cam' in!

I sent for the doctor, and bade him sit down;
He felt at my hand, an' he straiket my crown!
He ordered a bottle—but it turned out gin!—
Sae I've aye been fou sin' the year cam' in!

The Sunday bell rang, an' I thought it as weel
To slip into the kirk, to steer clear o' the deil;
But the chiel at the plate fand a groat left behin'—
Sae I've aye been fou sin' the year cam' in!

'Tis Candlemas time, and the wee birds o' spring
Are chirming an' chirping as if they wad sing;
While here I sit bousing—'tis really a sin!—
I've aye been fou sin' the year cam' in!

The last breath o' winter is soughing awa',
An' sune down the valley the primrose will blaw:
A douce sober life I maun really begin,
For I've aye been fou sin' the year cam' in!"

Church, but the most sacred mysteries of Christianity. There was in many places a traditional right to perform these fantasies within the churches, and even in their choirs; and the more blasphemous and brutal the exhibition was, the more was a sort of antithetic holiness attached to it.* The only necessary limit to the licence of the occasion was, that what was selected for ludicrous travestie must be something either in the Bible itself, or in the solemnities of the Church.

If advantage were taken of the excellent opportunity to make the foul fiend or the great traitor excessively ridiculous or offensive, it was, of course, a service to religion.† The animals mentioned in

* "Mais encore quelles folies? telles, en vérité, qu'elles seroient incroyables, si nous n'avions les evêques et les docteurs de ce tems-là pour témoins, qui disent que c'étoient d'horribles abominations, des actions honteuses et criminelles, mêlées par un infinité de folâtreries et d'insolences, car il est vrai que si tous les diables de l'enfer avoient à fonder une fête dans nos eglises, ils ne pourraient pas ordonner autrement que ce qui se faisoit alors."—Jean Beleth, cited by Du Tilliot, 'Mémoires pour servir à l'Histoire de la Fête des Foux, 1751,' p. 19. In the same book (p. 51), Gerson, the French Thomas-à-Kempis, is referred to as saying, "qu'on avoit prêché de son tems, que cette fête des foux étoit autant approuvée de Dieu, que la fête de la Conception de la Vierge Marie."

† "Nec prætermissus ipse Judas marsupii sollicitus custos. Perquam graphicè illic quoque sustinebat ejus personam valentissemus rusticanus, truci vultu, elato supercilio, torvo aspectu, flammantibus oculis, frendenti ore, gressu præcipiti, gestu feroci, aliisque multis truculentiæ

Scripture had their share in these ceremonies, and, according to some of the censorious, behaved themselves more discreetly than their human abettors. The whale which gave a lodging to Jonah, and the herd of swine which the evil spirit had entered into, were of course largely available for the objects of these entertainments. Balaam's ass had in some places a special festival of his own. The whole ceremonies attending it, with the ribald hymns and choruses, the processions and the costumes, are described at length by Ducange, under the head "Festus Asinorum;" and the description is almost as motley a contrast to his solemn comments on feudal usages and medieval dignities, as the scene itself must have been in the great Gothic churches where it was enacted. The "innocents"—that is to say, the children of the district—had their share in these mummeries, and no doubt enjoyed it. Their function was to pay off old scores with Herod, their great enemy; and when the whole of the "innocents" of a large town were let loose among the reliquaries, missals, paintings, and imagery of a cathedral, they were likely to leave some emphatic mark of their presence.*

---

signis, quibus se quandoque prodit nefarie subdola proditorum indoles."—Neurei Querela ad Gassendum, ibid., p. 38.

* "La fête des innocens ou la fête des enfans. . . . Mais cette fête meritait bien mieux d'etre appellé *la fête du diable*, à cause des insolences effroiables et des scandales horribles,

Among the strange shapes taken by these exhibitions, one is signally inexplicable as a feature of Catholicism—the exhibition of the *Mere folle.* It was, in fact, a travestie of the Virgin and Child, throwing, on her whom the Romanists are charged with venerating too much, a scurrility which even the most vehement Calvinists would scarce approve. In some places, round the title of the *Mere folle* there seems to have clustered a sort of body of revellers like the Calves' Head Club. They had banners, images, and paintings of the *Mere folle,* and various properties solemnly grotesque, which may be found represented in the curious plates of Du Tilliot, who also gives their macaronic poems, and the documents, in mockery of state papers and ecclesiastical edicts, contained in their muniments.*

In the fifteenth and sixteenth centuries there were many ecclesiastical denunciations of these practices. The following is the tenor of one of the most ample and descriptive of these documents—an ordinance by the Synod of Angers against the Aguillanneuf and its concomitants:—"Whereas the mortal enemy of mankind tries always with his usual

---

et des turpitudes execrables qui s'y faisoient."—Baptiste Thiers, 'Traité des Jeux,' &c., p. 441.

* For instance, 'Acte de reception de Henri de Bourbon, Prince de Condé, premier prince du sang, en la compagnie de la Mere-folle de Dijon, l'an 1626.' It begins, "Les superlatifs, mirelifiques, et scientifiques Loppinans de l'infanterie Dijonnoise, Régens d'Apollo et des Muses."

cunning to suggest to the minds of men, under the appearance of some good, things of which the fine and holy beginnings change afterwards into sad and wicked effects: Among the rest this instance is not to be despised, that by virtue of a certain custom of antiquity observed in some places in our age, principally in the parishes which are under the Deans of Craon and of Cand, the day of the Feast of the Circumcision of our Lord, which is the first day of the year, and others following, the young people of the said parishes, belonging to both sexes, go to the churches and houses, begging certain alms which they call Aquilanneuf, the proceeds of which they promise to spend on a candle in honour of Our Lady, or of the patron of their parish.

"Herein we are assured that under cover of some little good much scandal is committed. For, besides that of the said proceeds and other things accruing from the said begging, not a tenth part is spent in the honour of the Church, but consumed almost entirely in banquets, drunkenness, and other debauches, one amongst them, whom they call their *Follet*, under this name takes the liberty, as do also those who accompany him, to do and say in the church, and other places, things which cannot decently be uttered, written, or listened to, even often addressing themselves with great insolence to the priest at the altar, and imitating, by divers monkey-tricks, the holy ceremonies of the Mass and other observances of the Church; and under colour of the said Aquilanneuf, seize and take from the houses which they enter whatever seems good to them, of which people dare not complain and cannot prevent, because they carry sticks and offensive arms. And besides the above, there are a variety of other scandals. This having come to our knowledge by the remonstrances and complaints which have been made to us by certain ecclesiastics and others, we desiring, in the duty of our charge, to remedy such disorders, considering that our Lord severely, and with blows of a whip, drove from the Temple those who in it sold and bought things necessary for the sacrifices (how much less should they commit such wickednesses as those), reproaching them, that of the house of prayer they had made a den of thieves.

"Following His example, urged by His Holy Spirit, and by the authority which it has pleased Him to give us, we very positively forbid all persons, whether male or female, and of whatever quality or condition they may be, under pain of excommunication, to perform henceforth the said begging of the Aquilanneuf in the church, or in the manner above mentioned, or to make any assembly for this purpose of more than two or three persons at most, who, in performing it, shall be accompanied by one of the Procureurs de Fabrique, or by some other person of full age, not choosing that otherwise they shall perform the said begging, and under engagement to spend in wax for the service of the Church all the proceeds which shall accrue from it, not retaining nor spending a single farthing for any other purpose. We command and enjoin all rectors and curates of churches and parishes, and others having care of souls in this diocese, under pain of suspension *a divinis* for a month, and of greater penalties in future if this fails, that they neither have, nor permit, nor suffer such things to be done in their said parishes, otherwise than we have declared above." *

In defiance of repeated clerical denouncements, these practices retained so strong a hold, that a certain Mathurin de Neurě, who wrote a very angry Latin letter about them to Gassendi, already referred to, described the following as a scene to be witnessed in the middle of the seventeenth century:—

"Neither the priests nor the guardians go to the choir that day. The lay brothers, the porters, the scullions, the gardeners, the cooks and kitcheners, occupy their places in the church, and say that they perform the office suitable for such a festival, when they play at being fools and madmen, which indeed they really are. They dress themselves up in sacerdotal ornaments, if they can find them, but all torn, and turned outside in. They hold in their hands books upside down and absurdly, in which they pretend to read with spectacles, from which

* Du Tilliot, 68, 69.

they extract the glasses, substituting in their places orange-peel, which makes them look more hideous and frightful than one could believe without seeing them, particularly after they have blown the censers which they hold in their hands, which they do in derision, and made the ashes fly in their faces and cover each other's heads with them. In this guise they sing neither the usual psalms, nor hymns, nor the Mass; but they mutter certain confused words, and utter cries as foolish, as disagreeable, and as discordant as those of a herd of grunting pigs, so that brute beasts might perform the office of that day as well as they do. It would be better, indeed, to bring brute beasts into the churches to praise their Creator after their manner; it would certainly be a more holy custom than to permit such sort of persons to be there, who mock God by trying to sing His praises, and are more senseless and foolish than the most foolish and senseless animals." *

A certain 'Lettre Circulaire de la Faculté de Paris,' of the fifteenth century, in which the Fêtes des Foux are discussed, gives the following mildly-philosophic rationale of them: "Our predecessors, who were great people, permitted this feast; let us live like them, and do as they did. We do not do all these things seriously, but only for play, and to divert ourselves, according to the old custom; in order that folly, which is natural to us, and

* Querela ad Gassendum, cited in Du Tilliot.

which seems born with us, should escape and run away thereby at least once each year. Wine-barrels would burst if the bung or sluice were not sometimes opened to give them air. And we are old vessels, ill-bound barrels, which the wine of wisdom would burst if we were to let it boil constantly by incessantly addicting ourselves to devotion. We must give it some air and relaxation, for fear that it should be lost and spilt to no profit. It is for that that we give some days to games and buffooneries, that we may afterwards return with more joy and fervour to the study and exercises of religion."*

It is evident, however, that practices at once so offensively antagonistic to the prevailing sentiments of their times, and so obstinately retentive of life, must have had deeper roots than any such mild philosophy could nourish. Some seek for them in the Roman saturnalia, others in the heathenism of the northern nations. Both suppositions are mere guess-work, and the field appears to be open to the first thoroughly industrious inquirer. When it is undertaken, there will naturally be associated with it those relics of sculptural ribaldry, a sort of antithesis to all religious solemnity and reverence, to be found in the decorations of old ecclesiastical buildings. There is reason to believe that the relics of these stone caricatures, numerous as they are, are but a small percentage of the examples in the same

* Cited in Du Tilliot, p. 51.

spirit uttered by medieval art. Several of the ecclesiastical writs, denouncing the ribald ceremonies above referred to, are moved with equal indignation by indecent decorations in sculpture, painting, and tapestry.* It is quite natural, in the course of things, that the offensive paintings and tapestry

---

* In the statutes of the Synod of Angers (1678), an ordinance on reverent behaviour denounces, in the churches, "tapisseries qui representent quelquefois des choses si indécentes et si deshonnêtes, qu'elles ne sembleroient pas même assez modestes pour une salle de bal, ou un théâtre de comedie." In a manual of ceremonials it is laid down that, "Il faudra bien se donner garde qu'il n'y ait rien de profane ou d'indécent dans le peinture, ou dans le broderie qui sera sur ces tapisseries. . . . Sur tout on n'y mettra aucune image, si ce n'est des saints ou des souverains pontifs."—Passages cited by Thiers, 'Traité,' p. 473-4. The title of this book is, 'Traité des Jeux et des Divertissemens qui peuvent être permis, ou qui doivent être defendus aux Chrêtiens selon les Regles de l'Eglise et le sentiment des Pères, par M. Jean Baptiste Thiers, Docteur in Theologie, et Curé de Champroud. Paris, 1686.' The book must be rare, as it cost me a hard run to get a sight of it. It was not to be found in any library I had access to in Scotland, nor in the British Museum. An Edinburgh dealer, who sometimes remembers that his books are literature as well as merchandise, recollected that it had passed through his hands; and I thus traced it to the London Library in St James's Square, from which it was liberally lent to me. The author wrote other books on out-of-the-way matters, one of them a history of periwigs. There is much curious matter in his quotations, but he is a dry, stupid writer, and is addicted to carelessness and inaccuracies—privileges to which stupidity has no title, though it often usurps them. Du Tilliot corrects some of his blunders.

should disappear, while a portion of the sculpture remained.

I have enlarged on the French source of our New-Year's-Day rites because the matter seems to be curious, and the connection is peculiarly distinct. There are perhaps other features on the face of our national manners that might be traced to the same home, though with less certainty. Some have attributed the propensity in Scotland to indulge in territorial titles to the French connection. There was a long contest with the lairds to make them sign with the Christian and surname, instead of the name of the estate; and it was only accomplished by an Act rendering the territorial signature naught. The name of the estate still lingers in some districts, as a more courteous way of addressing its owner in familiar talk than by his own name; and in the same places formal communications are made to him by both names, with the "of" between them, like the "de" of France and the "von" of Germany. This is a matter in which the rights of women are stronger than those of men; for whereas, among brothers, the eldest, as proprietor, is the only one who can fitly take the name of the estate, it is common for elderly unmarried daughters of lairds to take the title of the estate which may belong to their brothers, or even to their nephews or grand-nephews.

It was natural that the Scots gentry, after the Union, proud and sensitive as they were, should keep up the foreign connection. So far as they differed from their English neighbours in home language and manners, they were provincial. A Continental tinge, on the other hand, removed the homespun characteristics, and perhaps gave them a touch of superiority. The five French Protestant universities—Montauban, Sedan, Montpelier, Nismes, and Saumur—were frequented by them till the revocation of the Edict of Nantes. The Protestants then flocked to Leyden, which sent many of them back as scholars and accomplished gentlemen. The foreign tone has been often observed by strangers in Scotland, and was thus especially noted by Defoe: "There was a consort of musick when I was at Stirling, where the ladies from the neighbourhood made a very good appearance. The young gentlemen in everything imitate the French, and have a hauteur which makes good the French saying—'*fier comme un Ecossais.*' Their education being in France, and the title of Laird—like Marquis in France—being their general appellation, gives them these French airs." *

Any one well acquainted with the Scotland of

* 'A Journey through Scotland, in Familiar Letters from a Gentleman here to his Friend Abroad,' by the author of the 'Journey through England,' p. 198. This book was so much altered in the subsequent editions—which are the easiest to be had—that it has become a mere statistical compilation rather than a book of travels.

that period will see in this, not that the Scots, as a people, had imbibed French manners, but that Defoe had met with many who had been themselves educated abroad, or had picked up their tone from assimilation to relations who had so acquired foreign manners. Here, as in all things, the influence of the French connection was superficial and incidental; and in nothing is this more distinctly perceptible than in the scraps of French preserved in the language of Scotland. As I have already remarked, it is of a purer Teutonic tone than the English, which took a tinge of French from the Norman influence. There are many good stories of Scotsmen wandering in Holland, or the Scandinavian countries, finding themselves direly perplexed for a medium of communication with the people, until, in their despair, they tried the broadest of broad "Buchan," and found that successful.

There are no such anecdotes of Scotsmen getting through in France by the aid of their peculiar dialect. The French terms, encased as it were in the common tongue of Scotland, are thoroughly exotic, and have been brought into it to express the special articles to which the foreigners applied them—like cheroots, mullagatawny, chatny, and suchlike terms, at the present day brought over with Oriental articles of luxury. There is something transcendentally Scotch about a haggis; and Burns, in his stalwart lines, has proclaimed its nationality in a defiant spirit, as if he had a misgiving that it might be questioned :—

"Is there that owre his French ragout,
Or olio that wad staw a sow,
Or fricassee wad mak her spew
Wi' perfect sconner,
Looks down wi' sneering, scornfu' view
On sic a dinner?

Poor devil! see him owre his trash,
As feckless as a withered rash,
His spindle-shank a guid whip-lash,
His nieve a nit;
Through bloody flood or field to dash,
O how unfit!

But mark the rustic, haggis-fed,
The trembling earth resounds his tread;
Clap in his walie nieve a blade,
He'll mak it whissle;
An' legs, an' arms, an' heads will sned,
Like taps o' thrissle.

Ye powers wha mak mankind your care,
And dish them out their bill o' fare,
Auld Scotland wants nae skinking ware
That jaups in luggies;
But, if ye wish her gratefu' prayer,
Gie her a Haggis!"

Yet there can be no question that this potent pudding, which I have heard likened to a boiled bagpipe, is the lineal descendant of the French *hachis*, which Cotgrave interprets as "a sliced gallimaufry, or minced meat."

Our hodge-podge is a gift from the same quarter. A term resembling it is in use in English law: but there is no resisting Cotgrave's "*hochepot;* a hotch-pot, a gallimaufry, a confused mingle-mangle of divers things jumbled or put together."* A special

---

* Oddly enough, this dish also is not without its sacred poet, vehemently protesting its Scotchness:—

"O leeze me on the canny Scotch,
Wha first contrived, without a botch,
To mak the gusty, good *Hotch-Potch*,
That fills the wame sae brawly:
There 's carrots intill 't, and neaps intill 't,
There 's cybies intill 't, and leeks intill 't,
There 's pease, and beans, and beets intill 't,
That soom through ither sae brawly.

The French mounseer, and English loon,
When they come daunderin' through our town,
Wi' smirks an' smacks they gulp it down,
An' lick their lips fu' brawly:
For there 's carrots intill 't, and neaps intill 't,
And cybies intill 't, and leeks intill 't,
There 's mutton, and lamb, and beef intill 't,
That maks it sup sae brawly.

And Irish Pat, when he comes here,
To lay his lugs in our good cheer,
He shools his cutty wi' unco steer,
And clears his cogue fu' brawly:
For there 's carrots intill 't, and neaps intill 't,
There 's pease, and beans, and beets intill 't,
And a' good gusty meats intill 't,
That grease his gab fu' brawly.

A dainty Dame she cam' our way,
An' sma' *soup meagre* she wad hae:
'Wi' your fat broth I cannot away,—
It maks me scunner fu' brawly:
For there 's carrots intill 't, and neaps intill 't,
There 's cybies intill 't, and leeks intill 't,
And filthy, greasy meats intill 't,
That turn my stamach sae brawly.

delicacy from the poultry-yard is known by the very Scotch-like name of howtowdy; and this is a special gift from the land of cocks, being no other than the *hutaudeau*, which Cotgrave says is "a cockerell, or big cock chick." In Burns's inventory of the contents of Grose's museum, we have

> "Parritch-pats an' auld saut-backets
> Afore the Flood."

The *saut-backet*, or salt-cellar, is from the French *bacquet*, just as our old term for a dinner-plate, an *ashet*, is from *assiette*, and *basnatis*, or small bowls,

---

> She gat her soup: It was unco trash,
> And little better than poor dish-wash;
> 'Twad gie a man the *water-brash*
> To sup sic dirt sae brawly:
> Nae carrots intill 't, nor neaps intill 't,
> Nae cybies intill 't, nor leeks intill 't,
> Nor nae good gusty meats intill 't,
> To line the ribs fu' brawly.
>
> Then here 's to ilka kindly Scot;
> Wi' mony good broths he boils his pot,
> But rare *hotch-potch* beats a' the lot,
> It smells and smacks sae brawly:
> For there 's carrots intill 't, and neaps intill 't,
> There 's pease, and beans, and beets intill 't,
> And hearty, wholesome meats intill 't,
> That stech the kite sae brawly."

These lines are taken from a privately printed collection of poems written by my late accomplished and venerable friend, Archibald Bell, the Sheriff of Ayrshire; and I think some of those who merely knew him as a man of business will be a little surprised, if not scandalised, to know that he was capable of such an effusion.

from *bassinet.* Among Grose's accomplishments as an antiquary,

> "The knife that nicket Abel's craig
> He'll prove you fully,
> It was a faulding jocteleg,
> Or lang-kail gully."

The origin of this word *jocteleg* was long a puzzle, until Lord Hailes solved it by attesting the existence of a large knife with the maker's name on it, "Jacques de Liege."

The ancient allies have left among us a more formidable memorial in the "bastle-house," or "bastle-tower," generally the name given to the small fortresses built for their protection by the inhabitants of small towns or hamlets near the border.

A considerable number of such coincidences may be found, but I shall content myself with one as a last word. I hope the novels of John Galt, and their descriptions of Scotch life—true, warm, and genial, like the pictures of David Teniers—are not yet forgotten. One of the best of them, 'The Ayrshire Legatees,' gives us the adventures of a country clergyman and his wife, who have gone to London to secure a large inheritance unexpectedly opening to them by the death of a rich relation. Among the many types of civilised comfort which Mrs Pringle left behind her when she sojourned in that "ausome place," she informed her favourite gossip, who was fortunate enough to be within reach of the luxuries of the nearest "burgh toon," that "there wasna a jigot o' mutton to be had within the four wa's o' Lunnon." It might, perhaps, have consoled her for the ridicule bestowed by her city friends on her barbarous method of applying for that universal commodity, a leg of mutton, had she remembered that her own special term for it was a bequest by the politest nation in the world, and was the way in which the French courtiers of Queen Mary would give their orders in the victualling-shops of Edinburgh.

END OF THE FIRST VOLUME.

PRINTED BY WILLIAM BLACKWOOD AND SONS, EDINBURGH.

CATALOGUE

OF

MESSRS BLACKWOOD AND SONS'

PUBLICATIONS.

HISTORY OF EUROPE,
From the Commencement of the French Revolution in 1789 to the Battle of Waterloo. By SIR ARCHIBALD ALISON, Bart., D.C.L.

A NEW LIBRARY EDITION (being the Tenth), in 14 vols. demy 8vo, with Portraits, and a copious Index, £10, 10s.

ANOTHER EDITION, in crown 8vo, 20 vols., £6.

A PEOPLE'S EDITION, 12 vols., closely printed in double columns, £2, 8s., and Index Volume, 3s.

"An extraordinary work, which has earned for itself a lasting place in the literature of the country, and within a few years found innumerable readers in every part of the globe. There is no book extant that treats so well of the period to the illustration of which Mr Alison's labours have been devoted. It exhibits great knowledge, patient research, indefatigable industry, and vast power."—*Times, Sept. 7, 1850.*

CONTINUATION OF ALISON'S HISTORY OF EUROPE,
From the Fall of Napoleon to the Accession of Louis Napoleon. By SIR ARCHIBALD ALISON, Bart., D.C.L. In 9 vols., £6, 7s. 6d. Uniform with the Library Edition of the previous work.

EPITOME OF ALISON'S HISTORY OF EUROPE.
For the Use of Schools and Young Persons. Fifteenth Edition, 7s. 6d., bound.

ATLAS TO ALISON'S HISTORY OF EUROPE;
Containing 109 Maps and Plans of Countries, Battles, Sieges, and Sea-Fights. Constructed by A. KEITH JOHNSTON, F.R.S.E. With Vocabulary of Military and Marine Terms. Demy 4to. Library Edition, £3, 3s.; People's Edition, crown 4to, £1, 11s. 6d.

LIVES OF LORD CASTLEREAGH AND SIR CHARLES STEWART, Second and Third Marquesses of Londonderry. From the Original Papers of the Family, and other sources. By SIR ARCHIBALD ALISON, Bart., D.C.L. In 3 vols. 8vo, £2, 5s.

ANNALS OF THE PENINSULAR CAMPAIGNS.
By CAPT. THOMAS HAMILTON. A New Edition. Edited by F. HARDMAN, Esq. 8vo, 16s.; and Atlas of Maps to illustrate the Campaigns, 12s.

A VISIT TO FLANDERS AND THE FIELD OF WATERLOO.
By JAMES SIMPSON, Advocate. A Revised Edition. With Two Coloured Plans of the Battle. Crown 8vo, 5s.

WELLINGTON'S CAREER:
A Military and Political Summary. By LIEUT.-COL. E. BRUCE HAMLEY, Professor of Military History and Art at the Staff College. Crown 8vo, 2s.

THE STORY OF THE CAMPAIGN OF SEBASTOPOL.

Written in the Camp. By LIEUT.-COL. E. BRUCE HAMLEY. With Illustrations drawn in Camp by the Author. 8vo, 21s.

"We strongly recommend this 'Story of the Campaign' to all who would gain a just comprehension of this tremendous struggle. Of this we are perfectly sure, it is a book unlikely to be ever superseded. Its truth is of that simple and startling character which is sure of an immortal existence; nor is it paying the gallant author too high a complement to class this masterpiece of military history with the most precious of those classic records which have been bequeathed to us by the great writers of antiquity who took part in the wars they have described."—*The Press.*

THE INVASION OF THE CRIMEA:

Its Origin, and Account of its Progress down to the Death of Lord Raglan. By ALEXANDER WILLIAM KINGLAKE, M.P. Vols. I. and II., bringing the Events down to the Close of the Battle of the Alma. Fourth Edition. Price 32s. To be completed in 4 vols. 8vo.

TEN YEARS OF IMPERIALISM IN FRANCE.

Impressions of a "Flâneur." Second Edition. In 8vo, price 9s.

"There has not been published for many a day a more remarkable book on France than this, which professes to be the impressions of a Flaneur. . . . It has all the liveliness and sparkle of a work written only for amusement; it has all the solidity and weight of a State paper; and we expect for it not a little political influence as a fair, full, and masterly statement of the Imperial policy—the first and only good account that has been given to Europe of the Napoleonic system now in force."—*Times.*

FLEETS AND NAVIES.

By CAPTAIN CHARLES HAMLEY, R.M. Originally published in 'Blackwood's Magazine.' Crown 8vo, 6s.

HISTORY OF GREECE UNDER FOREIGN DOMINATION.

By GEORGE FINLAY, LL.D., Athens—viz.:

GREECE UNDER THE ROMANS. B.C. 146 to A.D. 717. A Historical View of the Condition of the Greek Nation from its Conquest by the Romans until the Extinction of the Roman Power in the East. Second Edition, 16s.

HISTORY OF THE BYZANTINE EMPIRE, A.D. 716 to 1204; and of the Greek Empire of Nicæa and Constantinople, A.D. 1204 to 1453. 2 vols., £1, 7s. 6d.

MEDIEVAL GREECE AND TREBIZOND. The History of Greece, from its Conquest by the Crusaders to its Conquest by the Turks, A.D. 1204 to 1566; and the History of the Empire of Trebizond, A.D. 1204 to 1461. 12s.

GREECE UNDER OTHOMAN AND VENETIAN DOMINATION. A.D. 1453 to 1821. 10s. 6d.

HISTORY OF THE GREEK REVOLUTION. 2 vols. 8vo, £1, 4s.

"His book is worthy to take its place among the remarkable works on Greek history, which form one of the chief glories of English scholarship. The history of Greece is but half told without it."—*London Guardian.*

THE NATIONAL CHARACTER OF THE ATHENIANS.

By JOHN BROWN PATTERSON. Edited from the Author's revision, by PROFESSOR PILLANS, of the University of Edinburgh. With a Sketch of his Life. Crown 8vo, 4s. 6d.

STUDIES IN ROMAN LAW.

With Comparative Views of the Laws of France, England, and Scotland. By LORD MACKENZIE, one of the Judges of the Court of Session in Scotland. 8vo, 12s.

"We know not in the English language where else to look for a history of the Roman law so clear, and, at the same time, so short. . . . . More improving reading, both for the general student and for the lawyer, we cannot well imagine; and there are few, even among learned professional men, who will not gather some novel information from Lord Mackenzie's simple pages."—*London Review.*

THE EIGHTEEN CHRISTIAN CENTURIES.

By the REV. JAMES WHITE. Third Edition, with an Analytical Table of Contents, and a Copious Index. Post 8vo, 7s. 6d.

THE MONKS OF THE WEST,

From St Benedict to St Bernard. By the COUNT DE MONTALEMBERT. Authorised Translation. 2 vols. 8vo, 21s.

HISTORY OF FRANCE,

From the Earliest Period to the Year 1848. By the REV. JAMES WHITE, Author of 'The Eighteen Christian Centuries.' Second Edition. Post 8vo, 9s.

"An excellent and comprehensive compendium of French history, quite above the standard of a school book, and particularly well adapted for the libraries of literary institutions."—*National Review.*

LEADERS OF THE REFORMATION:

LUTHER, CALVIN, LATIMER, and KNOX. By the REV JOHN TULLOCH, D.D., Principal, and Primarius Professor of Theology, St Mary's College, St Andrews. Second Edition, crown 8vo, 6s. 6d.

ENGLISH PURITANISM AND ITS LEADERS:

CROMWELL, MILTON, BAXTER, and BUNYAN. By the REV. JOHN TULLOCH, D.D. Uniform with the 'Leaders of the Reformation.' 7s. 6d.

HISTORY OF THE FRENCH PROTESTANT REFUGEES.

By CHARLES WEISS, Professor of History at the Lycée Buonaparte. Translated by F. HARDMAN, Esq. 8vo, 14s.

HISTORY OF THE CHURCH OF SCOTLAND,

From the Reformation to the Revolution Settlement. By the Very REV. JOHN LEE, D.D., LL.D., Principal of the University of Edinburgh. Edited by the Rev. WILLIAM LEE. 2 vols. 8vo, 21s.

HISTORY OF SCOTLAND FROM THE REVOLUTION

To the Extinction of the last Jacobite Insurrection, 1689-1748. By JOHN HILL BURTON, Esq., Advocate. 2 vols. 8vo, reduced to 15s.

LIVES OF THE QUEENS OF SCOTLAND,

And English Princesses connected with the Regal Succession of Great Britain. By AGNES STRICKLAND. With Portraits and Historical Vignettes. Post 8vo, £4, 4s.

"Every step in Scotland is historical; the shades of the dead arise on every side; the very rocks breathe. Miss Strickland's talents as a writer, and turn of mind as an individual, in a peculiar manner fit her for painting a historical gallery of the most illustrious or dignified female characters in that land of chivalry and song."—*Blackwood's Magazine.*

MEMORIALS OF THE CASTLE OF EDINBURGH.

By JAMES GRANT, Esq. A New Edition. In crown 8vo, with 12 Engravings, 3s. 6d.

MEMOIRS OF SIR WILLIAM KIRKALDY OF GRANGE,

Governor of the Castle of Edinburgh for Mary Queen of Scots. By JAMES GRANT, Esq. Post 8vo, 10s. 6d.

MEMOIRS OF SIR JOHN HEPBURN,

Marshal of France under Louis XIII., &c. By JAMES GRANT, Esq Post 8vo, 8s.

WORKS OF THE REV. THOMAS M'CRIE, D.D.

A New and Uniform Edition. Edited by Professor M'CRIE. 4 vols. crown 8vo, 24s. Sold separately—viz.:

LIFE OF JOHN KNOX Containing Illustrations of the History of the Reformation in Scotland. Crown 8vo, 6s.

LIFE OF ANDREW MELVILLE. Containing Illustrations of the Ecclesiastical and Literary History of Scotland in the Sixteenth and Seventeenth Centuries. Crown 8vo, 6s.

HISTORY OF THE PROGRESS AND SUPPRESSION OF THE REFORMATION IN ITALY IN THE SIXTEENTH CENTURY. Crown 8vo, 4s.

HISTORY OF THE PROGRESS AND SUPPRESSION OF THE REFORMATION IN SPAIN IN THE SIXTEENTH CENTURY. Crown 8vo, 3s. 6d.

THE BOSCOBEL TRACTS;

Relating to the Escape of Charles the Second after the Battle of Worceste and his subsequent Adventures. Edited by J. HUGHES, Esq., A.M. A Ne Edition, with additional Notes and Illustrations, including Communicatio from the Rev. R. H. BARHAM, Author of the 'Ingoldsby Legends.' In 8v with Engravings, 16s.

"'The Boscobel Tracts' is a very curious book, and about as good an example of single subject h rical collections as may be found. Originally undertaken, or at least completed, at the suggestion of late Bishop Copplestone, in 1827, it was carried out with a degree of judgment and taste not always in works of a similar character."—*Spectator.*

LIFE OF JOHN DUKE OF MARLBOROUGH.

With some Account of his Contemporaries, and of the War of the Successio By SIR ARCHIBALD ALISON, Bart., D.C.L. Third Edition. 2 vols. 8v Portraits and Maps, 30s.

THE NEW 'EXAMEN;'

Or, An Inquiry into the Evidence of certain Passages in 'Macaulay's Histo of England' concerning—THE DUKE OF MARLBOROUGH—THE MASSACRE O GLENCOE—THE HIGHLANDS OF SCOTLAND—VISCOUNT DUNDEE—WILLIAM PEN By JOHN PAGET, Esq., Barrister-at-Law. In crown 8vo, 6s.

"We certainly never saw a more damaging exposure, and it is something worth notice that much of appeared in 'Blackwood's Magazine' during the lifetime of Lord Macaulay, but he never attempted make any reply. The charges are so direct, and urged in such unmistakable language, that no wri who valued his character for either accuracy of fact or fairness in comment would let them remain answered if he had any reason to give."—*Gentleman's Magazine.*

AUTOBIOGRAPHY OF THE REV. DR CARLYLE,

Minister of Inveresk. Containing Memorials of the Men and Events of h Time. Edited by JOHN HILL BURTON. In 8vo. Third Edition, wi Portrait, 14s.

"This book contains by far the most vivid picture of Scottish life and manners that has been given the public since the days of Sir Walter Scott. In bestowing upon it this high praise, we make no exce tion, not even in favour of Lord Cockburn's 'Memorials'—the book which resembles it most, and whi ranks next to it in interest."—*Edinburgh Review.*

MEMOIR OF THE POLITICAL LIFE OF EDMUND BURK

With Extracts from his Writings. By the REV. GEORGE CROLY, D. 2 vols. post 8vo, 18s.

CURRAN AND HIS CONTEMPORARIES.

By CHARLES PHILLIPS, Esq , A.B. A New Edition. Crown 8vo, 7s.

"Certainly one of the most extraordinary pieces of biography ever produced. . . . . . No lib should be without it."—*Lord Brougham.*

"Never, perhaps, was there a more curious collection of portraits crowded before into the same vass."—*Times.*

MEMOIR OF MRS HEMANS.

By her SISTER. With a Portrait. Fcap. 8vo, 5s.

LIFE OF THE LATE REV. JAMES ROBERTSON, D.D

F.R.S.E., Professor of Divinity and Ecclesiastical History in the Universit of Edinburgh. By the REV. A. H. CHARTERIS, M.A., Minister of Ne abbey. With a Portrait. 8vo, price 10s. 6d.

ESSAYS; HISTORICAL, POLITICAL, AND MISCELLANEOU

By SIR ARCHIBALD ALISON, Bart. 3 vols. demy 8vo, 45s.

ESSAYS IN HISTORY AND ART.

By R. H. PATTERSON. Viz.:

COLOUR IN NATURE AND ART—REAL AND IDEAL BEAUTY—SCULPTURE—ETHNOLOGY OF EUROPE—UTOPIAS—OUR INDIAN EMPIRE—THE NATIONA LIFE OF CHINA—AN IDEAL ART-CONGRESS—BATTLE OF THE STYLES—GENIU

NORMAN SINCLAIR.
By W. E. AYTOUN, D.C.L., Author of 'Lays of the Scottish Cavalie &c. &c. In 3 vols. post 8vo, 31s. 6d.

THE OLD BACHELOR IN THE OLD SCOTTISH VILLAG
By THOMAS AIRD. Fcap. 8vo, 4s.

SIR EDWARD BULWER LYTTON'S NOVELS.
Library Edition. Printed from a large and readable type. In Volumes o convenient and handsome form. 8vo, 5s. each—viz.:

THE CAXTON NOVELS, 10 Volumes:

The Caxton Family. 2 vols.
My Novel. 4 vols.
What will he do with it? 4 vols.

HISTORICAL ROMANCES, 11 Volumes:

Devereux. 2 vols.
The Last Days of Pompeii. 2 vols.
Rienzi. 2 vols.
The Siege of Grenada. 1 vol.
The Last of the Barons. 2 vols.
Harold. 2 vols.

ROMANCES, 5 Volumes:

The Pilgrims of the Rhine. 1 vol.
Eugene Aram. 2 vols.
Zanoni. 2 vols.

NOVELS OF LIFE AND MANNERS, 15 Volumes:

Pelham. 2 vols.
The Disowned. 2 vols.
Paul Clifford. 2 vols.
Godolphin 1 vol.
Ernest Maltravers—First Part. 2 vols.
Ernest Maltravers — Second Part (*i.e.* Alice) 2 vols.
Night and Morning. 2 vols.
Lucretia. 2 vols.

"It is of the handiest of sizes; the paper is good; and the type, which seems to be new, is very c and beautiful. There are no pictures. The whole charm of the presentment of the volume in its handiness, and the tempting clearness and beauty of the type, which almost converts into a sure the mere act of following the printer's lines, and leaves the author's mind free to exert its structed force upon the reader."—*Examiner.*

"Nothing could be better as to size, type, paper, and general get-up."—*Athenæum.*

JESSIE CAMERON: A HIGHLAND STORY.
By the LADY RACHEL BUTLER. Second Edition. Small 8vo, with Frontispiece, 2s. 6d.

SOME PASSAGES IN THE LIFE OF ADAM BLAIR,
And History of Matthew Wald. By the Author of 'Valerius.' Fcap. 8 4s. cloth.

CAPTAIN CLUTTERBUCK'S CHAMPAGNE:
A West Indian Reminiscence. Post 8vo, 12s.

SCENES OF CLERICAL LIFE.
The Sad Fortunes of Amos Barton—Mr Gilfil's Love-Story—Janet's Repe ance. By GEORGE ELIOT. 2 vols. fcap. 8vo, 12s.

ADAM BEDE.
By GEORGE ELIOT. 2 vols. fcap. 8vo, 12s.

THE MILL ON THE FLOSS.
By GEORGE ELIOT. 2 vols. fcap. 8vo, 12s.

SILAS MARNER: THE WEAVER OF RAVELOE.
By GEORGE ELIOT. Fcap. 8vo, 6s.

THE NOVELS OF GEORGE ELIOT.
Cheap Edition, complete in 3 vols., price 6s. each—viz.:

By JOHN GALT. Fcap. 8vo, 4s. cloth.

SIR ANDREW WYLIE.
By JOHN GALT. Fcap. 8vo, 4s. cloth.

THE PROVOST, AND OTHER TALES.
By JOHN GALT. Fcap. 8vo, 4s. cloth.

THE ENTAIL.
By JOHN GALT. Fcap. 8vo, 4s. cloth.

THE YOUTH AND MANHOOD OF CYRIL THORNTON.
By CAPTAIN HAMILTON. Fcap. 8vo, 4s. cloth.

LADY LEE'S WIDOWHOOD.
By LIEUT.-COL. E. B. HAMLEY. Crown 8vo, with 13 Illustrations by Author. 6 .

THE LIFE OF MANSIE WAUCH,
Tailor in Dalkeith. By D. M. MOIR. Fcap. 8vo, 3s. cloth.

NIGHTS AT MESS, SIR FRIZZLE PUMPKIN, AND OTH TALES.
Fcap. 8vo, 3s. cloth.

KATIE STEWART: A TRUE STORY.
By MRS OLIPHANT. Fcap. 8vo, with Frontispiece and Vignette. 4s.

PEN OWEN.
Fcap. 8vo, 4s. cloth.

PENINSULAR SCENES AND SKETCHES.
Fcap. 8vo, 3s. cloth.

REGINALD DALTON.
By the Author of 'Valerius.' Fcap. 8vo, 4s. cloth.

LIFE IN THE FAR WEST.
By G. F. RUXTON, Esq. Second Edition. Fcap. 8vo, 4s.

TOM CRINGLE'S LOG.
A New Edition. With Illustrations by STANFIELD, WEIR, SKELTON, WAL &c., Engraved by WHYMPER. Crown 8vo, 6s.

"Everybody who has failed to read 'Tom Cringle's Log' should do so at once. The 'Quarter view' went so far as to say that the papers composing it, when it first appeared in 'Blackwood,' the most brilliant series of the time, and that time one unrivalled for the number of famous maga existing in it. Coleridge says, in his 'Table Talk,' that the 'Log' is most excellent; and these have been ratified by generations of men and boys, and by the manifestation of Continental ap which is shown by repeated translations. The engravings illustrating the present issue are excellen *Standard.*

TOM CRINGLE'S LOG.
Fcap. 8vo, 4s. cloth.

THE CRUISE OF THE MIDGE.
By the Author of 'Tom Cringle's Log.' Fcap. 8vo, 4s. cloth.

CHAPTERS ON CHURCHYARDS.
By MRS SOUTHEY. Fcap. 8vo, 7s. 6d.

THE SUBALTERN.
By the Author of the 'The Chelsea Pensioners.' Fcap. 8vo, 3s. cloth.

THE BOOK-HUNTER, ETC.

By JOHN HILL BURTON. New Edition. In crown 8vo, 7s. 6d.

"A book pleasant to look at and pleasant to read—pleasant from its rich store of anecdote, its geniality and its humour, even to persons who care little for the subjects of which it treats, but beyond measure delightful to those who are in any degree members of the above-mentioned fraternity."—*Saturday Review.*

"We have not been more amused for a long time: and every reader who takes interest in typography and its consequences will say the same, if he will begin to read; beginning, he will finish, and be when it is over."—*Athenæum.*

"Mr Burton has now given us a pleasant book, full of quaint anecdote, and of a lively bookish tal There is a quiet humour in it which is very taking, and there is a curious knowledge of books which really very sound."—*Examiner.*

HOMER AND HIS TRANSLATORS,

And the Greek Drama. By PROFESSOR WILSON. Crown 8vo, 6s.

"But of all the criticisms on Homer which I have ever had the good fortune to read in our own any language, the most vivid and entirely genial are those found in the 'Essays, Critical and tive,' of the late Professor Wilson."—*Mr Gladstone's Studies on Homer.*

THE SKETCHER.

By the REV. JOHN EAGLES. Originally published in 'Blackwood's Magazine.' 8vo, 10s. 6d.

"This volume, called by the appropriate name of 'The Sketcher,' is one that ought to be found in th studio of every English landscape-painter. . . . . More instructive and suggestive readings for y artists, especially landscape-painters, can scarcely be found."—*The Globe.*

ESSAYS.

By the REV. JOHN EAGLES, A.M. Oxon. Originally published in 'Blackwood's Magazine.' Post 8vo, 10s. 6d.

CONTENTS:—Church Music, and other Parochials.—Medical Attendance, an other Parochials.—A few Hours at Hampton Court.—Grandfathers an Grandchildren.—Sitting for a Portrait.—Are there not Great Boaster among us?—Temperance and Teetotal Societies.—Thackeray's Lectures Swift.—The Crystal Palace.—Civilisation: The Census.—The Beggar' Legacy.

ESSAYS; HISTORICAL, POLITICAL, AND MISCELLANEOU

By SIR ARCHIBALD ALISON, Bart., D.C.L. Three vols., demy 8vo, 45s.

LECTURES ON THE POETICAL LITERATURE OF TH PAST HALF-CENTURY.

By D. M. MOIR. Third Edition. Fcap. 8vo,

"Exquisite in its taste and generous in its criticisms."—*Hugh Miller.*

LECTURES ON THE HISTORY OF LITERATURE,

Ancient and Modern. From the German of F. SCHLEGEL. Fcap., 5s.

"A wonderful performance—better than anything we as yet have in our own language."—*Quarterl Review.*

THE GENIUS OF HANDEL,

And the distinctive Character of his Sacred Compositions. Two Lectures Delivered to the Members of the Edinburgh Philosophical Institution. B the VERY REV. DEAN RAMSAY, Author of 'Reminiscences of Scottish and Character.' In crown 8vo, 3s. 6d.

BLACKWOOD'S MAGAZINE,

From Commencement in 1817 to December 1861. Numbers 1 to 554, formi 90 Volumes. £31, 10s.

INDEX TO THE FIRST FIFTY VOLUMES OF BLACKWOOD' MAGAZINE.

8vo. 15s.

And other Poems. By W. E[illegible]ONDSTOUNE AYTOUN, D.C.L., Prof of Rhetoric and English Literature in the University of Edinburgh. Fo teenth Edition. Fcap. 8vo, 7s. 6d.

"Professor Aytoun's 'Lays of the Scottish Cavaliers'—a volume of verse which shows that Scotland yet a poet. Full of the true fire, it now stirs and swells like a trumpet-note—now sinks in cadences and wild as the wail of a Highland dirge."—*Quarterly Review.*

BOTHWELL: A POEM.

By W. EDMONDSTOUNE AYTOUN, D.C.L. Third Edition. Fcap. 7s. 6d.

"Professor Aytoun has produced a fine poem and an able argument, and 'Bothwell' will take its stand among the classics of Scottish literature."—*The Press.*

THE BALLADS OF SCOTLAND.

Edited by Professor AYTOUN. Second Edition. 2 vols. fcap. 8vo, 12s.

"No country can boast of a richer collection of Ballads than Scotland, and no Editor for these Ball could be found more accomplished than Professor Aytoun. He has sent forth two beautiful volumes w range with 'Percy's Reliques'—which, for completeness and accuracy, leave little to be desired—w must henceforth be considered as the standard edition of the Scottish Ballads, and which we comm as a model to any among ourselves who may think of doing like service to the English Ballads."—

POEMS AND BALLADS OF GOETHE.

Translated by Professor AYTOUN and THEODORE MARTIN. Second Editi Fcap. 8vo, 6s.

"There is no doubt that these are the best translations of Goethe's marvellously-cut gems which yet been published."—*Times.*

THE BOOK OF BALLADS.

Edited by BON GAULTIER. Seventh Edition, with numerous Illustrations DOYLE, LEECH, and CROWQUILL. Gilt edges, post 8vo, 8s. 6d.

FIRMILIAN; OR, THE STUDENT OF BADAJOS.

A Spasmodic Tragedy. By T. PERCY JONES. In small 8vo, 5s.

"Humour of a kind most rare at all times, and especially in the present day, runs through and passages of true poetry and delicious versification prevent the continual play of sarcasm from ing tedious."—*Literary Gazette.*

POETICAL WORKS OF THOMAS AIRD.

Fourth Edition. In 1 vol. fcap. 8vo, 6s.

POEMS.

By the LADY FLORA HASTINGS. Edited by her SISTER. Second Editio with a Portrait. Fcap., 7s. 6d.

THE POEMS OF FELICIA HEMANS.

Complete in 1 vol. royal 8vo, with Portrait by FINDEN. Cheap Editio 12s. 6d. *Another Edition*, with MEMOIR by her SISTER. Seven vols. fca 35s. *Another Edition*, in 6 vols., cloth, gilt edges, 24s.

The following Works of Mrs HEMANS are sold separately, bound in cloth, edges, 4s. each:—

RECORDS OF WOMAN. FOREST SANCTUARY. SONGS OF THE AFFECTIC DRAMATIC WORKS. TALES AND HISTORIC SCENES. MORAL AND GIOUS POEMS.

THE ODYSSEY OF HOMER.

Translated into English Verse in the Spenserian Stanza. By PHILIP ST HOPE WORSLEY, M.A., Scholar of Corpus Christi College. 2 vols. cr 8vo, 18s.

"Mr Worsley,—applying the Spenserian stanza, that beautiful romantic measure, to the most poem of the ancient world—making the stanza yield him, too (what it never yielded to Byron), its sures of fluidity and sweet ease—above all, bringing to his task a truly poetical sense and skill,—has duced a version of the 'Odyssey' much the most pleasing of those hitherto produced, and which is lightful to read."—*Professor Arnold on Translating Homer.*

College, Oxford. Fcap. 8vo, 5s.

POEMS.
By ISA. In small 8vo, 4s. 6d.

POETICAL WORKS OF D. M. MOIR.
With Portrait, and Memoir by Thomas Aird. Second Edition. 2 vols. fcap. 8vo, 12s.

LECTURES ON THE POETICAL LITERATURE OF THE PAST HALF-CENTURY. By D. M. MOIR (Δ). Second Edition. Fcap. 8vo, 5s.

"A delightful volume."—*Morning Chronicle.*
"Exquisite in its taste and generous in its criticisms."—*Hugh Miller.*

THE COURSE OF TIME: A POEM.
By ROBERT POLLOK, A.M. Twenty-third Edition. Fcap. 8vo, 5s.

"Of deep and hallowed impress, full of noble thoughts and graphic conceptions—the production of a mind alive to the great relations of being, and the sublime simplicity of our religion."—*Blackwood's Magazine.*

AN ILLUSTRATED EDITION OF THE COURSE OF TIME.
In large 8vo, bound in cloth, richly gilt, 21s.

"There has been no modern poem in the English language, of the class to which the 'Course of Time' belongs, since Milton wrote, that can be compared to it. In the present instance the artistic talents of Messrs Foster, Clayton, Tenniel, Evans, Dalziel, Green, and Woods, have been employed in giving expression to the sublimity of the language, by equally exquisite illustrations, all of which are of the highest class."—*Bell's Messenger.*

POEMS AND BALLADS OF SCHILLER.
Translated by Sir Edward Bulwer Lytton, Bart. Second Edition. 8vo, 10s. 6d.

ST STEPHEN'S;
Or, Illustrations of Parliamentary Oratory. A Poem. *Comprising*—Pym—Vane—Strafford—Halifax—Shaftesbury—St John—Sir R. Walpole—Chesterfield—Carteret—Chatham—Pitt—Fox—Burke—Sheridan—Wilberforce—Wyndham—Conway—Castlereagh—William Lamb (Lord Melbourne)—Tierney—Lord Grey—O'Connell—Plunkett—Shiel—Follett—Macaulay—Peel. Second Edition. Crown 8vo, 5s.

LEGENDS, LYRICS, AND OTHER POEMS.
By B. SIMMONS. Fcap., 7s. 6d.

SIR WILLIAM CRICHTON—ATHELWOLD—GUIDONE:
Dramas by WILLIAM SMITH, Author of 'Thorndale,' &c. 32mo, 2s. 6d.

THE BIRTHDAY, AND OTHER POEMS.
By Mrs SOUTHEY. Second Edition, 5s.

ILLUSTRATIONS OF THE LYRIC POETRY AND MUSIC OF SCOTLAND. By WILLIAM STENHOUSE. Originally compiled to accompany the 'Scots Musical Museum,' and now published separately, with Additional Notes and Illustrations. 8vo, 7s. 6d.

PROFESSOR WILSON'S POEMS.
Containing the 'Isle of Palms,' the 'City of the Plague,' 'Unimore,' and other Poems. Complete Edition. Crown 8vo, 6s.

POEMS AND SONGS.
By DAVID WINGATE. Second Edition. Fcap. 8vo, 5s.

"We are delighted to welcome into the brotherhood of real poets a countryman of Burns, and whose verse will go far to render the rougher Border Scottish a classic dialect in our literature."—*John Bull.*

Queen for Scotland. A New and Enlarged Edition, consisting of 35 F Plates, and 27 smaller ones, printed in Colours, with 135 pages of Letterpr and Index. Imperial folio, half-bound morocco, £8, 8s.

"A perfect treasure of compressed information."—*Sir John Herschel.*

THE PHYSICAL ATLAS.

By ALEXANDER KEITH JOHNSTON, F.R.S E., &c. Reduced from Imperial Folio This Edition contains Twenty-five Maps, including a Pal tological and Geological Map of the British Islands, with Descriptive Le press, and a very copious Index. In imperial 4to, half-bound mo £2, 12s. 6d.

"Executed with remarkable care, and is as accurate, and, for all educational purposes, as valu the splendid large work (by the same author) which has now a European reputation."—*Eclectic*

A GEOLOGICAL MAP OF EUROPE.

By Sir R. I. MURCHISON, D.C.L., F.R.S., &c, Director-General of Geological Survey of Great Britain and Ireland; and JAMES NIC F.R.S E., F.G.S, Professor of Natural History in the University of Aberd Constructed by ALEXANDER KEITH JOHNSTON, F.R.S E., &c. Four Sh imperial, beautifully printed in Colours. In Sheets, £3, 3s.; in a Cloth C 4to, £3, 10s.

GEOLOGICAL AND PALÆONTOLOGICAL MAP OF T

BRITISH ISLANDS, including Tables of the Fossils of the different Epoc &c. &c., from the Sketches and Notes of Professor EDWARD FORBES. W Illustrative and Explanatory Letterpress. 21s.

GEOLOGICAL MAP OF SCOTLAND.

By JAMES NICOL, F.R S.E., &c., Professor of Natural History in the U versity of Aberdeen. With Explanatory Notes. The Topography by ALE ANDER KEITH JOHNSTON, F.R.S.E., &c. Scale, 10 miles to an inch. Cloth Case, 21s.

INTRODUCTORY TEXT-BOOK OF PHYSICAL GEOGRAPH

By DAVID PAGE, F.R.S.E., &c. With Illustrations and a Glossarial Ind Crown 8vo, 2s.

INTRODUCTORY TEXT-BOOK OF GEOLOGY.

By DAVID PAGE, F.R.S.E., F.G.S. With Engravings on Wood and Gl sarial Index. Fifth Edition, 1s. 9d.

"It has not often been our good fortune to examine a text-book on science of which we could exp an opinion so entirely favourable as we are enabled to do of Mr Page's little work."—*Athenæum.*

ADVANCED TEXT-BOOK OF GEOLOGY,

Descriptive and Industrial. By DAVID PAGE, F.R.S E., F.G S. Wi Engravings and Glossary of Scientific Terms. Third Edition, revised enlarged, 6s.

"It is therefore with unfeigned pleasure that we record our appreciation of his 'Advanced Text- of Geology' We have carefully read this truly satisfactory book, and do not hesitate to say that it is excellent compendium of the great facts of Geology, and written in a truthful and philosophic spirit." *Edinburgh Philosophical Journal.*

HANDBOOK OF GEOLOGICAL TERMS AND GEOLOGY.

By DAVID PAGE, F.R S.E., F.G.S. In crown 8vo, 6s.

THE PAST AND PRESENT LIFE OF THE GLOBE:

Being a Sketch in Outline of the World's Life-System By DAVID PAG F.R.S.E., F.G S. Crown 8vo, 6s. With Fifty Illustrations, drawn engraved expressly for this Work.

"Mr Page, whose admirable text-books of geology have already secured him a position of importan the scientific world, will add considerably to his reputation by the present sketch, as he modestly t it, of the Life-System, or gradual evolution of the vitality of our globe. In no manual that we are a of have the facts and phenomena of biology been presented in at once so systematic and succinct a f the successive manifestations of life on the earth set forth in so clear an order, or traced so vividly the earliest organisms deep buried in its stratified crust, to the familiar forms that now adorn and peo its surface."—*Literary Gazette.*

A Progressive Series of Questions adapted to the Introductory and Advanced Text-Books of Geology. Prepared to assist Teachers in framing their Examinations, and Students in testing their own Progress and Proficiency. By DAVID PAGE, F.R.S.E., F.G.S. Second Edition, 6d.

THE GEOLOGY OF PENNSYLVANIA:

A Government Survey; with a General View of the Geology of the United States, Essays on the Coal Formation and its Fossils, and a Description of the Coal-Fields of North America and Great Britain. By PROFESSOR HENRY DARWIN ROGERS, F.R.S., F.G.S., Professor of Natural History in the University of Glasgow. With Seven large Maps, and numerous Illustrations engraved on Copper and on Wood. In 3 vols. royal 4to, £8, 8s.

SEA-SIDE STUDIES AT ILFRACOMBE, TENBY, THE SCILLY ISLES, AND JERSEY.

By GEORGE HENRY LEWES. Second Edition. Crown 8vo, with Illustrations, and a Glossary of Technical Terms, 6s. 6d.

PHYSIOLOGY OF COMMON LIFE.

By GEORGE HENRY LEWES, Author of 'Sea-side Studies,' &c. Illustrated with numerous Engravings. 2 vols., 12s.

CHEMISTRY OF COMMON LIFE.

By PROFESSOR J. F. W. JOHNSTON. A New Edition. Edited by G. H. LEWES. With 113 Illustrations on Wood, and a Copious Index. 2 vols. crown 8vo, 11s. 6d.

NOMENCLATURE OF COLOURS,

Applicable to the Arts and Natural Sciences, to Manufactures, and other Purposes of General Utility. By D. R. HAY, F.R.S.E. 228 Examples of Colours, Hues, Tints, and Shades. 8vo, £3, 3s.

NARRATIVE OF THE EARL OF ELGIN'S MISSION TO CHINA AND JAPAN.

By LAURENCE OLIPHANT, Private Secretary to Lord Elgin. Illustrated with numerous Engravings in Chromo-Lithography, Maps, and Engravings on Wood, from Original Drawings and Photographs. Second Edition. In 2 vols. 8vo, 21s.

"The volumes in which Mr Oliphant has related these transactions will be read with the strongest interest now, and deserve to retain a permanent place in the literary and historical annals of our time."—*Edinburgh Review.*

RUSSIAN SHORES OF THE BLACK SEA

In the Autumn of 1852. With a Voyage down the Volga and a Tour through the Country of the Don Cossacks. By LAURENCE OLIPHANT, Esq. 8vo, with Map and other Illustrations. Fourth Edition, 14s.

EGYPT, THE SOUDAN, AND CENTRAL AFRICA:

With Explorations from Khartoum on the White Nile to the Regions of the Equator. By JOHN PETHERICK, F.R.G.S., Her Britannic Majesty's Consul for the Soudan. In 8vo, with a Map, 16s.

NOTES ON NORTH AMERICA:

Agricultural, Economical, and Social. By PROFESSOR J. F. W. JOHNSTON. 2 vols. post 8vo, 21s.

"Professor Johnston's admirable Notes. . . . The very best manual for intelligent emigrants, whilst to the British agriculturist and general reader it conveys a more complete conception of the condition of these prosperous regions than all that has hitherto been written."—*Economist.*

A FAMILY TOUR ROUND THE COASTS OF SPAIN AND PORTUGAL

during the Winter of 1860-1861. By LADY DUNBAR, of Northfield. In post 8vo, 5s.

THE ROYAL ATLAS OF MODERN GEOGRAPHY.

In a Series of entirely Original and Authentic Maps. By A. KEI JOHNSTON, F.R.S.E., F.R.G.S., Author of the 'Physical Atlas,' &c. W a complete Index of easy reference to each Map, comprising nearly 150, Places contained in this Atlas. Imperial folio, half-bound in russia or rocco, £5, 15s. 6d. (Dedicated by permission to Her Majesty.)

"No one can look through Mr Keith Johnston's new Atlas without seeing that it is the best which ever been published in this country"—*The Times.*

"Of the many noble atlases prepared by Mr Johnston and published by Messrs Blackwood & Sons, Royal Atlas will be the most useful to the public, and will deserve to be the most popular."—*Athenæu*

"We know no series of maps which we can more warmly recommend. The accuracy, wherever we attempted to put it to the test, is really astonishing"—*Saturday Review.*

"The culmination of all attempts to depict the face of the world appears in the Royal Atlas, which it is impossible to conceive anything more perfect."—*Morning Herald.*

"This is, beyond question, the most splendid and luxurious, as well as the most useful and comp of all existing atlases."—*Guardian.*

"There has not, we believe, been produced for general public use a body of maps equal in beauty completeness to the Royal Atlas just issued by Mr A. K. Johnston."—*Examiner.*

"An almost daily reference to, and comparison of it with others, since the publication of the first some two years ago until now, enables us to say, without the slightest hesitation, that this is by far most complete and authentic atlas that has yet been issued."—*Scotsman.*

"Beyond doubt the greatest geographical work of our time."—*Museum.*

INDEX GEOGRAPHICUS:

Being an Index to nearly ONE HUNDRED AND FIFTY THOUSAND NAMES PLACES, &c.; with their LATITUDES and LONGITUDES as given in KEI JOHNSTON'S 'ROYAL ATLAS;' together with the COUNTRIES and SUBD SIONS OF THE COUNTRIES in which they are situated. In 1 vol. large ‹

[*In the*

A NEW MAP OF EUROPE.

By A. KEITH JOHNSTON, F.R.S.E. Size, 4 feet 2 inches by 3 fee inches. Cloth Case, 21s.

ATLAS OF SCOTLAND.

31 Maps of the Counties of Scotland, coloured. Bound in roan, price 10s. Each County may be had separately, in Cloth Case, 1s.

KEITH JOHNSTON'S SCHOOL ATLASES:—

GENERAL AND DESCRIPTIVE GEOGRAPHY, exhibiting the Actual and C parative Extent of all the Countries in the World, with their pre Political Divisions. A New and Enlarged Edition. With a comp Index. 26 Maps. Half-bound, 12s. 6d.

PHYSICAL GEOGRAPHY, illustrating, in a Series of Original Designs, Elementary Facts of Geology, Hydrology, Meteorology, and Nat History. A New and Enlarged Edition. 19 Maps, including colo Geological Maps of Europe and of the British Isles. Half-bound, 12s

CLASSICAL GEOGRAPHY, comprising, in Twenty Plates, Maps and Plai all the important Countries and Localities referred to by Clas Authors; accompanied by a pronouncing Index of Places, by T. HAR M.A. Oxon. A New and Revised Edition. Half-bound, 12s. 6d.

ASTRONOMY. Edited by J. R. HIND, Esq., F.R.A.S., &c. Notes Descriptive Letterpress to each Plate, embodying all recent Discove in Astronomy. 18 Maps. Half-bound, 12s. 6d.

ELEMENTARY SCHOOL ATLAS OF GENERAL AND DESCRIPTIVE GEOGRAP for the Use of Junior Classes. A New and Cheaper Edition. 20 Ma including a Map of Canaan and Palestine. Half-bound, 5s.

"They are as superior to all School Atlases within our knowledge, as were the larger works of the Author in advance of those that preceded them."—*Educational Times.*

"Decidedly the best School Atlases we have ever seen."—*English Journal of Education.*

"The best, the fullest, the most accurate and recent, as well as artistically the most beautiful atlas can be put into the schoolboy's hands."—*Museum, April 1863.*

A MANUAL OF MODERN GEOGRAPHY:

THE BOOK OF THE FARM.

Detailing the Labours of the Farmer, Farm-Steward, Ploughman, Shepherd, Hedger, Cattle-man, Field-worker, and Dairymaid, and forming a safe Monitor for Students in Practical Agriculture. By HENRY STEPHENS, F.R.S.E. 2 vols. royal 8vo, £3, handsomely bound in cloth, with upwards of 600 Illustrations.

"The best book I have ever met with."—*Professor Johnston.*

"We have thoroughly examined these volumes; but to give a full notice of their varied and valuable contents would occupy a larger space than we can conveniently devote to their discussion, we therefore, in general terms, commend them to the careful study of every young man who wishes to become a good practical farmer."—*Times.*

"One of the completest works on agriculture of which our literature can boast."—*Agricultural Gazette.*

THE BOOK OF FARM IMPLEMENTS AND MACHINES.

By JAMES SLIGHT and R. SCOTT BURN. Edited by HENRY STEPHENS, F.R.S.E. Illustrated with 876 Engravings. Royal 8vo, uniform with the 'Book of the Farm,' half-bound, £2, 2s.

THE BOOK OF FARM BUILDINGS:

Their Arrangement and Construction. By HENRY STEPHENS, F.R.S.E., and R. SCOTT BURN. Royal 8vo, with 1045 Illustrations. Uniform with the 'Book of the Farm.' Half-bound, £1, 11s. 6d.

THE BOOK OF THE GARDEN.

By CHARLES M'INTOSH. In 2 large vols. royal 8vo, embellished with 1353 Engravings.

Each Volume may be had separately—viz.:

I. ARCHITECTURAL AND ORNAMENTAL.—On the Formation of Gardens—Construction, Heating, and Ventilation of Fruit and Plant Houses, Pits, Frames, and other Garden Structures, with Practical Details. Illustrated by 1073 Engravings, pp. 766. £2, 10s.

II. PRACTICAL GARDENING.—Directions for the Culture of the Kitchen Garden, the Hardy-fruit Garden, the Forcing Garden, and Flower Garden, including Fruit and Plant Houses, with Select Lists of Vegetables, Fruits, and Plants. Pp. 868, with 279 Engravings. £1, 17s. 6d.

"We feel justified in recommending Mr M'Intosh's two excellent volumes to the notice of the public."—*Gardeners' Chronicle.*

PRACTICAL SYSTEM OF FARM BOOK-KEEPING:

Being that recommended in the 'Book of the Farm' by H. STEPHENS. Royal 8vo, 2s. 6d. Also, SEVEN FOLIO ACCOUNT-BOOKS, printed and ruled in accordance with the System, the whole being specially adapted for keeping, by an easy and accurate method, an account of all the transactions of the Farm. A detailed Prospectus may be had from the Publishers. Price of the complete set of Eight Books, £1, 4s. 6d. Also, A LABOUR ACCOUNT OF THE ESTATE, 2s 6d.

"We have no hesitation in saying that, of the many systems of keeping farm accounts which are now in vogue, there is not one which will bear comparison with this."—*Bell's Messenger.*

AINSLIE'S TREATISE ON LAND-SURVEYING.

A New and Enlarged Edition. Edited by WILLIAM GALBRAITH, M.A., F.R.A.S. 1 vol. 8vo, with a Volume of Plates in Quarto, 21s.

"The best book on surveying with which I am acquainted."—W. RUTHERFORD, LL.D., F.R.A.S., *Royal Military Academy, Woolwich.*

THE FORESTER:

A Practical Treatise on the Planting, Rearing, and Management of Forest Trees. By JAMES BROWN, Wood Manager to the Earl of Seafield. Third Editio[illegible] ed with numerous En[illegible] on Wood. Ro[illegible]al 8vo

HANDBOOK OF THE MECHANICAL ARTS,

Concerned in the Construction and Arrangement of Dwellings and o Buildings; Including Carpentry, Smith-work, Iron-framing, Brick-m Columns, Cements, Well-sinking, Enclosing of Land, Road-making, &c. R. SCOTT BURN. Crown 8vo, with 504 Engravings on Wood, 6s. 6d.

PROFESSOR JOHNSTON'S WORKS:—

EXPERIMENTAL AGRICULTURE. Being the Results of Past, and Suggesti for Future, Experiments in Scientific and Practical Agriculture. 8s.

ELEMENTS OF AGRICULTURAL CHEMISTRY AND GEOLOGY. Eighth Editi 6s. 6d.

A CATECHISM OF AGRICULTURAL CHEMISTRY AND GEOLOGY. Fifty-sev Edition. Edited by Dr VOELCKER. 1s.

ON THE USE OF LIME IN AGRICULTURE. 6s.

INSTRUCTIONS FOR THE ANALYSIS OF SOILS. Fourth Edition, 2s.

THE RELATIVE VALUE OF ROUND AND SAWN TIMB

Shown by means of Tables and Diagrams. By JAMES RAIT, Land-Stew at Castle-Forbes. Royal 8vo, 8s. half-bound.

THE YEAR-BOOK OF AGRICULTURAL FACTS.

1859 and 1860. Edited by R. SCOTT BURN. Fcap. 8vo, 5s. each. 1861 1862, 4s each.

ELKINGTON'S SYSTEM OF DRAINING:

A Systematic Treatise on the Theory and Practice of Draining Land, adap to the various Situations and Soils of England and Scotland, drawn up the Communications of Joseph Elkington, by J. JOHNSTONE. 4to, 10s.

JOURNAL OF AGRICULTURE, AND TRANSACTIONS THE HIGHLAND AND AGRICULTURAL SOCIETY OF SCOTLANI

OLD SERIES, 1828 to 1843, 21 vols.	£3	3	0
NEW SERIES, 1843 to 1851, 8 vols.	2	2	0

THE RURAL ECONOMY OF ENGLAND, SCOTLAND, A IRELAND.

By LEONCE DE LAVERGNE. Translated from the Fren With Notes by a Scottish Farmer. In 8vo, 12s.

"One of the best works on the philosophy of agriculture and of agricultural political economy that appeared."—*Spectator.*

DAIRY MANAGEMENT AND FEEDING OF MILCH COW

Being the recorded Experience of MRS AGNES SCOTT, Winkston, Peeb Second Edition. Fcap., 1s.

ITALIAN IRRIGATION:

A Report addressed to the Hon. the Court of Directors of the East In Company, on the Agricultural Canals of Piedmont and Lombardy; wit Sketch of the Irrigation System of Northern and Central India. By LIE COL. BAIRD SMITH, C.B. Second Edition. 2 vols. 8vo, with Atla folio, 30s.

THE ARCHITECTURE OF THE FARM:

A Series of Designs for Farm Houses, Farm Steadings, Factors' Houses, Cottages. By JOHN STARFORTH, Architect. Sixty-two Engravings. medium 4to, £2, 2s.

"One of the most useful and beautiful additions to Messrs Blackwood's extensive and valuable lib of agricultural and rural economy."—*Morning Post*

THE YESTER DEEP LAND-CULTURE:

Being a Detailed Account of the Method of Cultivation which has been cessfull ractised for several uess of Tweeddale at Yes

A MANUAL OF PRACTICAL DRAINING.

By HENRY STEPHENS, F.R.S.E., Author of the 'Book of the Farm.' Third Edition, 8vo, 5s.

A CATECHISM OF PRACTICAL AGRICULTURE.

By HENRY STEPHENS, F.R.S.E., Author of the 'Book of the Farm,' &c. In crown 8vo, with Illustrations, 1s.

HANDY BOOK ON PROPERTY LAW.

By Lord ST LEONARDS. The Seventh Edition. To which is now added a Letter on the New Laws for obtaining an Indefeasible Title. With a Portrait of the Author, engraved by Holl. 3s. 6d.

"Less than 200 pages serve to arm us with the ordinary precautions to which we should attend in selling, buying, mortgaging, leasing, settling, and devising estates. We are informed of our relations to our property, to our wives and children, and of our liability as trustees or executors, in a little book for the million,—a book which the author tenders to the *profanum vulgus* as even capable of 'beguiling a few hours in a railway carriage.'"—*Times.*

THE PLANTER'S GUIDE.

By Sir HENRY STEUART. A New Edition, with the Author's last Additions and Corrections. 8vo, with Engravings, 21s.

STABLE ECONOMY:

A Treatise on the Management of Horses. By JOHN STEWART, V.S. Seventh Edition, 6s. 6d.

"Will always maintain its position as a standard work upon the management of horses."—*Mark Lane Express.*

ADVICE TO PURCHASERS OF HORSES.

By JOHN STEWART, V.S. 18mo, plates, 2s. 6d.

A PRACTICAL TREATISE ON THE CULTIVATION OF THE GRAPE VINE. By WILLIAM THOMSON, Gardener to His Gracé the Duke of Buccleuch, Dalkeith Park. Third Edition. 8vo, 5s.

"When books on gardening are written thus conscientiously, they are alike honourable to their author and valuable to the public."—*Lindley's Gardeners' Chronicle.*

"Want of space prevents us giving extracts, and we must therefore conclude by saying, that as the author is one of the very best grape-growers of the day, this book may be stated as being the key to his successful practice, and as such, we can with confidence recommend it as indispensable to all who wish to excel in the cultivation of the vine."—*The Florist and Pomologist.*

THE CHEMISTRY OF VEGETABLE AND ANIMAL PHYSIOLOGY. By Dr J. G. MULDER, Professor of Chemistry in the University of Utrecht. With an Introduction and Notes by Professor Johnston. 22 Plates. 8vo, 30s.

THE MOOR AND THE LOCH.

Containing Minute Instructions in all Highland Sports, with Wanderings over Crag and Correi, Flood and Fell. By JOHN COLQUHOUN, Esq. Third Edition. 8vo, with Illustrations, 12s. 6d.

SALMON-CASTS AND STRAY SHOTS:

Being Fly-Leaves from the Note-Book of JOHN COLQUHOUN, Esq., Author of 'The Moor and the Loch,' &c. Second Edition. Fcap. 8vo, 5s.

COQUET-DALE FISHING SONGS.

Now first collected by a North-Country Angler, with the Music of the Airs. 8vo, 5s.

THE ANGLER'S COMPANION TO THE RIVERS AND LOCHS OF SCOTLAND. By T. T. STODDART. With Map of the Fishing Streams and Lakes of Scotland. Second Edition. Crown 8vo 7s. 6d.

RELIGION IN COMMON LIFE:
A Sermon preached in Crathie Church, October 14, 1855, before Her Maj the Queen and Prince Albert. By the REV. JOHN CAIRD, D.D. Publisl by Her Majesty's Command. Bound in cloth, 8d. Cheap Edition, 3d.

SERMONS.
By the REV. JOHN CAIRD, D.D., Professor of Divinity in the University Glasgow, and one of Her Majesty's Chaplains for Scotland. In crown 8vo, This Edition includes the Sermon on 'Religion in Common Life,' preach in Crathie Church, Oct. 1855, before Her Majesty the Queen and the Prince Consort.

"They are noble sermons; and we are not sure but that, with the cultivated reader, they will rather than lose by being read, not heard. There is a thoughtfulness and depth about them which hardly be appreciated, unless when they are studied at leisure; and there are so many sentences so f tously expressed that we should grudge being hurried away from them by a rapid speaker, without allowed to enjoy them a second time."—*Fraser's Magazine.*

THE BOOK OF JOB.
By the late REV. GEORGE CROLY, LL.D., Rector of St Stephen's, Walbro With a Memoir of the Author by his SON. Fcap. 8vo, 4s.

LECTURES IN DIVINITY.
By the late REV. GEORGE HILL, D.D, Principal of St Mary's College, Andrews. Stereotyped Edition. 8vo, 14s.

"I am not sure if I can recommend a more complete manual of Divinity."—*Dr Chalmers.*

THE MOTHER'S LEGACIE TO HER UNBORNE CHILDE.
By MRS ELIZABETH JOCELINE. Edited by the Very Rev. Princi LEE. 32mo, 4s. 6d.

"This beautiful and touching legacie."—*Athenæum.*

"A delightful monument of the piety and high feeling of a truly noble mother."—*Morning Ad*

ANALYSIS AND CRITICAL INTERPRETATION OF T HEBREW TEXT OF THE BOOK OF GENESIS. Preceded by a Heb Grammar, and Dissertations on the Genuineness of the Pentateuch, and the Structure of the Hebrew Language. By the REV. WILLIAM PA A.M. 8vo, 18s.

PRAYERS FOR SOCIAL AND FAMILY WORSHIP.
Prepared by a COMMITTEE OF THE GENERAL ASSEMBLY OF THE CHURCH SCOTLAND, and specially designed for the use of Soldiers, Sailors, Colonis Sojourners in India, and other Persons, at Home or Abroad, who are depriv of the Ordinary Services of a Christian Ministry *Published by Authority the Committee.* Third Edition. In crown 8vo, bound in cloth, 4s.

PRAYERS FOR SOCIAL AND FAMILY WORSHIP.
Being a Cheap Edition of the above. Fcap. 8vo, 1s. 6d.

THE CHRISTIAN LIFE,
In its Origin, Progress, and Perfection. By the VERY REV. E. B. RAMSA LL.D., F.R.S.E., Dean of the Diocese of Edinburgh. Crown 8vo, 9s.

THEISM: THE WITNESS OF REASON AND NATURE AN ALL-WISE AND BENEFICENT CREATOR By the REV JO TULLOCH, D.D., Principal and Professor of Theology, St Mary's College, Andrews; and one of Her Majesty's Chaplains in Ordinary in Scotland. 1 vol. 8vo, 10s. 6d.

ON THE ORIGIN AND CONNECTION OF THE GOSPE

INSTITUTES OF METAPHYSIC: THE THEORY OF KNOWING AND BEING. By JAMES F. FERRIER, A.B. Oxon., Professor of Moral Philosophy and Political Economy, St Andrews. Second Edition. Crown 8vo, 10s. 6d.

"We have no doubt, however, that the subtlety and depth of metaphysical genius which his work betrays, its rare display of rigorous and consistent reasonings, and the inimitable precision and beauty of its style on almost every page, must secure for it a distinguished place in the history of philosophical discussion."—*Tulloch's Burnett Prize Treatise.*

LECTURES ON METAPHYSICS.
By SIR WILLIAM HAMILTON, Bart., Professor of Logic and Metaphysics in the University of Edinburgh. Edited by the Rev. H. L. MANSEL, B.D., LL.D., Waynflete Professor of Moral and Metaphysical Philosophy, Oxford; and JOHN VEITCH, M.A., Professor of Logic, Rhetoric, and Metaphysics, St Andrews. Second Edition. 2 vols. 8vo, 24s.

LECTURES ON LOGIC.
By SIR WILLIAM HAMILTON, Bart. Edited by Professors MANSEL and VEITCH. In 2 vols., 24s.

THORNDALE; OR, THE CONFLICT OF OPINIONS.
By WILLIAM SMITH, Author of 'A Discourse on Ethics,' &c. Second Edition. Crown 8vo, 10s. 6d.

"The subjects treated of, and the style—always chaste and beautiful, often attractively grand—in which they are clothed, will not fail to secure the attention of the class for whom the work is avowedly written. . . . . It deals with many of those higher forms of speculation characteristic of the cultivated minds of the age."—*North British Review.*

GRAVENHURST; OR, THOUGHTS ON GOOD AND EVIL.
By WILLIAM SMITH, Author of 'Thorndale,' &c. In crown 8vo, 7s. 6d.

"One of those rare books which, being filled with noble and beautiful thoughts, deserves an attentive and thoughtful perusal."—*Westminster Review.*

A DISCOURSE ON ETHICS OF THE SCHOOL OF PALEY.
By WILLIAM SMITH, Author of 'Thorndale.' 8vo, 4s.

ON THE INFLUENCE EXERTED BY THE MIND OVER THE BODY, in the Production and Removal of Morbid and Anomalous Conditions of the Animal Economy. By JOHN GLEN, M.A. Crown 8vo, 2s. 6d.

DESCARTES ON THE METHOD OF RIGHTLY CONDUCTING THE REASON, and Seeking Truth in the Sciences. Translated from the French. 12mo, 2s.

DESCARTES' MEDITATIONS, AND SELECTIONS FROM HIS PRINCIPLES OF PHILOSOPHY. Translated from the Latin. 12mo, 3s.

Lightning Source UK Ltd.
Milton Keynes UK
UKHW021419010219
336575UK00014B/979/P